THE SPY WORE RED

ALINE, COUNTESS OF ROMANONES

THE SPY WORE RED

My Adventures as an Undercover Agent in World War II

RANDOM HOUSE   NEW YORK

Grateful acknowledgment is made to Gilbert Keyes Music and Bantam
Music Publishing Co. and to Warner Bros. Music for permission to
reprint an excerpt from the lyrics to "It Had to Be You" by Gus Kahn
and Isham Jones. Copyright 1924 by Gilbert Keyes Music and Bantam
Music Publishing Co. pursuant to sections 304(c) and 401(b) of the U.S.
Copyright Act. U.S. rights administered by the Songwriters Guild of
America. Canadian and Open Market rights administered by Warner
Bros. Music. Copyright 1924 Warner Bros. Inc. (Renewed) All rights
reserved. Used by permission.

Library of Congress Cataloging-in-Publication Data
Aline, Countess of Romanones, 1923–
The spy wore red.
1. Aline, Countess of Romanones, 1923–
2. World War, 1939–1945—Secret service—
United States. 3. World War, 1939–1945—Secret
service—Spain. 4. Spies—United States—
Biography. 5. Spies—Spain—Biography. I. Title.
D810.S8A45   1987   940.54'86'73   86-29644
ISBN 0-394-55665-8

Manufactured in the United States of America
Typography and binding design by J. K. Lambert
89

For Luis:

For Luis, my husband

For Luis, my son

For Luis, my grandson

If the red slayer think he slays,
Or if the slain think he is slain,
They know not well the subtle ways
I keep, and pass, and turn again.

RALPH WALDO EMERSON
Brahma

AUTHOR'S NOTE

In the course of lecturing over the past eight years, I've discovered that people enjoy (and need) authentic, firsthand information about espionage, a topic on which reliable information is (understandably) difficult to come by. What I have attempted in this book is to inform and to entertain. My guide posts have been the events themselves, as well as I can reconstruct them from memory and from diaries, letters, snapshots, newspapers, and magazines of the period. There are, however, three limitations on the literal "truthfulness" of my memoir.

In the first place, many of the principals of the drama I recount are living and might conceivably be embarrassed or otherwise inconvenienced by my account of their activities. In order to protect their privacy, then, I have changed the names of some of the characters in the story. And in a very few cases, where a name change did not sufficiently conceal a character's identity, a composite character was created. The man I call Pierre has been disguised, I hope, as has the man code-named Mozart. But there was a Pierre, and there was a Mozart, as there were, in some fashion, all the others.

Secondly, I have occasionally omitted or altered insignificant incidents that would otherwise bore the reader and make the book cumbersome and dreary. Again, this has resulted in a composite character now and then, and in some cases the sequence of events has been slightly altered. The core of the story is accurate.

Finally, my efforts to reconstruct this period of my life from memory have been more successful than I had originally expected, but of course not perfect. Various documents, including reports and cables stored in the National Archives in Washington, D.C., have been of great help in refreshing my memory. But much of the dialogue in the book has been reinvented based on recollection. My intention throughout has been to capture the essence and flavor of the events and conversations that took place. If I have succeeded in doing that, the courage and dedication of my colleagues, and the excitement of the time, will speak for themselves.

ACKNOWLEDGMENTS

I would like to thank those who, over three and a half years, helped me in one way or another. First and foremost, my husband for his patience and his sense of humor. Then my grandchildren, Luis, Cristina, Juan, Carla, and Alvaro, whose complaints that I didn't have time to play with them on summer days in Spain when I was writing were flattering and whose high spirits brightened tired hours.

The mother of this book is Nancy Lady Keith, to whom I am immensely grateful for her prodding and warm, unwavering enthusiasm. The assistance of the Baron Guy de Rothschild helped especially in establishing the identity of one of my characters. The expertise, encouragement, and suggestions of Ken McCormick were indispensable. Tom Guinzburg sacrificed hours giving me advice. I want to thank Joe Hannan for his interest in the story and his worthy ideas. I am indebted also to John Taylor of the National Archives in Washington, to Peter Viertel, Lloyd Smith, the late Rudi Crespi, and to Frank Ryan, whose acquaintance changed the course of my life. Annie of Tighten and Tone kept me agile and optimistic despite many hours at the typewriter. William Rayner placed the manuscript in the hands of Random House. In Spain, Beltrán Domecq, Angel Alcázar de Valcarel, the Marqués of Santo Floro, the Marquesa of Quintanar, and Kay Denckla, the Countess of Yebes were all of invaluable assistance.

Dr. Anthony Nolke miraculously had preserved my letters and pictures, which helped to bring back the past. The enthusiasm and criticisms of my first editor, Jonathan Galassi, spurred me on. The patience of Jeff

Cohen of Random House, and of my editor there, Sam Vaughan, who put my manuscript into a better version of the queen's language and who tied the strings together, was notable. Bob Aulicino's jacket design was a welcome and lovely triumph.

There are others, indeed almost everyone with whom I came into contact during the last several years, who had to put up with some of sort of backlash and back talk as I worked on this story. Being able to talk with them about it helped me to finish the book—may they and I not regret it.

THE SPY WORE RED

Prologue: San Salvador, 1984

It was a trip to El Salvador several years ago that started this story. I had been lecturing on foreign affairs throughout the United States. At that moment, Central America and especially El Salvador were the areas my audiences were most interested in. But to be truthful, my motives for making the trip derived mainly from an unquenchable desire to be in the middle of whatever was going on. The fact that it would be warm and sunny there, in comparison to the ice and snow of Michigan, where I happened to be, and that I could eat mangoes might also have been a factor. At any rate, I indulged myself with the excuse that the visit would add credibility to my lectures.

The trip had ingredients that appealed to my sense of adventure. For example, I didn't know the name, telephone number, nor even the sex of the person who would meet me or where I would be staying. Arrangements had been made hastily through a telephone call to a Salvadoran friend in Washington who offered to find a private house where I could stay and friends who would take care of my needs. Since I had only a week free between lectures, he suggested I leave for Salvador immediately. "I'll have someone meet you at the airport who'll explain all the details," he said.

From the moment I boarded the plane in New York, I was, without being aware of it at first, on a trip back in time. That feeling took over in Miami, where passengers crammed on board with their belongings in cloth sacks, looking very much as the passengers had on Spanish trains in 1944.

In Panama, many disembarked, and in Tegucigalpa, almost all left. Our destination was now only minutes away. I looked down at the lush green valleys rolling into the volcanic mountain ranges which I knew harbored guerrilla groups, some at that moment in skirmishes with soldiers of the country's armed forces. Only one other passenger got off the large DC-10 to enter the empty, modern air terminal. Obviously the war had paralyzed tourism and discouraged foreign business.

My steps on the cement surface resounded along a passageway illuminated by shafts of sunlight coming through great glass windows. I peered over the heads of the officials examining my passport and luggage but could see no one waiting. Not until I descended the last step of the wide stone entrance did the discreet figure in black rise from a chair against the wall and approach. The smile erased my doubts. This was my friend's friend in El Salvador. She was of average height; either the few extra pounds or perhaps a touch of arthritis gave her a slight limp; she wore dark-rimmed glasses; an abundance of happy white hair framed a face full of friendship and goodwill. Then, as if by magic, a handsome, tall young man appeared smiling at my side.

"This is Bill Wallach," she explained in an agreeable Salvadoran accent. "He has volunteered to drive you into the city and to help any way he can. My name is María."

"Señora. We want you to be safe here." The young man spoke as he grabbed my suitcases and placed them in the jeep. "My father has sent this bulletproof car for you."

As we wound along the modern highway through open country, the twenty-five-year-old driver and my eighty-year-old hostess explained the latest developments in the civil war. After fifteen minutes, when we arrived at the outskirts of the city, I had learned that every road, especially those similar to the one we were on, could be dangerous. My companions showed no signs of fear, but I admit I was experiencing some apprehension.

"It's not safe in the city either," my new friend said. "Only two days ago, the house next to mine was bombed, and I do apologize for the unattractive sight when we arrive."

When I entered María's house, I was reminded of a small Roman abode, the rooms sprouting off from a central patio. An Indian woman was watering the plants, a child was seated on the tile floor in front of a color television screen banked by pink orchids.

"We will not be having dinner for a few hours yet," María explained. "Perhaps you would like to rest after such a long trip?"

"Not at all. I'm dying to see something of what's going on."

"That's not easy," she said. "Things happen sporadically, without notice, and one never knows where. A bus is burned, or someone is kidnapped, or a political center is attacked." She paused, considering the possibilities. "Unless you would like to go to the Camino Real Hotel, where the foreign press and television people spend most of their time. Something is usually happening there. The hour is too late to suggest anything else."

It was dark when the jeep entered the circular driveway of the large hotel. Nothing indicated that a war was being waged nearby. Several American television trucks almost blocked the entrance, and people sauntered in and out through the luxurious double glass doors.

A woman approached me as I entered. "Doña María called to say you were coming. I am the secretary of the hotel. We are so grateful that you are visiting our poor country to learn what is happening here. Unfortunately, I do not have the time to explain much now, but if you come with me, you can observe some interesting activities."

As we walked through the crowded foyer, she lowered her voice. "The foreign press gather around the bar, where they exchange news and are contacted by representatives of the guerrillas who provide reports in English of the recent battles and give tips as to where they might film a good scene."

The room was large and long, a bar at one end; round tables and comfortable armchairs placed at discreet distances from each other; a thick wall-to-wall carpet. Beyond open glass doors I saw a patio surrounded by flowers and plants, forming a sort of outdoor room with a turquoise oval pool in the middle.

"I will leave you here. If you want anything, look for me in my office."

I took a chair as close to the bar as possible, but couldn't hear a word. After about ten minutes I walked the length of the room, saw nothing of interest, and certainly could not distinguish any guerrillas. Some of the men appeared to be telling jokes, others looked bored to tears for lack of something to do.

I wandered onto the inviting patio. It was empty. Illuminated by mushroom lamps between tropical trees and rich foliage, there was an abundance of exotic flowers. The warm March night air carried the perfume of gardenias and jasmine. No longer could I hear the rumble of the voices of the men in bright cotton shirts with short sleeves, puffing on cigarettes in the room behind, only the slight gurgle of water filtering into the pool and the rustle of palm fronds above. I walked to the side of the pool, wondering why no one took advantage of it. Then I looked into the water for a while. Gradually I became aware that someone else on the opposite side was doing the same—the face disfigured by ripples in the water. Instinctively I looked up.

We recognized each other at the same moment, I think. I never had time to ask him later. We didn't speak, or call out. We merely stood transfixed in disbelief—almost forty years had changed so little. The same sly glint in that penetrating glance. The graying black hair added a smashing splash of glamour to the tanned skin. Even had I not known him, I would have been attracted by this unusual man.

We walked toward each other. As I looked at him, a great happiness came over me.

"Tiger," he said, taking my hands. I felt the pleasure in his eyes, the magnetism still there. His grin revealed those white teeth.

"How can this be possible?" was all I could say.

He was dressed in a white, stiffly starched *guayabera,* the creases around his eyes revealing years in the sun. He had always had that look. He led me to a secluded table near a huge banana tree. We sat.

"I know a bit about you, Tiger. I know who you married. Tell me, how do you like being a pillar of society in my favorite country?

I was so overwhelmed that I had to make a visible effort to answer.

"Of course I love Spain. I have children and grandchildren there. But I want to know about you. Tell me everything."

═══

Read my story, if you will, or you might not find our unexpected encounter as exciting as I did that night. Slide further back into time a bit with me. The story I want to tell begins one day in September in New York.

Chapter 1

The sign on the elaborate brownstone was delicately engraved: *Hattie Carnegie.* Leaving the sunny morning behind I flew up the narrow stairway and punched my time card. Nine-thirty.

Standing in the doorway of the dressing room, arms crossed on her tentlike smock, Hattie sighed abysmally. "Aline, there isn't a girl in this city who would come to work dressed like that." I looked down at mud-splattered saddle shoes and laughed. My red skirt was wrinkled from the high grass, wet with the early-morning dew, grass I had raced through in our apple orchard, an hour and a half before, to catch the bus.

Inside, my colleagues sat at the long-mirrored vanity chattering and applying masks of makeup. I hung my street clothes on a rack and squirmed into an ice-blue satin girdle, hooking up sheer silk stockings and stepping into spiky black pumps. After throwing on a wrapper I took the chair between Anne and Paula at the table. Both were sipping from cardboard containers of black coffee, painfully waking up.

"Morning, girls." Dabbing a sponge in water, I spread foundation on my face in a fine film. In the mirror I noticed that Paula looked exceptionally bleary; russet-haired, she was reputedly the most beautiful model in New York. "El Morocco?" I asked.

"Till three," she said, as if complaining, but clearly the fact thrilled her. She was the quintessential party girl of the moment.

"How do you do it? Every night at those clubs, with . . . *playboys.*" That was the kindest word I could think of to describe her dates—the kind of older men who get their names in the columns for a fourth divorce or a fortune squandered at the racetrack.

"Honey," Paula drawled, "why don't you let Buff and me take you out for a drink tonight and show you what you've been missing?"

I made a face in the mirror.

"Well, I don't see what your boring routine and the degree from that nuns' college have done for you."

"Face it, Aline," Amy put in, "Paula's right. You don't earn a dime more than we do. Don't you care about money?"

"Why do you think I work here? This is the highest-paying job I could find."

"Honey, she means *real* money," said Paula. "As in *rich*. And that means marrying it. Don't you want that?"

"I want to do exciting things. Maybe accomplish something worthwhile at the same time." My sigh was punctuation. "I guess what I want is adventure."

"All the more reason to come to Mike's tonight. You know his brother is coming into town." Amy had been pressing me to go for days. She was determined to marry Mike Derby, of the "Kentucky Derbys"—her joke, since his family was old, rich, and Southern—and he had asked her to get a date for his brother, who was in his mid-thirties; I was twenty and had never dated a boy more than two years older than me.

"It would mean catching a late bus home, and I have to get up at seven. But thanks a lot."

Now she sighed, weary of virtue. Mine.

By this time my hair was in a neat chignon, the tight roll centered in back, crowned in a pompadour. I rushed to the sink in the corner and filled my hands with soap suds with which I slicked up the stray strands.

For two hours I stood frozen as fitters pinned hemlines and tucked sleeves to the couturier's exacting specifications. Tossed on a chair in the fitting room was a copy of the morning *Journal American*—showing a beach strewn with the first soldiers killed in the landing on Sicily.

It was September 1943. My brother Dexter was a fighter pilot stationed in England, my brother Tom aboard a submarine somewhere in the South

Pacific. And I was standing like a brainless piece of furniture, being fitted in party dresses!

I stepped out onto the runway, into a blaze. Lights struck magnificent crystal chandeliers hanging from the high-ceilinged salon. Hundreds of smart hats were reflected in the mirrored walls. Spotlights and flashbulbs ricocheted from the glass, hurling sparks in my eyes. I paraded through the room a dozen times that afternoon. Soon I was ending the show.

Once back in the dressing room I yanked off the hat and veil and wedding dress and unpinned my hair until it tumbled to my shoulders. Over the commotion I heard Amy yell, "Aline, hurry up, get over here!" She stood at the wall phone in the corner, her hand covering the receiver.

"*Please,* be a good sport about tonight. I have to give Mike an answer. His brother has just come in from the airport—from overseas. I told you he does something or other in the War Department."

No, she hadn't. I was stung. *Overseas.* The *War Department.* The words worked on me, magically. Slowly, very slowly, I nodded. Okay.

=====

We arrived late.

"Come on in, come on in," Mike drawled. "Sorry, we'll have to eat immediately, because the spaghetti is just about ready."

We walked to a large table that dominated his bachelor's flat. The windows were shut on the sultry evening and covered with green shades for the blackout. Fans droned and so did the radio—it always seemed to be on everywhere one went, the war news a constant backdrop to conversation.

"Amy Porter, Aline Griffith, this is my notorious brother, John."

John Derby had a square face, striking blue eyes, fair scrubbed skin, prematurely silver hair. I guessed him to be thirty-five. His body was more solid than his brother's; Mike was a little pudgy, though more dashing. I sat on one side, Amy on the other, next to Mike. To my left were two other men, co-workers, Mike explained. He was in the research department of Standard Oil. I wondered why he hadn't enlisted.

John Derby turned to me. "Wine, Miss Griffith?" His manner was cool, detached.

"Thank you, no. I don't drink."

His eyebrow lifted in question.

"Ever," I said.

He turned away. It quickly became evident that neither Amy nor I was expected to participate as the men bantered and argued about the strategies of their heroes and villains of the war, from Patton to Rommel, Roosevelt to Hitler. They debated the use of the recently completed gargantuan Pentagon building and unanimously condemned union leader John L. Lewis and the United Mine Workers' strike.

Later, Derby turned to me and inquired, smiling, "Are you planning to become a famous model?"

I looked him full in the face. "Not if I can help it."

"Really? And why is that?"

"I want to get into the war—overseas."

John Derby glanced at me with curiosity. "How do you intend to do that?"

"I wish I knew. I've applied to Jacqueline Cochran's Flying Training Division, and every other group I can think of. I'm always told the same thing: too young. But there has to be a way."

"You could become a nurse."

"That would take years. I want to get in the war now—over there where the real fighting is going on."

"Now, why on earth would an attractive girl like you, safe and sound here in New York, want to go abroad to become embroiled in a bloody massacre? Someplace where your life could be in danger?"

I wanted to tell him I had three great-grandmothers who had braved crossing this country to lay down roots in the Midwest, despite Indian attacks, birth without doctors, sickness without medicine, helping to build homes with their own hands, but I was afraid he would laugh. Instead I said, "I love adventure. I like taking risks. All the men I know are eager to get over there. Why should it seem strange that a woman wants to also?"

I started to turn my back when he said, "Girls your age are usually dreaming of getting married and having children. Aren't you in love?"

It was beginning to be a boring evening. "What's that got to do with it?"

"Well . . . it *is* a factor."

"Well, it's not. As it happens, I'm not in love. But even if I were, it would make no difference." The first part may have been a lie: there was Tony, an intern at Bellevue, whom I liked a lot. But the second part was true.

John Derby studied me in silence. Then he said, "Do you know any foreign language?"

"In college I majored in French and minored in Spanish."

"Oh."

We smiled slowly at one another.

"Well, Miss Griffith, if you're really serious about a job overseas, there's a slight possibility I can help." I looked at him with new interest. "If you should happen to hear from a Mr. Tomlinson," he said, "you'll know what it's about."

Chapter 2

About two weeks later one Sunday at dinner, my father mentioned that an inquiry had been made at the bank concerning our family background. My mother was convinced it had something to do with my brothers, because they were in the service; my father, who managed a factory which manufactured folding machines for print plants (founded by my grandfather), worried about its connection to business. We were shaken somewhat, and didn't know what to think. But such a minor anxiety was eroded by the tedium of day-to-day existence, and our lives went on, as always, uneventfully.

The weather was still warm a week later—it was the last of September —when I came home from work. The light waned by degrees as I walked up the hill through the rustling wheatgrass, the wind entangling my hair.

As I entered the kitchen, my mother was holding the phone. "It's for you. Long distance."

"Miss Aline Griffith?" The voice was husky.

"Yes."

"This is Mr. Tomlinson. Can you be free for a few minutes tomorrow?"

"Yes."

"Then please be in the Biltmore Hotel lobby, at six o'clock. A man with a white carnation in his lapel will be looking for you. Don't mention this meeting to anyone. Is that clear?"

"Yes."

He hung up.

Servicemen streamed in and out of revolving doors or pressed against the bar of the cocktail lounge or took tea with young ladies in silk print dresses.

He was distinguished, medium height. Gray hair. Immaculately tailored suit. His manner was calm, gently commanding.

"We'll sit over there."

I followed him to an alcove and a ruby-colored banquette.

"I think we can speak comfortably here." Once seated, he explained, "I represent a section of the War Department. We may have some interesting work for you."

He smiled. His clear blue eyes inspired confidence. "We want to test you for a job. I can't tell you what it is just yet."

We were sitting side by side, protected by the noise and movement around us.

"Would I work overseas?"

"If you succeed in the tests, yes." His tone was polite but impersonal. "Can you come to Washington within ten days? It will mean taking leave from your job. You may never go back, if all goes well."

"I can be ready at any time."

"Good." He checked a pocket agenda. "Friday, October eighth. One week from tomorrow. Give your parents this phone number and address in case they need to reach you. You will not be here"—he tapped the card—"but mail and calls will be forwarded to you."

His expression now became severe.

"Tell your family you're being interviewed by the War Department for a job. Bring a suitcase of clothes suitable for the country. Remove all labels. Carry nothing with your initials nor papers or letters with your name. No one must be able to identify anything about you. Arrive in Washington by noon. Go directly to Q Building. Here is the address." He handed me another card. "Give a false name and home address to the receptionist. Do you have any questions?"

I shook my head.

A waiter came to take our order.

The gentleman said, "We won't be having anything today." He stood up.

So did I.

"Good-bye," he said. Again his reassuring smile. "And good luck to you."

As I bounced along Route 9W about an hour later, the exciting possibilities Mr. Tomlinson's words had opened up made my temperature soar. From the open window I saw only a blurred landscape, so concentrated was I on the immediate change of my humdrum routine for a future filled with uncertainties. It was foolhardy to accept the offer, but I couldn't resist. This was my chance to do something unusual at last. Overseas. In the war. Just what I had been struggling for. The secrecy Mr. Tomlinson had insisted upon implied something like espionage. No, I must not let my imagination run wild, but I would go to Washington to find out. My whole being was throbbing with joy.

Chapter 3

Have a seat, Tiger."

He was the man from the dinner a month ago, John Derby. I had never expected to see him again.

"As long as you're here that's the only name you'll be known by. You have a number also. Five two seven."

I sat in front of his desk. I put down my suitcase. I could hear my heart. Could he? He leaned forward, smiling.

"This is your first trip to Washington, isn't it?"

"Almost the farthest I've ever been from home."

"I guess the meeting in the Biltmore must have been pretty mystifying, but I can't tell you more at this point." His eyes engaged mine. "We need a special girl for a special job," he continued, very still at his desk, his large hands folded. "I've met and investigated many candidates, all highly recommended, and I've decided you are the one most likely to succeed in the tests which are a necessary preliminary. I've picked you because of your age, your college record, your languages, your looks, and your willingness to risk your life if necessary. We investigated you, back through your grandparents. Now we're going to see how you stand up to some specific training. I may be overestimating your possibilities. I hope not."

I studied his office. Stark gray walls, filing drawers built into a steel safe. From outside the new, ugly, single-story, prefabricated Q Building, the afternoon sunshine entered the sole window in the room. I sat perfectly erect in my chair.

"In the next few weeks you're going to have to adapt to unusual situations, and you'll be judged by how well you do. Nobody you're going to meet, not a soul, should know whether you're from Boise or Berlin, whether you prefer Cole Porter or Hegel. You must consider what you say and what you don't say, what you do and what you don't do."

His voice was low, soft, his manner calm, but each phrase contained information that was vital for me.

"From this minute on, you may be followed. And where you will be living your colleagues may go through your belongings searching for clues to your identity." That did not make my new associates sound particularly attractive.

John Derby spoke more slowly than before, as if to etch his words on my brain.

"Proceed to the Hay Adams Hotel. Wait at the main entrance for a black Chevrolet sedan—license number TX16248. Ask, 'Is this Mr. Tom's car?' " Derby handed me a narrow slip of yellow paper. "Here's the number in case you forget it. Destroy it afterward. It's a luxury for beginners."

======

Once on the street, I had difficulty feeling this was really happening—to me. I realized I had no idea how to get to the Hay Adams Hotel. Easy enough—I'd ask. No, he had said I might be followed. Behind me, Q Building squatted atop a shallow hill of lawn in the center of Washington. I tightened my grip on the suitcase, walked three blocks, went into a store, and telephoned the hotel for directions. It was much too far to walk and I had to take a taxi, in which I spent most of my time looking out the window to make certain we were not being followed.

When I reached the curved drive of the Hay Adams, a crowd was milling around in front, cars and taxis drawing up steadily. I hoped the bustle would make me inconspicuous. I took a place at the curb and began to watch every vehicle. Groups climbed in and out—and one girl with a huge yellowy gardenia behind her ear, and a young private in a wheelchair. Porters rolled and heaved baggage.

A bellboy grabbed my valise. We tussled with it. "But, miss . . ." I didn't know what to say; I'd never stayed in a hotel in my life. I hugged my suitcase closer and moved to one side, taking off my hat to smooth my hair, which had become damp. Was it unusually warm, or was I nervous? On the opposite side of the drive I noticed a man in a black overcoat, his face hidden by a newspaper, and another man a few steps away with sinister dark features.

Finally, a black Chevrolet appeared. Whirling around, I flung open my handbag and checked the number, aware that my clumsy gesture was not what was expected of me. When I turned around, the two suspicious-looking men were already in the car and the chauffeur was turning the motor on.

I rushed up. "Stop! Stop! I'm supposed to go with you."

The driver frowned. "What's your name?"

Trying to regain composure, I gave the passwords. "Is this Mr. Tom's car?"

He got out and placed my suitcase in the trunk, and I climbed in back, next to the black overcoat—a middle-aged man with thinning brown hair, whose fleeting smile was vaguely reassuring. The other man sat on his left. Directly in front was a fellow with thick black hair, but I couldn't see his face at all.

As we sped out the driveway, I thought of saying something like "Beautiful day," or "Washington is really prettier than New York"— no, not that. Hadn't Derby warned me a half hour ago not to say anything that could identify me? Wait for somebody else to start the conversation, I told myself. But to my increasing surprise as we wove through traffic in the sunny afternoon, no one uttered a sound.

It would be a short ride anyway, I figured—probably ten minutes to some government building—until I noticed that the city streets were giving way to thinning residential sections and finally wooded, two-lane country roads. For a moment, panic crept upward from my stomach. Was I in the hands of white slavers? Why not? Anything was possible. Here I was, not even Aline Griffith anymore, without a single piece of identification. I was only "Tiger," number 527.

We veered off the road into a long, dim drive under a tangled canopy of branches. By my watch we'd driven almost forty minutes, about twenty miles outside of the capital, and were somewhere in Maryland or Virginia. I had no idea. The house was enormous, rising above a hill of lawn with a gabled white brick front; the sun burnished dozens of windows. Surrounding its vast grounds was forest so vividly red and yellow it looked painted. The afternoon had reached its pitch, the autumn air crisp and sweet.

We came to a halt in front of a columned portico. I jumped out, followed by the three men. Quickly I straightened my skirt and smoothed my hair; the massive front door swung open. A hairy, muscled man in a red plaid sport shirt stepped onto the porch. Following him was a wiry fellow in a tight-buttoned Army jacket over black suit trousers, white socks, and shiny blunt-tipped shoes.

The larger one took my suitcase from the driver, who was unloading the trunk, and then walked over to me.

"Hello . . ."

He was waiting. I said, a little hesitantly, "Tiger."

"You're Tiger?"

Silently I nodded.

"Well, well." His smile was slow. "It just goes to show you. How misleading a name can be. I'm Whiskey." He stretched out a paw.

"Good afternoon . . . Whiskey." Shaking it, I thought the name fit. Something about his manner, his tone of voice, suggested liquor—strong, laced with a punch. I heard the sounds of birds, rustling trees, and—a muffled volley of gunfire?

"Hello, Pierre," Whiskey addressed the man who'd sat in front, the one I couldn't see.

"Hello, Whiskey. Good to see you again." The voice was clipped, with a British accent. I looked at him for the first time. Then I struggled, trying to show no reaction, for he was simply the most attractive man I'd ever seen. His dark skin was reddish tan, the look of an outdoor athlete, his hair blacker and thicker than it had appeared in the car. At that moment his brown eyes were penetrating, looking at me, a sudden smile revealing perfect white teeth. Not especially tall, but slim and vibrant. His black-and-white-check suit bespoke a cut and quality that matched its wearer.

Embarrassed and terribly aware of his presence, I walked up the steps to the house.

Still gripping my suitcase, Whiskey said to me, "Well, Tiger, you're a welcome sight. Come on in." As we walked up onto the porch, the ground felt as unsteady as sand beneath my feet. The short, wiry creature had stood in motionless silence, witnessing the proceedings like one of those small jockey statues that often grace entrances. Now Whiskey gestured for him to enter also.

"Sphinx, why don't you take this young lady's suitcase and show her to her room."

For a second, the little man eyed me. His taut features and carved eyes were almost attractive, but his momentary glance chilled me and dissolved the spell the handsome stranger had cast. Taking my suitcase from Whiskey's hand, Sphinx took small, militant steps into the large front hall. I looked around and saw—men, only men, mostly in their forties or fifties, dressed in a random assortment of attire, boxy business suits or slacks and sport shirts, while others—like Sphinx—wore a mix of Army uniforms and civilian clothes.

Whiskey pointed his huge hand. "To the left is the dining room. Dinner is at six, sharp. There'll be a meeting for newcomers in the library at seven."

Dumbly I nodded and turned to follow the smaller man up the curving staircase. His precise wooden-soldier steps led down a hall to a door designated with the number 3.

"This is where you bunk." His high voice was as taut as his drilled gait.

Sphinx opened the door. The room was small, austere—twin beds, one bureau against a white-painted wall, two straight chairs, a green shade covering the lone window. On one of the beds a startled young woman looked up from the book on her lap.

"You could have knocked." She directed her words to Sphinx.

"Not a chance, Magic. You're not in a luxury hotel. You're working for the U.S.A." His voice was unemotional, cold.

Somewhat cautiously, she stood up, facing me as though waiting for

Sphinx to make the introduction. By conventional standards she wasn't pretty—a long horsy face, shiny brown mane, and unusually thick glasses. But her high cheekbones and pale, thick-lashed eyes gave her an undeniable attractiveness. The long green wool skirt and navy sweater revealed a sturdy, athletic figure. We studied each other while Sphinx placed my suitcase on the floor and then left the room without a word.

I started to speak, but she put her finger to her lips, indicating silence, and pointed to a corner of the ceiling. I saw only an air vent.

"Not a word you don't want overheard," she whispered. "This room is wired for sound." Her muffled voice was thick with a guttural foreign accent. "My name is Magic."

"I'm Tiger."

She clasped my hand in a warm welcome. "That fellow is the bane of my life," she whispered again, gesturing toward the door. "He doesn't think women have a right to be here. A lot of the men feel the same way, but at least they are courteous. Ninety-nine out of a hundred women wouldn't want to be here even if they could. You'll see tomorrow what I mean. But it is fascinating despite the toughness of the schedule. Only two women to over thirty men!"

"Only you and me?"

"Aren't two more than enough?" One of her myopic eyes winked. "I've been the only woman in the group since I arrived three weeks ago. New recruits arrive on Fridays with some of the old ones who've been given time off. We're all at different stages in this training program."

She glanced at her wristwatch. "I must go." She dashed to the closet, exchanged her low-heeled oxfords for a pair of high-heeled pumps, rushed past me, saying *"A bientôt,"* and left.

I walked to the window. In the distance the fiery woods cast lengthening shadows on vast lawns, and there were glimpses of golden fields through the trees. Below, a group of men played touch football. Leaning closer, I recognized the handsome Pierre standing under a large maple tree, and Magic appeared to be running in his direction.

I turned away and began to unpack and then waited impatiently for six o'clock.

====

The group in the dining room resembled a fraternity reunion—men were seated eight at each rectangular table, laughing and talking as boisterously as if the war had nothing to do with them. Whiskey beckoned.

"Tiger, I'd like you to meet those at our table." He introduced Bluejay, Francis, Popoff, Lucky, and two others.

Lucky and Popoff had been my silent companions in the car. Taking the chair between Whiskey and Lucky, I limited myself to saying hello and smiling. I was determined not to make unnecessary slips. Whiskey turned to me, amiable, alert. "So, Tiger, what do you think?"

The men were scrupulously attentive.

"Of these digs, I mean. Not bad, huh?" he went on.

"Just great." I smiled again, the only safe ground I could think of at that moment.

"I sure hope you like tough steak. Because you're going to see a lot of it around here."

"In this place you need it," a man across the table added good-naturedly. "You have to be as tough as this steak to survive."

Glancing around, Lucky and I exchanged a look. He had remained as silent too.

"And don't forget the potatoes," Bluejay put in. "They must be the only crop for a hundred miles. Breakfast, lunch, and dinner. Ugh."

"Now, what's wrong with potatoes?" asked Whiskey heartily. "Our boys overseas love their potatoes mashed, boiled, baked, hash-browned, and pan-fried, in that order."

I did not dare join in the conversation, afraid of revealing that I'd never been anywhere and knew nothing of the world. Yet everyone else, except Lucky, bantered freely—skimming from Mark Clark's assault on Naples and MacArthur's drive on New Guinea to the season's football scores.

====

In the library a fire sparked, shedding a gleam over paneled walls and leather-bound books. Lucky was already there. I sat down next to him. In five minutes twelve of us were gathered in a silent group. Whiskey appeared, attended closely by Sphinx.

"Make yourselves comfortable, please. There's scotch and bourbon over there"—pointing to a table against the wall—"and cigarettes in the boxes."

Nonchalantly, our host, sitting on the large mahogany desk, arms crossed on his chest, waited until every glass was full, every cigarette lit, every seat resumed. I remained glued to my seat. He seemed to thrive on prolonging our suspense. Sphinx leaned against the same desk to Whiskey's right, and the way he surveyed each of us I thought he was deciding which one he should choose to pummel first. Uncrossing his arms, Whiskey waited until you could hear the proverbial pin drop.

"Well. I think you deserve to know exactly what is going on, and why you're here."

Whiskey shifted position, waited, enjoyed the silence. "This is the first school of espionage in the United States. And you're here to be converted into . . . S . . . P . . . I . . . E . . . S." Each letter took a second.

No one moved. In the fireplace an ember ignited, hissed, died. Ice clattered in a glass. Matter-of-factly now, with unaffected heartiness, Whiskey continued.

"If you can pass the training, you'll be the employee of a brand-new service, the Office of Strategic Services, and we're accountable to only one guy—General Wild Bill Donovan. No government department has jurisdiction over our operations—except the President."

Whiskey paused only a second while glancing at us one by one. "The FBI is responsible for intelligence gathered within our borders—and right now they're also helping us out in South America. We can't train recruits fast enough. That leaves us the rest of the globe to cover—and it's plenty." A grunt of accord. "OSS has five sections. MO, Mobile Operations, coordinates agent activities behind enemy lines. There's the propaganda section. R&A, Research and Analysis, collects and sifts strategic war data. CE, Counterespionage, deals with gathering foreign intelligence while overseas. And SI, Secret Intelligence, handles agents assigned special missions in countries abroad. Donovan is the overall chief, but each of the five sections has a boss with authority worldwide for that department's activities. Each will be assigned one section in particular."

Just as affably, Whiskey continued, "That's if you pass the training. I hate to be the one to tell you, guys—and gal—but some of you won't even last two weeks."

So this was the catch. How could my inexperience prove a match for these worldly men?

"For a few, your memory won't be sharp enough. Or your responses too slow. Or the fatigue will grind you down—I'd better tell you right now you're going to be put through some pretty rough tests—and you're going to have to follow every order whether you like it or not. You're going to have to be a champ just when you think you're too tired to stay awake another minute—and then you'll have to make split-second decisions."

Whiskey said, glancing at each of us in turn, "If you don't like what I've said, or if you think it's too much for you to handle, there's the door. No hard feelings.

"As long as you sign a paper and swear under oath never to repeat a word you've heard in this room, you can leave now and be driven back to Washington in an hour. And forget you were ever here."

No one moved.

"And here's another thing. There's always the chance—and not a bad one either—that an enemy agent may have wormed his way in here. That's one of the reasons your code name is your only name as long as you're here. I'm only going to say that once. But I want you to remember it: keep your identity to yourself. That means from your roommate, your teacher, your buddy."

I never took my eyes off our speaker. Whiskey had none of the refinement of John Derby. His stance, his walk were pugilistic. John Derby might have been a lawyer, Whiskey a Marine. They were about the same age and they shared one observable characteristic—each seemed to me methodically playing a hand of cards, choosing exactly which one to play, which one to withhold.

"Forget your past. Forget you ever had one. Only the present counts. And the future. Now you'd better get a good sleep tonight, my friends —it may be your last. Tomorrow, breakfast is at seven, your first lecture at eight sharp—I'll have the pleasure of delivering it. From then on, your schedule will be nonstop. I think that's about it for now.

"Oh, by the way, welcome to RTU-11, also known as the Farm."

I left the library in a daze. Was all this really happening? I was climbing the stairs when I heard: "Tiger, I have something for you."

Turning around, I saw Whiskey holding a parcel. He advanced until he stood one step below. "You can see by now there's no standard uniform here. But you might find these practical."

I opened the box to discover two pairs of Army dungarees with drawstring waist. "Thank you."

"They're not stylish enough for you by a long shot, and I hope you don't mind the color."

We looked at one another. I finally said what I'd been thinking all evening: "If I told you, wouldn't I be giving away something about myself?"

His smile was slow. His unshaven beard was like infinite dots engraved on his rugged face. "That's the way, Tiger. I think you're going to do all right here."

———

Promptly at eight, Whiskey appeared—alert, stolid, amicable as an old friend, resolute as a Sherman tank. Right behind him tagged Sphinx. Two middle-aged men in Army uniforms took seats at the back of the room while Sphinx and Whiskey proceeded to a table in front, where they placed a metal rod and what appeared to be rolls of film.

Lucky, who had taken the seat next to me, confided: "Last night one of the fellows told me that Whiskey is quite a guy. He's a West Pointer, also did one year at Saint-Cyr, the French military academy. Then England for further training, where he became the instructor in hand-to-hand combat for the Canadian and English agents who were being sent behind enemy lines. Nobody knows if Whiskey has done service 'out in the field,' but it's possible. He didn't take charge here until two months ago."

Whiskey's physique was not immediately noteworthy, but as I focused on him, he appeared more impressive—and lethal. His body was not especially tall or broad, but had a quality that revealed unusual physical ability. His manner also reflected confidence in that ability.

I asked Lucky, "Do you know how long the training period for us is?"

"There's no definite time. Some men have been here over a month, others after a few weeks are sent to another training camp to learn parachuting and other skills. Every student is prepared for a specific mission. We're sort of custom-made by the time we leave, if we're not bounced." He shifted in his chair uncomfortably. "I don't like not knowing what I'm going to do or where I'm going to be sent, do you?"

Before I had a chance to answer, Whiskey, who by now was standing in front of a portable white projection screen which had just been set up, began to speak. "Anybody know what our most dangerous secret weapon is?" With a smile he scanned the room. Not a peep. "You're in it."

I felt Lucky's glance. To my left one of the men who had entered in uniform was walking to the front.

"Our friend here"—Whiskey pointed to the approaching officer—"will be one of your instructors. He's going to give you a briefing. Refer to him as Captain, but don't think he is one just because you see that rank on his uniform. Remember, from now you must get accustomed to questioning all evidence. We'll ask for your opinions later. And I can tell you your instructors have some pretty good laughs with the mistakes you fellows make—and, pardon me"—he glanced in my direction—"you gals."

The captain patted Whiskey on the back and without preface began. "The first thing you'd better get in your heads is that this is a *secret* intelligence agency, not a public information service. The intelligence we provide to the military is *top* secret. Know what that means? It means you can be shot just for knowing it yourself. In other words, one ear doesn't even tell the other. Now, we're as serious about our secrecy as the German Abwehr or the Russian NKVD. Repeat one word you've heard in this place to anybody without consent—I don't care who he is or what his rank—and you'll be tried for treason. That applies to every one of you —whether or not you pass the training. Get it, friends?" A quick smile.

"We're here to save lives. That will be our prime effort. The information our agents obtain of the enemy's forces, their coastal emplacements, their troop movements, roadblocks, antiaircraft guns, their mines—together with knowledge of their intentions—all is indispensable.

"And we have problems. Stalin does not want Allied troops in Eastern Europe. He has plans for controlling those countries bordering Russia. That makes our work in that area critical, because if our agents could convince those governments that we will not abandon them to the Bolsheviks after the war, some would join our side now. At the moment they are less afraid of the Nazism of Hitler than the communism of Stalin.

"There are rumors of assassination plots by the German military conspiring against Hitler, but even if successful such a possibility would not end our problems. If the Führer is eliminated, Heinrich Himmler would step into his place, and he's equally dangerous.

"And then there's Italy, where we've been having trouble precisely because of lack of information on German strength and because no one can tell us yet what Kesselring has in mind for the future. Will he retreat? Will Rommel send him more troops? These are the questions our OSS men over there are trying to answer right now. So far Kesselring is hanging on somewhere between Naples and Rome and one thousand American men have been lost. We hope OSS will reduce casualties, will show the way to victory. Now do you understand how strategic is the part each of you is going to be prepared for?"

The captain continued, sketching a brief picture of current events in the Pacific. When he finished, Whiskey came to the table. "What do you say, Captain? Time for a few pictures?"

A young man began to prepare a movie projector. Meanwhile, Whiskey addressed us in his usual informal manner. "You know, the boys in Washington say there's a joke going around about us—about what the letters OSS stand for." He snickered. "Oh, So Social. Just because some of our members' names come from social registers. Now do you think that's fair, Sphinx?" He turned to the little fellow sitting behind him. "When they're lucky enough to have such tough guys as you and me?"

"What does 'social' mean, anyway?" Sphinx joked in his remarkably humorless voice.

Our speaker laughed heartily. "Well, this little home movie will show you what we're working to stop—and it'll take more than social graces to do it." With a nod, the lights went dark, all window shades drawn.

The projector lurched with a screech, the projectionist adjusting its focus. The footage was black-and-white, grainy, often blurred. Whiskey explained that much of it had been smuggled out of enemy territory. First a capsule history of the war, including the German bombing of Rotterdam, destroyed not for military reasons, explained Whiskey, but in revenge for Dutch resistance, and intended to annihilate the victims' will; the execution of Polish patriots en masse by a Nazi firing squad before a gaping cavernous grave; the brutal rounding up of Jews in Amsterdam, Vienna, Bucharest; the combined German and Russian carnage in Stalingrad, reduced to rubble in front of our eyes.

"Now for matters closer to home," our lecturer said. "The next stars you're about to see worked for one intelligence service or another— unfortunately some of our own. A lot of Brits. A Swede. A Greek girl working for the Russians."

What we saw now was unspeakable. Whether slashed to ribbons by knives, hung on lampposts, disfigured by human hands or machine-gun fire, the result was always the same—death. At the end, Whiskey's smile was gone. He merely gave a nod of dismissal.

Lucky and I walked out side by side. I was trembling, but making an effort to disguise my emotions, because I noticed the two officers, as well as Whiskey and Sphinx, observing each of us as we left through the one narrow door.

"Tiger, this work we are in could become pretty grisly," Lucky mumbled. He was especially shaken; no one else spoke.

———

Next we were directed to a room where a big, gangling man named George awaited us surrounded by safes and freestanding doors fitted with a variety of locks. All smiles, he said by way of introduction, "Before you get your hands on the enemy, you have to break into his house, ha-ha-ha. And I'm here to teach you exactly that. For once you've broken into his house, you can break into his safe. Hold out your hands." He examined the skin on the tips of our thumbs and forefingers. "Tsk, tsk. All virgins; that's easy to see." Laughter. He produced a file. "Now, every morning the first thing you'll do after you brush your teeth is to file the skin on your fingertips—thumb and forefinger will be sufficient—both hands. Why? To increase your sensitivity when trying to detect key markings on combination locks. Today's subject is a fine art—in my humble opinion, the finest there is."

That day George also taught us the techniques of picking door locks and pickpocketing.

Magic and I walked out together. This was the only opportunity to chat so far.

"Tiger, you've found your profession. You were terrific. My hands are like two left feet."

"It's George. He's a great teacher, and what a charming man!"

"Charming? He's what the Americans call a 'safecracker,' evidently the best in this country. They say he was broken out of jail just to teach us."

====

The handsome Pierre was by my side for the field exercises. He helped me enormously, because the tests were grueling. We climbed stone walls, waded through a muddy stream, crawled through weeds on our bellies. "Come on, Tiger." He knew my name! "Only two more hurdles to go. Don't get discouraged, and don't worry about not making it. You're doing fine."

When I couldn't move, he pulled or pushed me, until we completed the obstacle course. Our reward was Sphinx, waiting with arms crossed. Glumly he surveyed us, muddied, perspiring, gasping for breath. "Lousy. All of you. You'd never last a day in the field. Remember one thing— if you're not in top shape, exhaustion will make a coward out of you." He turned around, and I thought with relief that at least this test was over. Then, as he walked away, I heard, over his shoulder, "Okay, once more. Take it from the top."

Pierre and I traded winces. I was almost too exhausted to care that he was seeing me filthy and exhausted while he was apparently as fresh as when we began.

═══

After dinner we assembled in a sitting room; a visitor in a gray business suit and tie checked his wristwatch. "Make yourselves comfortable, friends. I'm just back from out in the field and have only one hour to tell you everything I know."

I leaned forward, fascinated.

"When working behind enemy lines, money is needed to recruit new agents. But beware. You'll be traced like a bitch in heat unless you master the finesse of such transactions. I'm here to teach you how to negotiate. Some agents blow their covers merely because they're tempted to squander their expense accounts too freely. If you can, when you recruit a subagent, the first rule is to defer payment until the end of the war. In case you haven't learned by now, the common proverb is true—everyone does have his price. And it isn't always money. It can be a guarantee of medical treatment, an immigrant visa, a job after the war.

"Just make sure the price isn't your life."

═══

I had not seen Pierre for several days, and then he turned up in front of me at the long lab table where we were concocting invisible inks. They were clear, traceless, impervious to heat, cold, and light; either dry powder, or alcohol- or water-based. Using one such powder encapsulated, Pierre stuck a toothpick into the capsule, then wrote on a sheet of paper brushed thoroughly clean with a wad of cotton. When he caught me watching, I blushed. He just smiled, went on with his note, and then handed his message to me. I began to develop it by sprinkling the paper with a red powdery compound containing ampthalene. Then I heated it over a lighter flame and exposed the sheet to a portable ultraviolet lamp. Letter by letter, Pierre's words swam into view.

Tiger, Have You Noticed This Isn't Washington—It's Hollywood! Rumors Circulate That There's A Former Nazi Spy Here. Do You Like Popovers For Breakfast?

Pierre

I read his message and realized immediately he was referring to Popoff, who seemed to be my roommate's closest pal. With her accent, Magic could be a German defector herself.

My turn to respond. First I mixed a most peculiar solution in an ink bottle—a yellow chemical, water, and schnapps! Then I dipped a pen into the mixture:

Pierre, there may be more than one. How about the following cast:

POPOVERS

THE TRUE STORY

Claude Raines. . . . . Popoff
James Cagney . . . . Whiskey
Boris Karloff. . . . . Sphinx
Shirley Temple . . . . Tiger
Charles Boyer . . . . Pierre

He treated my reply to the implausible solution of water and cigarette ashes, and as the letters began to appear I saw his amusement. When we walked out the lab door minutes later, he asked, "What about Magic? How can you forget our star?"

"Whom do you have in mind?"

Pierre retorted in a blink, "Norma Shearer."

I felt a pang of regret that I was not as sophisticated as my roommate, but Magic did resemble that famous actress, even to her manner of stalking into a room and her tone of voice. I had been very much aware that Pierre often sat next to Magic in the dining room and seldom made an effort to join me, yet he made himself charming and fun in a class we shared learning how to roll a newspaper into a point so fine that in lieu of a better weapon, it could function as a knife—if you pierced your foe in the soft fleshy recess under the chin. Skeptically, as we worked, Pierre looked at me. "It doubles as a tickler," he remarked under his breath. "Your victim dies laughing."

Chapter 4

After about ten days of close-combat classes, our skill was tested by assigning each of us an opponent from the more advanced students. Pierre was to be my adversary.

Closely, silently, we watched each other. The coach shouted the signal to begin. Instantly the field was full of gladiators. We stepped toward one another in our dance. Pierre lunged with the agility of a professional, his right arm grabbing me and hurling me to the ground. The bare trees loomed above my eyes.

I leaped to my feet. Although his next punch was light, it jabbed my ribs, robbed me of breath, flung me to the ground again. I lashed out with my left leg, but he moved back, and I missed. The pain was agonizing, but in one elastic motion I sprang to my feet and out of his range. Panting, sweating, I resolved to deal him at least one blow.

He was circling, stalking me—there was no time to think. Before I could edge nearer, his strong right leg and arm in expert jujitsu threw me flat on my back. Damn! Again I attempted to scissor my leg in a swift kick; but he skirted backward. I stumbled to my feet. Never give up . . . never.

Our eyes met. He was smiling! Easy triumph curled his mouth. Pierre closed in, ready to pounce, and I spun around as if to run. Now was my chance: that one staccato blow to the groin we'd been taught so well. With every ounce of remaining energy I gyrated to thrust my leg at him. His hands cupped my foot just short of its mark. Grazing my cheek, his other hand jerked back my shoulder—I tumbled to the ground.

I gazed up at the pale gray sky, drenched from head to foot. My breath, my strength were gone.

Pierre's face leaned over me. "Are you all right?" He was hardly out of breath. "An unfair match from the beginning. One I wouldn't choose, given the chance."

I heard my own breath rattle. I couldn't speak, but I nodded.

"You're doing fine, Tiger."

"Fine?" I breathed through my teeth.

"Why not? You almost made it. You're beginning to get the idea."

Looking up at him, I tasted salt.

"Your last kick was nearly lethal. Had I not expected it, you'd have disabled me."

Holding my hands, he lifted me to my feet. As he did our contact transmitted something sensuous—startlingly agreeable. I tried to hide my reaction, busying myself brushing off dirt, twigs, leaves. He watched until I turned away.

———

Each slide flashed for twenty seconds on the screen.

The first slide—a man's face. Beside it—name, age, occupation, place of residence. The second, another man. Four slides in all.

The first scene flashed on once more, this time only the face. I dredged my memory to quickly supply the corresponding data. Ten seconds later the second slide was repeated on the screen. And so on.

Then slides of maps. First designated by the names of strategic cities, towns, rivers, highways. But when the slides were replayed, the identical maps showed nameless terrain. The instructor's teaching stick tapped certain points on the barren maps—and it was up to me to recite the names.

Again and again these tests. What was impossible gradually became routine.

Twenty-one days straight without a break—twenty-one days from dawn to midnight, of being relentlessly trained, stretched, molded. The longest, hardest, most revolutionary days of my life. There were times I was so tired that telegraphing the Morse code and firing a machine gun sounded the same.

Then I was given one free day. I spent fourteen hours sleeping!

═══

The books were tightly packed in their shelves. Prying out one, I fumbled —it fell to the floor with a thud. I turned to descend the ladder. A hand lifted the book up to me.

"Yet another effective way to eliminate the enemy?" I hadn't seen Pierre come into the library. Again I experienced that feeling of—what could I call it?—awe mixed with a tense alertness.

He glanced at the title as I stepped down. Then at me. I wore a short wool dress and high heels, my hair in a low bun at the nape of my neck. For the second time in two weeks—it was the middle of November— we stood face to face. Only scattered lamps around the room emitted soft light. The coved ceiling loomed above us like a dome.

"What is your interest in France, exactly? Perhaps I can help you."

I hoped France would be my assignment, French being my foreign language. "I'm interested in studying the country's mountain borders," I replied, true in part.

"Oh, I say, you may have just blown your cover, but don't fret. I won't give you away."

"Worry about your own cover, Pierre. You make more slips than you think. This book, for example"—I shook the red-bound volume in front of his eyes—"may tell me something about you." I smiled sweetly as I edged closer to him and held him in my gaze. He appeared confused. "It's quite simple to uncover your secrets, if I care to."

He smirked to show his slight amusement with my childish remark.

Then I whipped my left hand in the air, displaying my trophy in the light—a waferlike leather cigarette case I had just extracted from his jacket pocket.

Pierre's astonishment flickered for a moment. Then he smiled. "From now on, I see I must keep my eyes on you."

Taking the book from me, he thumbed through it. "There is another with more detailed maps, which clearly charts mountain access routes by train and highway." Climbing up, then down the ladder, he brought it to me. We walked to a table and drew up two chairs.

"The Juras, the various Alps, the Pyrenees." He traced a tanned finger over their spines. "You'd be surprised what I used to shoot here." He pointed to the Loire Valley. Glancing up, "No, not that. Birds—pheasants —wild boar."

Just who was this man? I felt the gulf of our different worlds, our closeness, and the intensity of his gaze. He inhaled his cigarette and then said, "Did I give you that?"

I put my hand to the small bruise by my ear, the blue flesh still sore. "You were only doing your job," I said, "and you did it well." My body was covered with bruises. He gazed at my cheek as though he could heal by sight.

A familiar voice made me start. "Whiskey has been looking for you, Tiger." She threw me a glance.

"Thank you, Magic."

I stood up, wondering if Magic had a special interest in getting me away from Pierre. How could I tell her he meant nothing to me . . . especially since I had just realized he did.

―――

I could smell Whiskey's cologne, or was it his shaving lotion? Whatever, it was too strong and a mistake. Once or twice before I had known Whiskey was near because of that particular scent. I made a mental note never to use perfume. Was he doing this on purpose—to see if any of us would notice the danger of being identified by a familiar odor? I couldn't believe Whiskey would make a slip like this but dared not mention it.

Our chief was nearly engulfed by stacks of papers piled on his desk. A still life, a cornucopia with fruits and vegetables, hung on the wall behind him, probably a remnant of the former inhabitants of this beautiful old house.

"Ready for a couple of trial missions, Tiger?"

"You bet I am."

I sat down, leaning with both arms on his desk; perhaps these missions would decide my fate.

"Tomorrow morning at eight you'll be out front—for a day's excursion. You'll be driven to Union Station, from which you'll catch the twelve-o'clock Penn Central to Richmond, Virginia. You have six hours to deliver this message." Reaching over, Whiskey handed me a small vellum envelope. "Return to Washington on the five-o'clock train and you will be met at the station."

As I picked it up, I felt that Whiskey, our pal, was in abeyance—I was facing his great guns.

Next he scrawled something on a piece of paper. He held it up to my vision. "Memorize this." He crushed the paper into a wadded ball, pocketed it. There had been a name and an address. It sounded too simple. "Your objective is to deliver the envelope without its being . . . intercepted, confiscated."

I should have known. I'd be tailed.

In the station the next day I did the only thing that had occurred to me. Equipped with the carryall I'd brought into the lavatory, I emerged with the high collar of Magic's fur coat and the veil of my own toque concealing my face, in my Hattie Carnegie suit (its label excised) and high skinny heels. As I stepped out and walked toward the tracks I hoped I had changed my appearance sufficiently.

It didn't take long to see the man who had been trailing when I got on the train. And I had not fooled him! During an anxious twenty minutes, the train rolled on. Then the conductor passed through announcing Fredericksburg, the next station stop. I got up, walked in the direction of the lavatory, opened the door, and went in. Only when the train started to move out of the station did I open the door, rush for the steps, and jump off onto the platform. Finally I had slipped my tail. But how was

I going to get to Richmond in time? There was no train until four-thirty. No bus until later. I did not have enough money for a taxi, even if there had been one. With gasoline rationed, they were hard to find.

I hitchhiked. The address turned out to be a small hotel. When I asked for the man whose name I had memorized, the woman said he was not in, but was coming back at any moment. She then proceeded to chat—insistently. Where had I come from? Was I a relative? How long had I known the man? How long could I wait?

I did the best I could, but even after the woman had ceased questioning me, my troubles continued, because the time for the five-o'clock train back to Washington was drawing near. I knew I couldn't leave the envelope there—that was against the rules. At four forty-five, I left for the station, constantly checking to see if I was being followed. Several times I called the hotel, but not until eight minutes before five did the man—who identified himself correctly—answer the phone. I told him to go to the telephone booth I was in and look under the R pages for the envelope. Did he think it would be safe? He said that was an excellent solution, and I then ran, just barely catching the five-o'clock.

=====

The next time the routine was reversed; I had to follow a fellow. He seemed to disappear into thin air. Although I learned a lot, I failed that test completely.

=====

On a fresh-mown field close behind the main house sat a stack of wooden poles and blocks.

"Make an enclosure with those poles. You have a man to help you and just ten minutes to do it. Go."

As fast as I could—under the scrutiny of two psychiatrists—I started to construct a boxlike enclosure by fitting four wooden poles into the blocks. I saw that Sphinx was the person assigned to assist me. He stood around idly while I inserted three poles. But as soon as I'd thrust the fourth pole in place, Sphinx began to take out the others and toss them away.

It took only a moment to see what was up. His face was expressionless; only his tight eyes registered undisguisable glee.

Redoubling my efforts, I worked furiously—and got nowhere. Sphinx detached the poles quicker than I could join them, making a shambles of my efforts. After five minutes I'd had it. There was only one thing I could think of. Without waiting, I gyrated with the pole in my hand and delivered a swat to Sphinx that drove the little man to his knees. The next second I thought: Oh, God, what have I done? Yet it was a fun moment.

The two psychiatrists watched me like hawks—and time was running out. With a brief respite from Sphinx's interference I raced to rebuild the skeletal box, and when he began to menace my work I whirled to threaten him again. I was able to construct about half the structure—when I heard "Stop!"

One of the doctors—his spectacles were thicker than Magic's—motioned me over. With a coolness Freud himself might have applauded, he regarded me and said, "Your patience . . . leaves something to be desired."

I smiled.

"Fortunately you were also being tested for determination and stamina."

As I turned around I almost caught Sphinx smiling.

=====

"Your next mission is a bit more complicated, Tiger. You are supposed to get a job in a plane-parts factory outside of Pittsburgh without using any identification. Unfortunately you won't have the pleasure of enjoying it for more than forty-eight hours. During that time, however, you'll have procured a conspicuous envelope containing delicate information from the office safe." Whiskey gave me a roll of tracing paper. "These are blueprints of the office, including the safe location. Just use your initiative —you'll find a way to open it. By the way, here's the number to call if you land in jail."

Handing me a small white card, he saw my look of concern. "Don't worry, Tiger, we're getting the unlucky ones released all the time. They go to jail, we get 'em out. Bound to happen to you on one of these trips."

My trip to Pittsburgh was moderately successful. The security check admitted me without much difficulty, but I opened the wrong safe in the wrong office, which also set off an alarm. Nevertheless I returned to the Farm without a police escort. Whiskey said I only got a C-plus on that one.

===

I lowered the gun and peered at the target. Bull's-eye. Not a chance. The bullet had bored into a tree trunk next to the target. Damn! The .45 with its chunky butt made my grip ache. My muscles quivered; the backs of my knees, my buttocks also.

I broke position slowly, wiping thin drizzle from my eyes. After five weeks of training this was still my favorite lesson—the sounds, the smells, the sense of competition; one thing a woman could learn as quickly as a man. I sensed a presence behind me. Some yards off, Whiskey stood observing beneath an umbrella. Though the surrounding trees were nude, the sky, the clouds, the light itself were underwater green. He came over and scrutinized me.

I looked at myself. After morning exercises—push-ups and sit-ups on soggy fields—after jujitsu and now target practice, not only my clothes but my hands and face were caked with mud, dirt, and grass. Sweat steamed off me; my hair was streaming, loose strands pasted to my cheeks. Whiskey held the umbrella over us, his bulky frame close to me. How long had he been there? Long enough to witness my shots.

"Come back to the house, Tiger, and change. In an hour you're going to Washington. You have a meeting this afternoon with Jupiter."

Jupiter? Who was Jupiter?

I deposited my gun with the rangemaster and walked beside Whiskey under his umbrella. As we crossed the wet lawns he said, "By chance I happened to spot you horseback riding the other day. Where did you learn to ride like that?"

"On a horse."

Whiskey laughed. "Good. No slipups, Tiger. I ride, too. Maybe when the weather permits we'll take a ride together."

How strange that I should look up at that moment. We were near the house and I glanced at a bedroom window on the second floor. From it Pierre watched us approach the terrace.

=====

I smoothed my dress in the backseat, running my fingers up my legs to make sure my seams were straight. My suitcase was next to me. Whiskey had informed me that after my meeting with Jupiter I had a free weekend. The drive through country roads and the dismal weather affected my mood. I began to wonder if this meeting was a good sign or a bad one. Despite all I had gone through, had they decided I was not the one for the job?

It seemed strange to be back in a city, a hub of life, where streets were full, where traffic blared. The Farm was a bizarre dream. I was dropped in front of ugly, squat Q Building, then ushered by an aide waiting at the entrance into the office of—John Derby. Jupiter!

I tried not to appear worried. Nervously I adjusted an earring, sitting down in front of him. Having stood to greet me, Derby now sat. A smile crossed his face. "Well, Tiger, you've fared better than some of us expected."

There was a photograph—face up—on his desk. Jupiter saw my glance. A young woman who was emaciated, naked, and bloody implored her photographer with horrible eyes. Without a word he tilted the picture so I could see it clearer. "The SS having a field day," he drawled. It was all premeditated, I realized. Every move of Derby-Jupiter was measured, calibrated in advance.

Then he said softly, "Are you sure you're willing to risk your life, Tiger?"

"Yes."

"Then we have an assignment for you."

I waited. He paused. It seemed a long time. I held on to the chair.

"We need you in . . . Spain."

Spain? Is that what he said? My shock was total. France, yes. Sweden, Switzerland maybe, but I had never thought of Spain.

"Then I have passed the tests?"

"Yes, but you will need more preparation before we can send you over there. Apart from the normal routine, you will have to study up on your destination. In the library at the Farm there is abundant information on the countries where our agents will be sent. Be careful no one notices you are interested in Spain. You will have to pick two other countries and study them as well, so as to make it impossible for your colleagues to determine where you are going. You must become familiar with Spain's geography and history, and be able to recognize the current political personalities. By now your memory training should help you to absorb a surprising amount of material in a short time."

"Which of the five sections of OSS have I been assigned to?"

"You will be in SI—Secret Intelligence. But I cannot tell you what your mission will be. Only the worldwide chief of SI, Whitney Shepardson, can tell you that. Shepardson likes to explain personally the missions to his agents going into delicate situations. So you will have to wait until he's ready."

I wondered what it could be—my mission. No chance of parachuting into Spain. I was a bit disappointed.

"Is there any real excitement there?" I asked. My strenuous training had made me want an active mission. "I hope it won't be too soft." I was striving for clues.

He just laughed. "Don't worry. Believe me, the key to the success of the war is in Spain." He leaned back, interlacing his fingers under his chin.

"On the surface, the country declares itself neutral," Jupiter continued smoothly. "Politically, emotionally, it is aligned with Hitler. Spain is precarious, volatile. Franco won his civil war with German and Italian money, troops. And the country is still bleeding from its aftermath. One million Spaniards died in their war."

I had studied that devastating war in college and remembered that the

Spanish King Alfonso XIII, because of violent disturbances and to avoid bloodshed, had gone into exile in 1930. In 1931, elections brought to power communists, socialists, and anarchists, who, by 1936, had the country in such a state of unrest that the aristocracy, the Catholic church, and the fascist Falange party rebelled against the Republican government. The ensuing war, which had ended only three years before with gigantic human suffering, became the worst in Spain's long history.

Jupiter continued, "Spain is still a jumble of factions. Many of those Republicans who lost the war are diehard communists—some are our closest allies because of their hatred for the Germans and their alliance with Russia. For those reasons, we recruit subagents there only among those who were on that side."

I remembered that some brave Americans had volunteered to fight in Spain in that war—a group called the Abraham Lincoln Brigade. They, too, had been on the Republican side. It was confusing. Americans helping communists.

"Everything about Spain is pivotal for our war," he said. "The Germans obtain tungsten for their armament industry from northern Spain; they ship it in Spanish boats over the Bay of Biscay to France, from where it is transported by rail into Germany. Without that, their arms factories would be in trouble. The safety of our troops in North Africa and those now being sent to Italy depends upon Spain's maintaining its neutrality. There is always the possibility Franco could join Hitler. Imagine how disastrous that would be!

"Also, two invasions of the Continent are being planned right now. One is for the north, and one for the south. The Germans are mighty worried about exactly where those invasions will take place. OSS Spain will be responsible for the southern attack. The outcome of the war hinges on those invasions.

"Then there are other reasons Spain is important. Admiral Canaris, the head of German intelligence, the Abwehr, is a close friend of Franco and visits him regularly. Himmler is trying to discredit Canaris with Hitler, claiming Canaris influences Franco not to join the Axis. We are anxious that Himmler not eliminate Canaris from his job because our agents in other countries inform us that Canaris is backing plots to assassinate Hitler. Ironic, isn't it?" Jupiter chuckled. "To be protecting the head of our enemy's intelligence service?"

I was digesting his information as well as I could. Although confused, I realized Spain could be the exciting assignment I had been hoping for.

Chapter 5

Only when the train was churning out of Union Station did I have time to think of the future. Jupiter's briefing had changed the direction of my life—pointing it toward Spain. I savored its tantalizing appeal as I stood in the small entrance to the coach, looking out absently at the buildings flashing by. Finally, I began to walk unsteadily through the rocking train and entered the first, almost-empty compartment. The only occupant was peering intently out the window. I placed my suitcase on the floor and sat down. Then I had a shock.

Was he incredulous, too? If so, he showed no emotion, but for a spark in his eyes. Pierre asked, "Would you like me to put your suitcase on the rack?"

"Oh, no." I jumped up. "I'll have to go to another coach. You know we're not allowed to speak to colleagues outside the Farm."

He grabbed my valise and stowed it above. "Don't worry about that. Nobody we know is on this train." He sat down and lit a cigarette. "Are you following me, Tiger?"

My expression caused him to laugh heartily. I didn't know what to do and remained standing. Abruptly he pulled me down to the seat next to him.

"What are you doing here?" I said without moving.

"And you?" He gave me his sly, sinuous smile.

Barren trees shot by. The locomotion continued to rock us. I had to say something—anything. "Do you think we will finish our training before the war is over?"

Totally composed, he said, "Naturally, I don't see any end in sight."

"But we're winning," I retorted, trying to reclaim self-possession.

"We're still climbing the mountain," he contradicted. "Italy is a disaster. German armament production is at an all-time high. The whole Pacific is ahead of us. And then there's Stalin."

"Stalin?" It was impossible—he never took his eyes off me.

"Stalin is insatiable," he replied. "And Russia inexhaustible. Determined to become the world's next empire."

"Empires are finished. The war has seen to that."

"What an optimist you are, Tiger."

"What a pessimist you are, Pierre."

"We're very different," he declared simply.

I don't know why—I felt regret.

"I've wanted to be alone with you for a long time." He leaned toward me. The light on the wall of the compartment glowed, making a yellow sheen behind his head.

Pierre heard steps in the hallway and leaned back. We gave the conductor our tickets, and before he closed the door, a disheveled woman with a child in her arms installed herself in our compartment. A minute later, an Army officer entered. They sat across from us the remainder of the trip.

Pierre and I did not exchange another word until hours later, when the train drew into Pennsylvania Station.

He stood up and reached for my suitcase. The others were putting on their coats; the child whined. Pierre whispered, "You will have dinner with me?"

I knew I couldn't, but I regretted it. "I can't." The confidence invested in me these last six weeks held me back.

"Don't be ridiculous," he said moodily.

I looked at him. His expression was indecipherable. Just as we were about to step off the train, I grabbed my valise from his hand and dove into the throng, running, bumping everyone in my path.

═══

On Sunday night I was back at the Farm, but Pierre was not. He had not returned late Monday either when I began my last class of the day.

Blindfolded, I groped and fumbled with the revolver, disassembling it piece by piece, hammer, barrel, muzzle, heel. It had an acrid, metallic smell. When it was completely disassembled, Sphinx scattered the parts around me. Then, trying to put it back together as fast as possible, I dropped the empty clip—it banged on the wooden floor. Groping sightlessly while Sphinx looked on, I finally retrieved it and proceeded. Would I ever have to assemble a revolver in the dark in Spain? When he made me repeat the process, I slowed down and was more successful. Sphinx had told us, "Control your nerves, and your head and hands will do the work they're supposed to."

=====

The sound awakened me from a dead sleep—what was it? At first I thought Magic was talking to someone else in the room. I got up and tiptoed to her bed. She was babbling to herself in her sleep, her voice eerie, full of fear and anger, bordering on hysteria—in German or Polish. I couldn't tell. She repeated something like "sorg-liet." Gently I shook her shoulder. She sat up with a start, letting out a pitiful wail.

"You're all right. Just dreaming." I switched on the lamp next to her bed. She breathed deeply.

"Thanks, Tiger. I get these nightmares ever since—" She caught herself in time. "Sorry to wake you. I hope you'll never have to go through some of the experiences I have had."

I knew that night Magic had been someplace terrifying. I suspected she had been in Europe near the trouble and that each day she was probably making a valiant effort to appear carefree. Her tenacity and good humor became another incentive for me to withstand the grueling regimen.

=====

Sitting at the table in front of a small electrical box, I was trying to concentrate as best I could on learning Morse code. After that I received lessons in ciphering. We were told code rooms were off-limits for everyone except the code clerks in OSS offices abroad, since they handled all messages relayed to and from Washington. After focusing on the combination of letters and memorizing many, we each had to choose a personal code—a piece of prose or poetry—in case we ever had to transmit a message outside normal channels.

I worked on the Morse, juggling the tiny lever till my wrist ached, then practiced coding until I thought I couldn't absorb another letter. I found myself repeating letters over and over, trying to inscribe them on my brain. Memory was all-important, and we were taught how to improve it through such devices as associating picture images with numbers. With perseverance, this became my best class, the one in which I most excelled.

=====

This time on my belly, in the windy fields, flanked by my group, waiting for another machine-gun lesson to commence. My hands were frigid—why hadn't I worn gloves? Behind me footsteps crunched leaves.

"Let me show you." Pierre dropped to the ground beside me.

One full week of anguish—I hadn't seen him since that night on the train. In that moment, I was happy again—merely because he was there, lying beside me on the cold ground, so close. "Don't worry; I'll teach you. You're not going to miss a bull's-eye, not once. I'll do the reloading."

With Pierre at my side, it was easy. He was expert at everything. In front, yards away, bullets riddled the target, right on center. The wind whipped the mown fields. After six rounds, I turned to him. "Did you come merely to improve my aim?" My defenses were under control again.

"I've been away at another training camp, and I'm leaving for good in a few days. I suspect you get a free weekend Friday. Please meet me in New York on Sunday morning, eleven o'clock, at the Plaza Hotel, the entrance in front of the square. It will be my last opportunity to see you."

I started to protest.

"No excuses," he said. "You wouldn't want me to think you are afraid. Would you?"

=====

That week, the strain was beginning to tell. The remaining nine men in my group—Lucky and two others were gone—looked haggard; I did also. Thursday night we had an "uncover" session, orchestrated by Whiskey and Sphinx to discover security risks. The object was for us to unmask our colleagues. By turns, we were each in the "hot seat," grilled pitilessly.

Whiskey and his assistant had selected three of the most advanced— and sharpest—recruits for me to face. They couldn't have chosen more formidable and less desirable foes: Pierre, Popoff, and the Farm's own uncover queen, who stole the show every time she performed—my roommate.

It was Magic who now surveyed each of us as though prepared to disrobe the entire group on the spot. "Well, well, well." She smiled, licking her lips. "What could be more fun than to expose one's dearest friends?" Her gaze abruptly concentrated on the oldest participant. *"You, Popoff, I know as well as the back of my hand."* She waved to him.

Whiskey half smiled, while Sphinx remained characteristically true to his name. Pierre had turned to stone, but the mild man across from Magic chirped sweetly, "No, you don't."

Magic sighed regretfully. "Do you like tulips, Popoff?"

"Tulips?" He bent his ear forward with a finger, as though to hear better.

"Tulips," Magic emphatically repeated. "You know. Those lovely bulbs that bloom in such profusion every spring. In Holland. Particularly near The Hague. The estate called Park Zorgvliet must be a garden of earthly delights in the spring, huh, Popoff?"

I looked at my roommate with incredulity. What was she talking about? Then I remembered the night she had been dreaming. Those were the words she repeated—"Park Zorgvliet." Now I had no doubts about Magic's having been "over there" during this war. Maybe she had come from Europe directly to the Farm. That would explain those foreign-looking shoes and clothes.

Magic didn't wait for an answer. "Tell us, my dear Popoff, about Agent School West, the best German spy school in Europe."

"Wrong," Popoff declared.

"Wrong?" The queen regarded her prey with satisfaction.

"What makes you think I'm German? Could it be that birds of a feather . . . ? My guess is your youth was spent near Leipzig. Perhaps as the daughter of a famous concert pianist who conducted some of Hitler's favorite symphonies? Who was denounced to the Nazis for helping Jews flee Germany?"

"Your imagination, my dear Popoff, is boundless, and a delightful fiction." Nevertheless, the star had faltered a little. *"Everybody* knows, Popoff, so what is the use of hiding it? How did you feel when you defected? Why did you do it?"

"You're psychic. You tell me." The little man seemed to have lost some of his cheer. "Were those *your* motives when *you* escaped?"

I wondered if they had really known each other over there. Probably they were both guessing, but there was no doubt that each had much knowledge of what happened abroad. That left me out of the game for the time being.

"Tell us about those tulips, Popoff—and stop beating around the bush."

"A bird in the hand is worth two in the bush, my dear Magic," Popoff replied. "Just what do you know about Pierre?"

Somewhat repentant, perhaps, she looked at the handsome foreigner. "Rich. Very rich."

"As rich as Tiger?" volleyed Pierre, speaking for the first time.

And for the first time also, the star considered me. Not unkindly, I thought. "Richer."

"Just where is Tiger from, do you think?" Pierre now asked.

I stiffened.

"Rhode Island," Magic decreed.

"Ohio," said Popoff.

"Manhattan," corrected Pierre. "Or thereabouts."

"An only daughter," Magic informed them.

"Of a banker." Pierre looked at me. "She was educated abroad, in Switzerland."

"No wonder she speaks fluent German," Popoff surmised. "She'll be dropped by parachute into the Rhineland!"

This was blindman's buff, being played with words. I looked at each of them in turn. "How did you all know?"

"It was nothing," said Popoff with a toss of his hand.

"Speak up, Tiger," Whiskey now ordered. "What do you think of these characters?"

I didn't possess subtle aptitudes for exposing my companions' identities, but I now felt confident that I had at least managed to conceal my own. I turned to Magic. "You're—Austrian. Popoff is right. You've been involved in something frightening."

She looked back. "Maybe someday after the war I'll tell you."

"Popoff, I've heard you were . . . you are . . . a . . . former German spy?"

"So young." Popoff shook his head. "And so ignorant."

I faced Pierre, trying to hide my agitation. "You're Belgian. A playboy who likes to shoot—anything."

He grinned. "Go on."

"You're the one who's going to be parachuted behind enemy lines, where I think you've already been."

Now it was Pierre's turn. "I've been watching Magic—very closely."

The queen responded with a quick bat of her eyelashes.

"Magic is unmistakably a woman . . . of valor and very feminine. I recognize a Flemish accent. She would have learned English at the University of Brussels around 1938. I believe she has been married—to a German army officer, because she carries a German army insignia in her handbag."

It was no mistake—our highness colored. I wondered when Pierre had gone through the bag she always kept locked.

Magic glared at Pierre.

"I hope her affairs of the heart don't interfere with her affairs of the moment," Pierre added.

"Love is a game, just like this one, my dear Pierre. You know that better than I."

"Touché!" Whiskey beamed. "The party's over," he announced as he stood up.

Were we learning too much? I wondered. Some of those guesses must have been close to the truth.

=====

Sunday, Pierre was late. I stood in front of the Plaza Hotel hoping the wind wasn't making a mess of my pageboy hairdo, shivering in what I considered my smartest outfit, a blue tweed Carnegie suit with matching cape and hat. Finally I saw him weaving through the traffic, a beige polo coat hanging from his shoulders. Soldiers, officers, bellboys with bulky packages kept obscuring my view.

He raised my hand to his lips, his eyes warming mine. When he took my arm, pulling me close, and we started to walk, my qualms about breaking rules evaporated entirely. And after all, he had said he had only this one day to see me before going overseas. He might be killed. I might never see him again.

"Do you feel guilty about meeting me today?"

"Naturally. I don't like breaking rules."

"They chose you well, Tiger." His eyes were smiling, but he suddenly looked unhappy.

"Not at all. I wouldn't be here if I were the perfect agent."

"You're not going to worry about that now. We have only five hours together." He directed our steps toward the park. But the spell was broken, and we walked in silence for some time, wrapped up in our separate thoughts.

"Come, Tiger," he pleaded. "This is not the proper way to help a chap have a good time in his last moments of freedom."

I looked at him and felt sad. His mission would probably be far more dangerous than my own. He was certainly going to be behind enemy lines —in danger every moment. I smiled.

"Look," he said, "I've always dreamed of seeing an American Indian. How about going to that museum across this park, where I've been told there are hundreds. Not very talkative ones, but anyhow I only want to talk to you."

No shadow lurked for the rest of the day; sheer joy seemed to spark off in each of us at the same moment.

We had lunch at the Stork Club, a first for me. Champagne. Another first. The sharp, dry bubbly appeared at the same moment Pierre withdrew from his jacket pocket a red, beribboned Cartier box. He placed it in front of me on the table.

"Open it," he said.

I untied the ribbon. Resting on a black velvet lining was a ring—a twisted knot of gold encircling a single sparkling blue sapphire, and a set of identical earrings. Intently I looked at Pierre, screening that marvelous face for an explanation. "I don't think I can accept such a valuable gift."

"Of course you can. I want you to remember me."

"I'll remember you no matter what. And, who knows, we may even meet over there. After all, we are in the same business."

"Put them on."

Shyly, I extracted the ring. It fit perfectly. Then I put on the earrings.

Before I could react further, Pierre stood up and took me to the dance floor. From someplace there was music, just enough, playing softly. The season's hit, "As Time Goes By." It was about four o'clock in the afternoon and we were almost alone. Until then dancing for me had been mostly jitterbugging at college hops, one sweaty face next to the other. Pierre held me close, his arm tight around my waist. His cheek barely touching mine felt like satin.

We were both close to missing our trains, mine from Pennsylvania Station to Washington and his leaving from Grand Central to—I dared not ask where. In the street he hailed a cab. As I turned to say good-bye, he started to raise my hand to his lips and then dropped it; he pressed me to him and we kissed.

Chapter 6

W e ducked under branches as our horses cantered through the woods. "I have some odd news for you, Tiger."

I pulled up short, my horse whinnying.

Whiskey viewed me uncertainly. "You're going to Washington again today."

Why? It was only two days after Pierre had left and I was already depressed enough. The smell of the horses, the wintry mold of leaves beneath my feet, reeked suddenly in my nostrils. I reined in my horse, close to Whiskey. "Why is that odd?" Already fear stabbed my chest.

"Because this time you're going to see the big boy, Shepardson." He dismounted. I followed suit. "Maybe it means you're on your way. Or maybe something's gone wrong. Anything unusual happen lately?"

"Nothing." Did they know about my date with Pierre?

With the reins in our hands, we traipsed through the grove of trees, spraying leaves with our boots.

"You still should have at least two more weeks here," said Whiskey pensively. "Shepardson never sees people until they have finished training. I don't understand. It is unusual."

Again, the long drive to Washington. . . . The bleak landscape of early December underscored my apprehension. I thought of Pierre. This Chevrolet sedan was the same that had brought both of us to the Farm that September day.

The minute I saw Jupiter, I knew everything would go well. He was enthusiastic as he stood up to welcome me.

"I guess this is our last meeting, Tiger. You're on your way."

I gave a sigh, a surge of relief.

Jupiter grinned. "You certainly wanted to get into the war badly that night I met you at my brother's house. Well, you're in it and you've earned your way. Here's what you're going to do."

Jupiter and I sat facing each other. I felt, for the first time, prepared.

"You're one of the key persons we're using to ensure that when Operation Anvil—the invasion of southern Europe—takes place, there will be nothing the Germans are doing we don't know about. Also, you will help us befuddle them about our plans."

How could I accomplish such things?

"Tiger, we've got a lot of other people out there. Some may be working with you and you won't even know it. But I assure you the job we have picked for you is critical. If you bungle, you can mess up the work of a number of other agents and the landings could be a disaster. Have I made myself clear?"

Nothing was clear. Nevertheless, I nodded.

"When I met you in New York, I had just come back from one and a half years in Spain. I'm the guy who recommended you for this role, and I'm still the guy. You fit into the scenario as if made for the part. But if you fail, it'll be my failure also."

The significance of his words sank in. What a responsibility John Derby was putting on my shoulders. He must have read my mind. "You're not having second thoughts?"

"No. I'm scared, excited, but dying to go. I just hope you haven't overestimated me."

"Look, Tiger. You've done a hell of a job at the Farm. You'd never be sent if we didn't know you were capable. I'm proud of you." He paused. "Okay, that rolls it up. Shepardson is waiting for you now. He's the one who gives the final briefing."

He picked up the telephone. "Whitney, I have Tiger in my office. She's on her way."

Jupiter put down the receiver. "Quick. Everybody's in a hurry today. Down the hall to the end, then right."

I rushed along the corridor, rubbing my lipstick off on the back of my hand. My brown tweed suit and oxfords had been selected to help me look serious and older when I met the famous Whitney Shepardson. At the Farm I had heard that this was the man who held the most power in OSS after General Donovan.

The chief of Secret Intelligence, distinguished, heavyset, silver-haired, stood as I was ushered into the room, walked around the table and the huge American flag, and shook my hand. He directed me to a corner.

"Please take a chair, Miss Griffith."

I hadn't heard that name in a long time.

"I hope you will speak to me freely. Personal contact with my agents is worth ten of these reports." He indicated the papers in his hand. "You have made an excellent impression on your teachers." He offered a cigarette. I declined. After lighting his own, he said, "Tell me just why you are so anxious to get into this war—in a perhaps hazardous situation."

His charming manner and calm voice put me at ease.

"Mr. Shepardson, every boy I know is in, including two of my brothers —both younger than I. Naturally, I love my country as much as they do and I am just as willing to risk my life. It's not fair that only men should be allowed to fight for this great country." I paused.

He smiled. "You'll have plenty of opportunity to do something for your country, Miss Griffith. Perhaps more than you realize. The job you have been selected for is vital. Too dangerous to entrust to a woman so young. But ironically, that is one of the reasons you are our candidate." He studied me. I wondered if he was changing his mind. "Listen carefully."

He needn't have said that. I was already on the edge of my chair.

"A contact inside the Gestapo in Berlin informs us that Himmler has one of his most capable spies operating out of Madrid, running a network —a particularly effective one—for uncovering Allied plans related to Operation Anvil. Your mission is to discover who that person is. Our Berlin agent has given us the names of four people in Madrid, one of whom he believes is the person we're looking for. All move at a level of international society which precludes easy surveillance. We need an agent there who can fit into that group."

He took a slow drag on his cigarette. "We hope you are the one."

I waited silently, then jerked inadvertently when two of the telephones on his desk began to ring at the same time. Mr. Shepardson walked across the room and picked up both phones. "No calls for the next ten minutes, please."

When he sat down again, he pulled his chair closer.

"One of our agents will meet you on arrival in the Palace Hotel in Madrid. He'll introduce you to a few people and give you advice. In Spain no one expects a woman, much less a young girl, to be doing anything of that type. But you must realize your enemy will be clever and dangerous. Fortunately, you have been well prepared in self-defense. If you find yourself in a tight spot—" He paused and shook his head in a manner that encouraged me to ask.

"You're implying that I should kill an opponent if necessary?" I hoped my voice sounded properly nonchalant.

A trace of compassion crossed Shepardson's face.

"You can eliminate the enemy in any way convenient at the moment. Regrettably, history knows of no more satisfactory solution. We don't have to like it. We just have to do it."

I looked at Whitney Shepardson without speaking.

"Are you willing to give it a try?" he asked.

My throat was parched. My words almost stuck in it. "Oh, yes."

"You'll get to see a *corrida de toros.*"

I looked blankly.

"A bullfight," he explained. "You'll have to improve your Spanish."

I nodded.

His smile expanded. "As a matter of fact, that's what I call your mission."

I was still blank.

"Operation Bullfight. Your chief in Madrid will inform you about the four suspects when you arrive."

"I'll do my best, Mr. Shepardson. When do I leave?"

"Young lady, almost immediately. You'll be working against time."

He smiled encouragingly. "Your cover will be the American Oil Mission, which is the same for many of our agents there, although we have others using the cover of international companies with offices in Spain. Tell your family and friends to write you through your APO number. All letters you send will be censored."

All Shepardson said when I left was "God bless you."

———

For three days and three nights I waited in a room on the fifteenth floor of the Biltmore Hotel in the middle of Manhattan. Only Jupiter and Shepardson knew where I was. My orders had been "Don't leave the room until we call." I had been given a number-one priority and would be on the first plane leaving for Europe. The fact that I had been assigned to one of the famous Pan American flying boats, the only air service across the Atlantic, underscored the importance of my assignment.

Wrapped in a blanket in the chair next to the window, I watched the snow drifting softly and looked down at the Christmas Eve traffic jams and endless scurrying below. Then night came and Manhattan faded into a blackout, its shadowy silhouettes becoming ominous.

I remembered things I hadn't thought about for years. Especially my childhood, when Pearl River, only thirty-eight miles north of New York City, had been a really small town. My mother was born there, but my grandparents came from the Midwest. My father's family had been farmers in Maryland. Except for my grandmother Griffith, my ancestors were American "way back."

My mother had been indignant when I told her I was leaving for Spain to work in the Oil Mission. "Absolutely a sin for a young woman to travel so far and to live alone," she complained. Ever since I could remember, sin had been a preoccupation in our family. When I was four years old, I was punished for taking a pear from Mrs. Maloney's yard, despite the fact that it had already fallen to the ground. At about the same period Joe Kohler, who lived nearby, used to say "shit" all the time. When I copied him, that was another sin and my mother washed my mouth with soap.

Hemingway's *For Whom the Bell Tolls* occupied me for a while, but then I went back to daydreaming. I knew I was leaving for a long time and might not come back. Those summer days when I was about eight years old, we used to pick violets in the woods. Then the Sundays when we walked up the hill to Grandma Griffith's house, where she served us delicious long strips of coffee cake at the kitchen table. . . .

I loved that cake and her and those moments. Once I made the mistake of buying several bright red balls of chewing gum. But they turned out to be sinful, too. "Only hussies chew gum," Grandma said. What were *hussies*? I wondered, and longed to see one.

When I came in, whistling, Grandma called, "Aline, stop that noise. A whistling woman and a cackling hen never came to any good end."

Now I was wondering what kind of end I might come to when, like a bullet, the phone rang. It was eleven-thirty, the end of the third night.

=====

It was pitch-black. The only sounds were waves slapping the moldy wooden platform. Down below a motor's whining drone. I'd been driven across Manhattan, then through numerous foggy streets to the foggy end of an empty wharf. A chapped-faced man in a woolen cap materialized out of the fog.

"We've been waiting for you, miss," he wheezed. With one hand I clutched my handbag, with the other I accepted his assistance down a ladder into a launch. The beam of his flashlight revealed two figures; one tall man stood up just as the boat lurched forward, hurling us both onto the opposite bench.

"More dangerous than the front line," he joked. "Are you all right?" On the shoulder of his greatcoat were the four silver stars of a full general. I nodded and smiled. The craft skimmed the choppy water. The bitter wind encouraged me to turn up my coat collar and pull my hat down. In no time we pulled up to a shadowy hulk and stepped onto a gangplank.

Inside was a huge salon like those on ocean liners, drapes and carpets, polished hardwood paneling, with upholstered sofas, armchairs, and a bar at one end. We were thirty-two on board. I had been told that was the maximum for transatlantic flights. The Pan American Clipper floated like a duck on the sea as the general escorted me through the cabin. Three men rushed to his side; none were in uniform. "What kind of secret weapon have you here, General?" asked one.

"Don't even know her name, Russ. But I have no doubt you'll find out."

A steward announced takeoff. The man called Russ guided me to an upholstered armchair, sitting down in one facing mine. We fastened our seatbelts. One by one, the engines roared. The plane began to move, gaining momentum as it plowed through the water. With a shattering sound, wobbling from bow to stern, the flying boat lifted and slowly surged into the air.

No sooner had we ascended than a voice from behind said, "Russ, you and the lady are invited to dine with us, at the general's request."

I couldn't believe my eyes. The man with the white carnation from the Biltmore so many months ago!

Russ spoke up. "Larry Mellon, this is . . ."

"Aline Griffith," I mumbled.

Larry Mellon warmly shook my hand. "A pleasure to meet you, Miss Griffith." We followed him to an upper deck to a room resembling the dining coach in a train, but much better, and took seats at a table gleaming with crystal and starched white damask. Larry Mellon and the general sat across from a fellow who was introduced as Bill Casey.

As I took a seat next to the general, a steward appeared. "Two and a half hours to Bermuda, gentlemen. After refueling there, we go directly on to Lisbon."

I was amazed, since the last two weeks had been filled with shots against diseases that ranged from sleeping sickness to malaria and the black plague. I turned to the general. "My trip to Europe was planned to route through Brazil and Morocco. The number of visas in my passport make it look like an accordion."

The general explained, "The route is changed for extra precaution. The Germans attack everything crossing the Atlantic. Not long ago, they downed a plane from Lisbon with Leslie Howard aboard. They were after a friend of mine, an English general. Unfortunately, he was a friend of Howard's, too. We suspect the German agents were able to trace his whereabouts because of the movie star's publicity." The general shook his head. "Flights in and out of Lisbon have lost several planes."

"We shouldn't frighten our only lady on board," Larry Mellon observed.

"I watched this young lady during takeoff, and I don't think she frightens easily," Bill Casey remarked. "I'd be more worried if I were you, General, going back to the front."

Chapter 7

Lisbon lay below, dazzling in a diamond horseshoe of lights. It was as if we were arriving at a gigantic party in full swing; gaiety seemed to beckon in the velvet night from the shimmering bay. Perhaps it was the contrast with the blackout in the United States or that this was my first plane trip, but I was spellbound as I stood in the captain's cockpit watching the Clipper descend onto the water, splitting the waves into peaks of creamy froth.

Motorboats manned by jabbering Portuguese in long red-tailed woolen caps transported us to the dock.

"Look!" Larry Mellon pointed to some rowboats nearby. "The Japanese. Their intelligence center operates out of Lisbon and Madrid. When a Pan Am Clipper crashed a month ago, the Japs were cruising the wreckage before anyone could get to the scene, picking up pouches destined for Allied embassies, leaving wounded passengers to drown while salvaging top-secret documents. Beware," he said, seriously. "Under Lisbon's frivolity lurks a city of deadly intrigue."

He had informed me that his orders were to present the new agent to the SI staff in Portugal before I went on to Madrid.

A taxi took us along the coastal highway to the Hotel Palacio in Estoril, about half an hour away. While the reception clerk thumbed through passports, I marveled at the ornate carpet, the Louis XVI furniture, the antique baroque wall clock, the quality and elegance of the old world.

Larry glanced at his watch. "Can you change into evening clothes in twenty minutes? I must go to the casino, and you should see it, too."

The idea of seeing a casino charmed me, and I was dressed in fifteen minutes flat.

The gambling palace's bronze-embossed mahogany entrance doors were attended by footmen in livery. Inside the scene was breathtaking, because of the sheer scale of its opulence. From cavernous ceilings, crystal chandeliers were suspended on ropes of bronze poised above a bank of game tables. Enormous arched windows were cloaked with fringed burgundy velvet; red carpeting absorbed our steps. The clatter of chips and whirr of roulette wheels could be heard as we entered.

"Prenez vos places. Rien ne va plus," the croupiers shouted. Muffled voices spoke in many tongues. Larry pointed to the Japanese milling about. "Again, watch those fellows. Here in Lisbon they receive information about troop departures from seaports on our West and East coasts, which is relayed to Tokyo and Berlin. The Japanese have an excellent worldwide espionage network. They're contacting agents here in the casino, picking up messages, including dates and hours transmitted by the numbers played at the roulette table—right under our noses."

By now we were next to a chemin de fer table, where eight players were seated and over twenty stood watching, some in evening dress, others quite shabbily clothed.

"Never speak audibly near a game table," whispered Larry. "Gamblers are superstitious, especially when the stakes are high. There are over ten thousand dollars in escudos and chips on that table right now."

A plump lady in red lace with a diamond-and-ruby brooch pinned above her monumental bosom was about to pull cards from a wooden box in front of her. A red-nailed finger slid card after card over the green felt surface, facedown—two for her opponents and two for herself.

"A gut-grabbing game," Larry murmured. "Not to be compared to roulette. The winner is the one whose cards add nearest to nine, not more. Kings, queens, and jacks count zero. Aces, one. Look, she's turned up one of her two cards—a three. Now the opponent has the chance of deciding if he wants a third card." A hush engulfed the group. "Ah, he's having difficulty making up his mind." Larry's whisper was getting louder. "He probably has five, maybe even six." The player gave a minute negative shake of his head. "See, I was right. He doesn't want to take the chance. Another card may raise his count over nine." I watched as the lady pulled a third card for herself.

"That's Madame Lubescu, and the jewels she is wearing represent all that is left of an enormous fortune given her by King Karol of Rumania. If she loses tonight—!"

My eyes were glued to the pile of chips. Would she win? After a split second, she flung the cards down on the green felt with an obvious sigh of relief—echoed by the surrounding crowd. Her opponent got up without a word, and she waited until the croupier shoveled the chips and bills into a neat mound in the center of the table. Her hand wavered over the box for a moment. She was tempted to try again. If she won she could double her money. Slowly she began to slide the chips into her purse. Most of us watched as the bills were stuffed in also. Then she stood up and left.

We wandered through the game rooms for a while, Mellon scanning the faces. Then he guided me down a wide corridor to the WonderBar, the nightclub "famous," he said, "for its cuisine." At midnight the crowd was at its peak and every table was taken; the floor was filled with couples moving to the music of a rumba band.

After a few minutes at the long crystal bar, we were seated near the dance floor. Larry leaned close. "The man dancing with the lady in the silver dress. You'll be seeing a lot of him in the future. That's Top Hat, one of the best agents we've got."

My first impression was: Top Hat the cat. He was sleek and feline; thick eyebrows and a narrow mustache gave him a slippery air. His glamorous partner was obviously enjoying his conversation.

"One of Mr. Top Hat's attributes appears to be his charm for women," I commented.

"Charm?" Larry returned dryly. "He doesn't just charm them—he slays them."

After dinner, we strolled back toward the game rooms through the high-ceilinged hall, chatting about the contrasts with life at home. Suddenly the piercing shriek of a terrified woman resounded through the wide corridor. In an instant the scene before us became a bedlam of people running. Larry sprinted ahead, and I followed just as fast. By the time we reached the end of the long passageway, a crowd was gathering around something on the red-carpeted floor. I stared down at the crumpled body of a man lying facedown. Larry, who was just to my right, gripped my arm. Then I saw why. A knife protruded from the center of the man's black dinner jacket! We remained frozen. More screams from behind us. A woman fainted. Kneeling down, Larry felt the man's pulse while the crowd pushed and shoved to get a better look. It had happened too fast for me to digest its meaning—the scene had the unreality of opera. Then my companion turned the body over, just enough to see the face.

The ashen countenance of the stricken man confronted me. Color had faded from the big nose and jowls. Mellon appeared struck by a revelation. I knew in that moment that Larry recognized the man on the floor.

What snapped, there and then? What delusion of mine? This was the difference between textbook medicine and the operating room. The contorted face, frozen in pain, awoke me to the reality of what I was in for. Blood now was staining the thick carpeting, beading my black satin pumps with tiny droplets. When I looked up, a mass of bewildered faces —ladies in jewels, some of the uniformed staff, and a few croupiers— were staring.

Straightening, Mellon braced his hands on my shoulders and pivoted me around, propelling me with an energetic stride through the crowded hall toward the entrance.

"Is he dead?"

"Very much so."

"Do you know him?"

"Of course not. Come on, we can't get involved."

"How can we not get involved? Won't we be questioned?"

"Aline, where do you think we are? Wake up—this is Lisbon. The only thing anybody in there cares about is getting rid of the body so they can get back to the tables. Some of those gamblers may look opulent, but most of them are betting tomorrow's breakfast."

On the ride back, each in our own worlds, we barely spoke. I was thinking how fast death can come. The sumptuous hotel lobby was deserted, and the ancient clock above the concierge's desk ticking its steady monotone marked three-thirty. Mellon left me at my door. "Try to put it out of your mind, Aline—get some sleep. Wait for my call in the morning."

I nodded.

In my room I opened the balcony doors and listened to the ocean splash in the distance, saw a few straggling lights flashing like beached stars. The cold moonless night brought me back thirty hours to a Brooklyn pier. Already my universe had changed. I had tasted the excitement, but also the horror. Nevertheless, I was able to sleep soon afterwards. Was it fatigue or my new callousness?

=====

The next day Larry avoided any reference to the night before as we careened along the rugged ocean highway to Lisbon.

Soon the road sprouted tributaries—the snaky narrow streets that braided the steep hills of pink-and-dusty-beige Lisbon. In a cobblestoned square near the docks, fishermen and their wives were selling shiny codfish from crude stands of wooden crates, the men in baggy black corduroy trousers and blouselike jackets, the women in ankle-length skirts, fringed black shawls, and black head scarves. A few cars circulated, but many people thronged the streets on foot, and a small red trolley rattled by.

Just in front of a fortress rising in craggy splendor above the bay, Larry told the taxi driver to stop. Paying him, we got down and walked toward a side street. He pointed to the large structure above us. "That was one of the few buildings to withstand the earthquake of 1755. Voltaire was here then and described the holocaust in *Candide*. Remember?"

The street was narrow and steep, bordered by old gray apartment houses with balconies where clothes hung to dry and waved with the salty sea wind. At number 16, Larry opened a door and led me through the small patio, then down an ancient stone staircase.

The cellar room, windowless except for one grated aperture up high, was engulfed in clouds of the cigarette smoke created by the ten men who sat in a circle. I recognized Bill Casey and Russ Forgan from the plane; otherwise, the assortment was a melting pot. One looked like an academic, another was a Mediterranean type, another with a British accent offered me a chair.

Larry went to the center of the circle. The group, reseated, shifted collectively in their chairs. The damp cellar room became silent.

"The news stinks," Mellon announced in his slow drawl. "The head of one of our MO teams was captured and our transmitter reports the Krauts began the torture by pulling out his fingernails one by one."

I did my best to hide my revulsion. MO agents were those behind enemy lines, spreading psychological warfare in southern France, sometimes blowing up bridges and sabotaging enemy routes. He went on, "One of our colleagues dropped in the Pau area in France was picked up on arrival. Pretty bad, eh? That might indicate a double agent someplace." Mellon waited a few moments to let his information sink in. "If so," he continued, "Operation Anvil is being sabotaged from within."

"How about our agent bumped off last night in the casino?" asked a skinny young American seated next to me.

"Forget that incident," Mellon advised sharply.

So the corpse had been one of us. That made the scene I had witnessed still more appalling. While Larry was relaying technical data, I decided the best thing I could do was to hope no one would become aware of the depths of my insecurity at this moment. Last night had been a warning of situations we might face in the future. And what I had heard this morning was proof that our business would necessitate more skills than those taught at the Farm.

Chapter 8

The lush green valleys of Portugal were left behind. Soon I was gazing down on the gray, barren fields of Castile. The land below appeared more hostile than inviting. Mountains loomed into view, then more rolling prairies plowed in symmetrical stripes of reds, browns, grays. After crossing a snow-capped mountain range, the plane descended in a birdlike arc along the course of a sinuous river on a high plateau. Where were the people? Only a tiny village now and then with little houses squeezed together dotted the checkered landscape. So this was my destination? As I gazed down, I prayed that I would be worthy of the mission which had been entrusted to me.

The small Iberian aircraft landed in the midst of a windstorm on a field where a fat-bellied Junker bearing a black-and-red swastika on its wing was the only other plane.

In the garagelike room that composed the entire air terminal, two customs officials, Civil Guards in ankle-length olive capes, greeted me with smiles. *"Buenos días, señorita."* After stamping my passport and briefly inspecting my luggage, they kindly escorted me to a taxi. Some enemy, I thought, but then I remembered the scene in the Lisbon casino and realized I shouldn't be overly confident.

The taxi bounced through the outskirts of Madrid on a pitted dirt road with scarcely any traffic, passing a spectacular bullring and then streets lined by shabby buildings. A few minutes later we arrived at a tree-lined boulevard where well-dressed children played under the vigilance of governesses in picturesque plaid skirts, fringed woolen shawls, and large globe-shaped gilt earrings.

"La Castellana," the driver announced proudly.

Like Lisbon, the city was almost bereft of autos; a few bicycles, some dilapidated carriages drawn by bony horses—no policemen or traffic signals at all. At one point, the driver sideswiped an approaching taxi, whereupon both drivers rolled down their windows and shouted *"Idiota!"* Every few blocks we passed a plaza with barren trees and waterless fountains adorned by gigantic statues; bordering the boulevard were granite palaces, their iron-grilled walls enclosing gardens. The peaceful wide avenue with its surrounding residences had an air of old-fashioned opulence and dignity. According to my watch, we turned into the curved drive of the stately Palace Hotel at twenty minutes to five in the afternoon, December 31, 1943. In the lobby I filled out forms at the reception desk. This was the moment planned in Washington for me to meet, in a seemingly accidental manner, the agent who would assist me "on the outside," Shepardson had said.

As I turned around, a man emerged from behind a marble column, striding toward me exactly according to the predetermined arrangements. The feline gait registered even before the exotic, high-cheekboned face. Top Hat!

At the same moment, something else happened. Behind Top Hat, a good-looking young man was approaching also. Which was my contact? When I dropped my handbag as foreordained, both men darted for it. I looked from one to the other. Then Top Hat, with a polite "excuse me" to the younger man, took my purse and handed it to me.

"The historical way to meet a lady." His words, although the correct code, were pronounced with the affected air of a bad actor. At close range, his features appeared tinged with a slightly sinister cast; maybe it was the gangster's mustache over the seductive smirk of his mouth. He had thick black hair shiny with brilliantine, graceful fingers, extremely white teeth.

"Edmundo Lassalle's my name. Would you do me the honor of joining me for a drink in the bar this evening?"

Now I answered with a previously planned sentence: "How kind of you to invite me."

We exchanged a few more words before I put my hand out to say good-bye. Top Hat bowed slightly, kissing my hand, his air still theatrical.

When I reached the elevator I was surprised to find the same handsome young man awaiting me with my two suitcases in his hands. His presence as we ascended made me nervous, and I was relieved when the door of my room closed behind me.

I looked around. The oak flooring was only partly covered by a tattered red carpet, yet the apartment was spacious, high-ceilinged, with mahogany scroll-worked furnishings and armoires instead of closets. I pumped the long round bolster on the bed—hard as a rock. Next I went to the windows and parted the heavy red velour, then the lace curtains. In front, an imposing edifice with two carved stone lions adorning the wide steps; over the entrance was inscribed "Las Cortes"—the Spanish Parliament, no less.

One taxi beetled around the plaza to my right, where a statue of Neptune decorated another dry fountain; a yellow trolley rattled by. On the sidewalk below, an old man waved pieces of paper. *"Lotería,"* he squawked in a rasping voice. Lottery and all, the city possessed a slow, pacific rhythm, light-years away from the commotion of Manhattan.

═══

At nine-thirty I walked into the Palace Bar. Edmundo Lassalle raised my hand to his lips while bestowing a stunning smile. Once we were seated he asked, "What will you have? Here everybody takes dry sherry or a gin fizz."

"I don't drink."

"Divina," he purred. "Better for your work, my dear." His smile still embraced me.

"Do you have any idea who that good-looking young man was in the lobby this afternoon?" I inquired.

He shrugged. "Just an admirer, I presume. Your entry caused quite a sensation."

I looked at him dubiously. "Do you know, he took my bags up to my room, and when I offered him a tip, he wouldn't accept. He spoke perfect English. I suppose he could just as well be German?"

"Don't worry about it. You're new. You will be under observation for a while."

"Since we will be working together, don't you think I should know what your cover is?"

"My cover is that I am a Mexican." I tried not to laugh. What else could he have been? "The representative of Walt Disney in Spain. This gives me the possibility of appearing neutral and enables me to see people of both sides. The plan is to take you to a reception given by the Marquesa of Torrejón, where you'll meet Spaniards—foreign ambassadors, a few enemy spies, also many rich, beautiful women from other countries. Only women with influence today can obtain exit permits from the countries at war. Madrid is considered the paradise of Europe right now. This will be the ideal opportunity to introduce you to the social world of the city."

A short plump man accompanied by a blond woman stopped at the table to speak to Edmundo. My companion stood up, mumbling a few words to the man, and quickly sat down again. "A friend of mine from the secret police. Couldn't introduce you because he's with his mistress. Mistresses and respectable women have no contact here," he explained.

I took another look at the lady, wondering how I would ever distinguish the difference.

"My dear, you're going to adore this city," he went on. "Everyone here is worth taking note of. Over there," he indicated with a nod, "are the Italians. Next to them the Germans. Just behind, Rumanians, Poles, and Bulgarians. The Japanese stay in that corner."

"Are some enemy spies?" I asked.

"Some?" He laughed. "They're *all* spies. Not a reliable person in the place."

"Does that include you?" I smiled.

"Absolutely not." Again a flash of teeth. Something about the sly smirk, his patois, the squeaky giggle, made me feel he was as shady as anyone he had pointed out.

"Who is the Marquesa of Torrejón?"

"She is the most popular social leader, and her gatherings the spiciest. I hope you have a wardrobe to meet the demands of Madrid's social life. If not, I recommend a visit to Balenciaga. Women in Madrid are especially chic, but Ambassador Hayes's wife is, frankly, dowdy, while the German ambassador's wife has a flair that makes her most popular. The majority of Spaniards are pro-Allies, politically. But darling, much as I love the Americans—and work for them—their social graces don't hold a candle to the Europeans." His eyes darted from one end of the room to the other. Each newcomer was closely appraised, but Top Hat's glib conversation never stopped.

"The partridge shoots are very grand. The banquet tables are set up out in the field with silver and crystal, served by white-gloved men in livery. When the shooting season ends, carnival begins, with the masked balls and parties. The whole city used to go masked in the streets, but Franco put an end to that. A pity. It would have been so useful for our business. I love disguises, don't you?"

He crunched a potato chip as he spoke, seldom waiting for me to respond. His foreign accent made everything he said sound alluring. "Lent is a letdown. They play a lot of cards in their chilly palaces. You know, there is a lack of coal. That's why most of Balenciaga's dresses are of wool and with long sleeves. During Lent the ladies have tea and say the rosary a lot; the men gamble and brag about their *conquistas,* their seductions. Franco outlawed public casinos. Probably a good thing. Spaniards are natural-born gamblers. Betting is permitted at the jai-alai court on Calle Hermosilla. You've got to see with what speed the bookies take the bets and then stuff their betting slips into slit tennis balls and toss them up to the stands. Jai-alai is the fastest ball game in the world, you know. The players are usually Basque. With any luck, Lent will be pepped up by some romantic scandal. There is no divorce, and adultery is an inevitable game."

Edmundo arose again, this time to bow to a particularly attractive woman who proceeded to the table behind us. "The *guapísima* Marquesa of Córdoba," he muttered to me as he sat down. But even she had not distracted him from his determination to inform me totally on life in Spain. He continued his diatribe more or less where he had left off.

"The grandees rarely go to their country estates, although they possess enormous properties. The ration of petrol is thirty liters a month, so most travel by train when they are obliged to make a visit to their farms and ranches. But they all prefer the gaiety of the capital to the country—unless there is a shoot, of course. Rural life in Spain is hard. No electricity, no plumbing, no heating, not even decent roads. The civil war didn't help that situation, either."

Edmundo gesticulated frequently with his graceful fingers. Often his voice rose in a squeaky crescendo at the end of a sentence. I couldn't make out yet what kind of person my new colleague was, but he was bizarre.

"A formal dinner invitation reads ten-thirty, but you may not get served until an hour later. But then the Gypsies for the entertainment don't arrive until two, so why begin earlier? Anyhow, no one awakes at dawn. And remember, it's bad manners to telephone a lady before noon."

He asked for another gin fizz.

"After Lent and Holy Week comes the Fair in Sevilla in April. What magnificent carriages and horses—the harnesses are always decorated with pompons and bells! The sound of castanets and dancing in the streets night and day for one whole week! And, my dear, Spaniards are really democratic people. The *most*. The Gypsies, the poor, the rich, the grandees, the shepherds and the cowherders all dance and drink together whenever they are celebrating a holiday. They are proud and individualistic. No inclination for regimentation, like the Germans. They envy each other but would die for a friend. Hate to obey the laws and are completely ungovernable. They enjoy especially complaining about their government, whatever it might be—monarchy, republic, democracy, and they've had them all."

He ceased talking for a second while he searched his pockets for another pack of cigarettes. "Really, Aline, you will have to make me a gift of some of those cartons you have available in the office to help make friends. These black Spanish *cigarillos* smell terrible." He waved to a waiter, gesturing expressively with his hand to his mouth to indicate what he wanted, and then turned his attention again to me.

"May is the month of the Fair of San Isidro, patron saint of Madrid. Bullfights for seventeen days straight. When June rolls around, the wives and children are packed off to the north. The husbands stay here, presumably to work, but the order of the day is to play—with their girlfriends, of course. The weather in Madrid is dry and hot but never unbearable in the summer."

The waiter appeared with an assortment of cigarettes and cigars. The transaction absorbed the attention of my colleague for a full five minutes. At last he seemed satisfied and returned to his self-imposed task of making me the best-informed newcomer in Madrid.

"There will be a smattering of Axis and Spanish personalities at the marquesa's. Concentrate on the women, the only way to get invited inside a Spanish home. The idea that Spanish women are submissive is ridiculous." He pulled a gold chain and watch out of his vest pocket. "You must be starved. We have a reservation at Edelweiss."

"A German restaurant?"

"Yes. To see more of the enemy. Edelweiss is the favorite of German diplomats and sympathizers."

=====

A crowd was waiting inside the door, but Edmundo and I were led to a table immediately. The room was unpretentious, overcrowded, and buzzing with voices. I watched the waiter fluttering around Edmundo. If he's on the payroll, he's overdoing it, I thought. "Would Señor Lassalle care for some pickled herring just flown in from Berlin? Tonight we have wiener schnitzel or venison." I felt like laughing. Here I was already feasting on provisions from the enemy's capital.

Edmundo lit a long, thin cigarette. "You must understand the quality and pace of the world you are entering. Right now we are in the shooting season. Partridge and wild boar, my dear. You rarely get anything else when you dine at the home of an aristocrat. Especially at the dinners given by one of the grandees who are the cream of the nobility. They live in splendor, but they certainly don't squander. Not one peseta! They shoot four days a week and eat the fruit of their efforts seven. Work is always secondary to enjoying life in this country. That goes for all levels of society."

He abruptly ceased speaking. Then he said, "Look at the tall blond fellow in the corner to your left."

Casually I glanced. All I could see was the profile of a young man with a scar near his left eye and his arm in a sling. Questioningly I looked back at Top Hat.

"Constantin von Weiderstock, a favorite disciple of Admiral Wilhelm Canaris, who controls the Abwehr. You should be aware that a power struggle rages now in Berlin between Himmler and this young fellow's boss, who also happens to be his godfather. Himmler wants to get rid of Admiral Canaris and absorb the Abwehr, the best espionage service in the world today, and meld it into the Gestapo, which is under his command. He is trying to convince Hitler that Franco has not joined them in the war because Admiral Canaris, who is a friend of Spain's dictator, advises Franco not to."

I had heard part of this before, of course, and he must have sensed it. He looked at his watch. "Almost midnight. We must run to catch the New Year across the street in the Teatro de la Zarzuela. The stars, Lola Flores and Manolo Caracol, are friends, and quite useful—also the best flamenco artists in Madrid."

As we entered, on the stage a beautiful Gypsy girl with long, abundant curly black hair, enormous eyes, and a curvaceous body was stamping her feet and snapping her fingers to eerie, contagious music played by two guitarists. A man, thickset, in a black, wide-brimmed hat, tight black pants, and red silk shirt, was singing "La Niña de Fuego"—"The Girl of Fire."

She moved, wildly, lustily, her frenzy growing with the crescendo of the rhythm. When the song came to an end, the curtain rolled down to tremendous applause, but no one moved. It was about ten minutes to twelve. Ushers hurriedly passed tiny baskets of yellow grapes down the long rows. On the stage, each artist was holding a similar basket. The audience concentrated on a huge clock onstage. Then a loud, solemn gong began to mark slow booms. Each head bent. The artists gobbled their grapes, the audience did the same. All around me I heard their sputterings, chokings—Top Hat too was frantically consumed in the effort, swallowing even skins and pits before the last stroke. When it did come, the theater echoed with screaming and laughing.

Edmundo turned to me and planted a damp kiss on both my cheeks.

"Feliz año nuevo, Aline—Happy New Year." Then he looked down at my half-filled basket. "You didn't finish your twelve grapes. That's a bad omen for your 1944," he added. In all seriousness.

Chapter 9

The next morning, a soft but persistent knock awakened me. I threw on a robe. "Who is it?"

"*El mozo de espadas.*"

Man of swords? Cautiously, I opened the door. Three men in black suits bowed respectfully. One supported the biggest basket of flowers I'd ever seen—bright red carnations. The other two held sparkling costumes draped over their arms.

"Señorita Griffith, I am the man of swords of Don Juan Belmonte, who sends you these gifts."

"Belmonte?"

"Yes, señorita." He beamed at me.

"If you please, who is Belmonte?"

"The señorita must have heard of the great Belmonte?"

I shook my head. "There is some mistake."

"No mistake," the man replied politely. "Don Juan beheld the señorita last night in the Teatro de la Zarzuela."

I pointed to the elaborate garments. "But what is this?"

"Señorita, the *traje de luces,* suit of lights, that Don Juan wore in Toledo when he got two ears."

The clothes were beautiful—hand-embroidered pink satin pants and a matching short jacket and vest paved with gold threads and sequins. Before I realized it, an elaborate cape was in my arms—so heavy with the rich embroidery of glittering stones that I could barely hold it.

"Tell Mr. Belmonte I am grateful and will accept his flowers, but not his clothes!"

"Señorita, do not refuse, *por favor.* Don Juan would . . . would never forgive us."

"I'm sorry, it's completely out of the question."

It still took five minutes to convince the trio to leave.

I called Top Hat.

"Edmundo, it's Aline. I'm sorry to wake you. Thanks so much for last night. Just tell me one thing, then go back to sleep. Who is Don Juan Belmonte?"

"A top matador, and the son of the greatest bullfighter in history. I'll call you later, *guapa.*"

I bathed, dressed in a somewhat plainer costume—slacks and a plaid shirt—devoured the crunchy bread with marmalade, and sipped tea while studying a Madrid street map, looking for 4 Alcala Galiano—the American Oil Mission—where I would start work the next day. Throwing on a long overcoat, I ran out.

Early New Year's Day the city was mine. I took a yellow trolley up the Castellana to the Plaza de Colón where a statue of Christopher Columbus looked down on the world. Despite the cold winter air, two men were seated at a café in the sunlight, taking coffee. I walked up the Calle Alcala Galiano to number 4, an old stone building where a chauffeur in a modern black Packard stared at me, as had the people in the hotel lobby and the trolley. When I passed by, he leaned out the window.

"Why does such a pretty girl want to wear men's clothes?"

I pulled my coat closer. At least I had learned why people had been staring and that it would be better not to wear slacks in Madrid again.

Quickly I changed my direction and headed toward the center of the city. The shops on the narrow streets, as in Lisbon, were small and specialized. Streets carried the names of their wares: La Calle de la Plata, the Street of Silver. And the Street of the Harness, the Street of the Capes, the Street of Bookbinders. The products on display appeared to date fifty years back—thick-boned corsets and bulky brassieres, top hats, copper household utensils.

Urchins on the sidewalks begged for money, and when I sat on a bench in the Plaza Santa Ana, a bootblack pulled up a stool and began to shine my shoes. The women were dressed in black with woolen scarves tied under their chins; the men wore long voluminous capes or coats hung from their shoulders. The horse-drawn carriage to the hotel cost only ten cents, although the ride up the Calle Alcala and down the Gran Vía took half an hour. Mule-drawn wagons and carts interfered with the old automobiles, many of which functioned thanks to a stove in the back trunk burning charcoal. The coachman explained these *gasógenos* were a solution because of the price of gasoline.

When I entered the Palace lobby, the three men awaited with still more flowers and the sparkling costume. Once more I accepted the flowers and refused the bullfighter's outfit. My room now resembled a funeral parlor. A half hour later the phone rang.

"Señorita Griffith?" He pronounced it "Greefeet."

"Yes."

"I am Juan Belmonte, and I would like the privilege of taking you out to buy a box of chocolates."

I tried not to burst out laughing. The incredible invitation encouraged me. "When would you like to buy these chocolates, Señor Belmonte?"

"As soon as possible, señorita. This afternoon would be perfect. I could pick you up around five. Would that be possible?

Since I had nothing better to do, I agreed. "But how will I know you?" There was a pause before he answered.

"It is not a problem, señorita. I will know you."

Morguelike in the morning, the lobby at five stirred with commotion. One cause seemed to be a dark-haired youth signing autographs. I looked around—no one was waiting for me. Then the center of attention walked toward me. So this was my bullfighter. I had imagined a matador would be tall and strong, like a football player. He was short, skinny, and olive-skinned, with a pleasant smile.

"Señorita Griffith," he said, raising my hand to his lips. "I cannot think of a more promising omen than to spend the first day of the New Year buying you chocolates."

I wondered if this was another Spanish superstition.

"May I call you by your first name?"

"My name is Aline."

Belmonte took my arm and escorted me to a car surrounded by fans in the middle of the circular drive. The doorman shooed the throng away, and we drove off in the cream-colored Bugatti convertible.

"You are the first American girl I have seen in Madrid." Belmonte had alert dark eyes and long thick lashes. "To what do we owe the honor of the señorita's visit?"

"I'm going to be working in Madrid, Mr. Belmonte."

"Please—call me Juanito. Everyone does." The matador's expression brightened. "So you will be with us for a while? Long enough to see me in the ring? The season opens in March, but the best fights don't begin until May." He slowed down as we turned off the Gran Vía. "And what is your work here?"

"I'm in the American Oil Mission."

"Wonderful. Please use your influence so we get more gasoline. The black-market prices make it every day more expensive to operate this car. Now that you are here, I am sure things will improve."

He brought the car to a halt on the Calle Peligros in front of a shop with "La Mahonesa" scrawled above the door on shiny tiles and gallantly walked around to my side to lead me into the store.

"Thank you for opening on this holiday, Don José, and a Happy New Year to you." The owner, obviously delighted to receive the famous bullfighter, bowed repeatedly and then began to compliment him on one of the fights of the past season. Juanito interrupted to introduce me. Don José bowed from the waist several times.

"Señorita, it is an honor to have you visit this shop. For one hundred and sixty-six years, my ancestors and I have made Spain's best chocolates. We have served the royal family and the country's most illustrious citizens. The señorita shall have a box just like the ones we used to prepare for Queen Victoria Eugenia." He produced a box lined with pink silk, and taking some tongs from the counter, he began to select candies from each group in the vitrine.

We watched for a few minutes, then Belmonte took my arm and turned to leave, calling out to the busy merchant as we reached the door, "Don José, we will be in the car."

"But what about the chocolates?" I asked. "Shouldn't we wait?"

"Certainly not," he answered. "In Spain gentlemen do not carry packages."

A few minutes later Don José appeared bearing a silver tray on which rested a box. "The señorita's chocolates," he announced proudly, beaming again at us both.

Driving back to the hotel, Juanito recited the names of the tree-lined boulevards, and the people who lived in the palaces and embassies along the Castellana. Many pedestrians waved to him as we passed.

"Juanito! Juanito!" Two beautiful girls, dark and slender, called from a café with the name "Chicote" over the door.

"Happy New Year, Juanito!"

"Happy New Year, Carla. Happy New Year, María," Juan replied.

"Admirers?" I asked, smiling.

"Uh, yes, in a way."

"Is Chicote a popular bar?"

"Not a place for you, Aline," Juanito answered.

"Why?"

"Well, it isn't respectable, that's all. These girls are models."

I stared. "What's wrong with that?"

Now he looked at me in surprise. "Everybody knows that models are not respectable. A girl like yourself would never go to Chicote."

The Spanish mentality was definitely different.

———

As we approached the hotel a black Mercedes with a small German flag flying on the hood passed us on the way out. A veiled woman from the backseat waved at Juan.

"That's the German Countess Podevils. She's very beautiful and very brave—and not a bad bullfighter."

When he asked me a second later to dine with him the following week, I accepted. He was a friend of everyone in the city and could be useful.

"That would be fun. Call me."

I rushed into my room—the telephone was ringing while I unlocked the door.

"Where have you been all day?" Top Hat asked.

"Sightseeing with that bullfighter. I called you this morning."

"The crack of dawn, my dear. Now, how did you ever meet Belmonte?"

I told him about my day.

"Delicious," he exclaimed. "I knew it the minute I met you—you are the most refreshing American I have met in a long time." He paused, then continued. "By the way, I have something for you. Will you meet me for dinner Monday night? And whatever you do, save me a chocolate, my dear. They're my favorites."

Chapter 10

The crude cardboard sign on the elevator read *No funciona*. The sign, like the bullet-marked walls of many buildings, reminded me I was in a country that was still recovering from war and many things did not function. I climbed chipped marble stairs to the second floor, where a sign on a door read OIL MISSION OF THE UNITED STATES OF AMERICA. A woman led me into the office of Walter Smith, who I had been told in Washington was the authentic representative of the Oil Mission, not part of our OSS operations. He kindly took me up another stairway and knocked on a door. A booming masculine voice told us to enter.

Behind a desk sat a gigantic man. He stood up and seemed to grow taller still as he shook my hand.

"Miss Griffith, I've been expecting you."

He returned my smile only fleetingly, his manner formal. Hulky, big-boned yet angular, his face jagged, his eyes brown—almost black— an abundance of dark hair.

"I'm Phillip Harris. Sit down, please."

I took the only chair in the room. Sealed shutters barred the sunny morning and noises from below.

He thumped back to the other side of the table.

Without recourse to any amenities, his small eyes avoiding mine, his voice quiet, controlled, without inflection, he went directly to business.

"Fortunately you're finally here. I've work for several like you. We're understaffed since a triple agent burned half our group—and the ambassador does all that's possible to make it difficult for us to get recruits. That damned agent was working for the Germans, the Spaniards, and us, all at the same time. When he started to swing around town in a new car and with an expensive mistress, we knew he didn't get all the dough from us. You can never be too careful. Remember that."

The wooden swivel chair squeaked as Harris's massive frame overflowed into it. The arms he crossed in front of him on the desk top made the room and the furniture seem minute. Could this man walk down a street unnoticed?

"We've barely twelve U.S.-trained agents in all Spain. The Germans have literally hundreds. That gives you an idea of what we are up against." He changed position. I thought the chair would break.

"I trust your encounter with Top Hat went as planned?"

"Yes. We had dinner together."

"That's good. Remember, in Madrid I alone know of Operation Bullfight. You will be the contact between Top Hat and myself. Also he will work with you whenever convenient, but be aware that he has his own mission. No unnecessary confidences. All information must be given to me. Only I put the pieces of the puzzle together. Is that understood?"

"Certainly."

His air was pompous and intimidating. But I listened with interest.

"Your orders are to uncover Heinrich Himmler's top agent here. There's no time to be lost. Operation Anvil is expected to take place about one week after Overlord, which could occur at any time."

He still did not look at me as he spoke. He concentrated on a yellow pencil which he rolled between the fingers of both hands. "The success of the southern invasion depends principally on the intelligence provided by OSS Madrid. Some of our information on German troop movement is brought here by agents coming across the Pyrenees. Also we receive reports through our radio rigs. Our transmitters, although small, reach Madrid. We relay on to headquarters. This is the spot"—he dropped the pencil and pounded a fist on the table—"from where the safety of Operation Anvil will be secured." Now he looked up. "Miss Griffith, if you do not follow orders strictly, you could be responsible for hundreds —or thousands—of deaths of American soldiers."

The abruptness and the magnitude of his statement, the gruff tone, made the silence that followed as intimidating as his words. I dared not speak. He picked up some papers. "Read these reports now and try to memorize them."

The first sheet concerned Ramón Serrano-Suñer. The paragraph was short.

====

Ramón Serrano-Suñer, Franco's brother-in-law, ex-minister. Friendly with Hitler, Himmler, Goering, and most of the top officials in Germany. Rumored Franco removed him from his cabinet post because of his efforts to have Spain enter the war on side of Axis.

Prince Nikolaus Lilienthal, a Czechoslovak citizen until 1925, later used a German diplomatic passport, active in Nazi-Sudeten movement in Czechoslovakia during the Munich period 1938–1939. Since then in close touch with Berlin, particularly with Himmler and Goering. Currently seeking to transfer the capital of his German friends in the Hermann Goering group from Germany to Spain. He is obliged to repay the economic assistance received from Himmler by rendering political services in cooperation with the Gestapo. Berlin authorities value Lilienthal highly due to his social position and influential relations in Spain. The attitude he usually adopts in Spain is of presenting himself as anti-Nazi and monarchist, whose only preoccupation is the Moscow communist danger.

Countess von Fürstenberg, with residence in the Palace Hotel in Madrid, recently arrived from Berlin, is in contact with Walter Schellenberg, Gestapo official, favorite of Himmler. No obvious means of support in Madrid, other than possible assistance from Gestapo.

Franz or Hans Lazaar, press attaché of German Embassy in Madrid, at present responsible for effective work with Spain's correspondents.

When I looked up, Phillip Harris was studying me.

"May I ask Top Hat for further information on these people?" I ventured.

"Yes, but I don't want him cozying up to any of these suspects. He's not the type who will be able to pull off the ultimate role we have in mind for you. He excels in a slightly different circle, but he will be able to get you into one or two of the large receptions where you will meet these people. Then you will have to progress on your own."

He took the papers I had placed on the table and put them in a drawer. "Obviously, I can't tell you everything right now, but I assure you your mission will become more vital as you proceed."

So this was going to be the preparation for something still more important. What could *that* be?

"Your other obligations, Miss Griffith, will be varied. You must protect your cover, above all. Not doing so would jeopardize the rest of us. That means you will keep normal office hours. Give the impression you are an authentic member of the Oil Mission. Keep away from embassy personnel. They don't have your security training and unwittingly could be dangerous. We will use your apartment—when you have one—to hide female agents who bring Order of Battle information from France. Here in the office you will be a code clerk. But you have one principal purpose: to uncover Himmler's special agent in Madrid." He paused. I awaited his encouragement to ask questions. A hundred occurred to me.

"Use the telephone with care. The equipment to record conversations is nonexistent, and even if the enemy brought in their own, the static and constant cuts on the line make tapping impossible. But don't take unnecessary chances.

"There is another matter, Miss Griffith, about which I must speak." He stiffened in his chair and began to toy again with the pencil. "At the slightest indication you are becoming involved romantically, you will be sent back to Washington. Only yesterday in Lisbon, a female member of our staff committed suicide. She had broken these rules by having a love affair with a Portuguese subagent who sold to the enemy information she unwittingly provided. We don't know how much damage has been done, but do you know how she killed herself?" Again I did not have time to answer. "She put her head in the oven in her kitchen and turned on the gas. Quite a mess, no? And another thing to be aware of is that the Spanish social circles in which you are supposed to move would never admit an unknown American girl whose reputation was not impeccable. This is Spain, not the United States."

I blushed—partly from indignation. "You need not worry, Mr. Harris."

He opened a drawer in his desk, handing me a little Beretta .25. "I suggest you get accustomed to carrying this at all times." Opening my bag, I dropped the familiar weapon inside. "Don't forget the ammunition," he added. As he handed me the small box, he stood up. I gathered our meeting was over and after thanking him turned to leave.

I can't imagine my expression on closing the door. Whatever it was, the young man who greeted me let out a bark of laughter. "Why, hello, Aline. I'm Jeff Walters. Welcome to Madrid."

We shook hands. His face was smiling and attractive; he chatted comfortably while leading me down the hall. The room we entered had two large desks, on which coding boards were set up. Jeff became my friend immediately, telling me all about our colleagues. According to him, everybody in the office was easy to get along with—except the chief. Phillip Harris—code name Mozart—watched everyone like a hawk, and laxity in security regulations was severely condemned. Jeff also confessed he was fascinated by a beautiful Swedish girl, daughter of the Swedish consul. He went on to inform me that all the men in our office were married, but since no wives had been allowed to accompany them, many were enjoying their freedom with the beautiful Spanish models and musical-comedy dancers. "They call this post 'the gravy train,' and it is, until one of us agents gets killed. During the five months I've been here, one of our subagents was found dead with a wire around his neck and our former radioman was tortured in ways I couldn't tell you."

I attempted to give Jeff the impression that I was not especially intimidated, shrugging my shoulders and turning to the work on my desk. Actually I was remembering the sight of the knife protruding from the black tuxedo and the blood running in rivulets on the carpet in Lisbon, and I was trembling inside. I'd have to toughen up in a hurry if this sort of thing was going to be routine.

In the middle of my table was a paper containing the now-familiar five-letter coded words.

"Try that one first," said Jeff. "I decoded it over the weekend, but before you start on today's stuff, I want to see if you'll need any help." He grinned. "Don't get your feelings hurt. Washington informed us you're tops at that, but I'm not sure you were taught on the same-style boards."

The cardboard tablet, about thirty inches high and fifty wide, was sitting in front of me much like a huge picture. Tapping the plaque covered with a jumble of letters of the alphabet, I said, "Don't worry. Although the board is larger than what I worked on in my classes, it'll be easier."

The message was from Lisbon. Jeff continued to provide general information while I decoded. "The embassy offices are four blocks away on Calle Miguel Angel, but we try to avoid them. . . ." Suddenly I wasn't listening. The information in the cable absorbed my attention.

TO MOZART FROM ZEBRA STOP   SUBAGENT SOCRATES CAUGHT SELLING
INFORMATION TO AXIS STOP   SOCRATES HAS BEEN ELIMINATED STOP

"What's the matter?" Jeff asked. "Having trouble?"

"No, the coding is easy, but I think this cable refers to a fellow who was murdered when I was in the casino in Estoril."

"You'll never know. Mozart tells us only what is indispensable."

Dimly I nodded. So the corpse had a code name. Socrates. Had he also been the lover of the girl Mozart referred to?

=====

The signs were subtle, but not subtle enough. My room had been searched with precision. Fortunately, I had laid traps, a thread here and there, inspired not only by our training but also by the Japanese who had squeezed into the small elevator with me twice that day and who had gotten out on the fifth floor also. No doubt about it, I would have to find an apartment soon.

Edmundo phoned.

"Listen, my dear. Meet me in the lobby at eleven. Put on your dancing shoes. We're going nightclubbing."

I took it for granted that the evening was planned for work, but forgot to ask if the late hour meant I was expected to have eaten before. Spanish hours were going to make it difficult for me to get sleep, so to be on the safe side I went to bed for two hours rather than wait for food to be delivered to my room. Top Hat roared when I told him my dilemma later.

"Only a barbarian eats before eleven in Madrid, my dear. We'll dine where we're going. No restaurant, good or bad, will serve before ten, and in the nightclubs much later."

We were going up the Gran Vía in a taxi. "Edmundo, my room was searched today. Who do you think is responsible—Franco's secret police, the Japanese, or the Germans?"

"It could be the Americans," he answered, giggling.

He seemed to be in an anticipatory mood but did not tell me the purpose of our date.

On the Gran Vía we entered a canopied doorway and descended a wide, red-carpeted staircase into an ostentatious room. Pasapoga rivaled the WonderBar for glamour. Shining bronze reflected in the mirrored walls, marble columns, crystalline chandeliers. A large band played Guy Lombardo music.

"Isn't it *wonderful*?" Edmundo beamed. "So gaudy, so baroque. The favorite spot for Spaniards to take their mistresses."

Every few steps he smiled or nodded at someone, enjoying his role of man about town. After we were seated and he had ordered something to eat, the band took a break and the orchestra leader came over. Edmundo introduced him. "Aline, I want you to meet René Blum." He lowered his tone. "René is French and came here a year ago from Paris, barely escaping capture by the Gestapo. Thanks to his efforts, we help many Jews escape into Spain."

The musician took a seat next to me. I liked him the minute I saw his round smiling face. "You will be my contact with René when I am out of town, Aline. He is the best agent I have."

Blum laughed. "Edmundo exaggerates. Anybody in my position could give reports on foreigners in Madrid. They all come here. Many get drunk and reveal confidential matters. I merely pass on what I see and hear, and naturally I am in contact with my Jewish friends back home. We all work together to get them out."

When the waiters left, Top Hat set up procedures for the bandleader to contact me when Edmundo might be traveling or unavailable during an emergency. Once telephone numbers and hours were exchanged, René went back to direct his orchestra.

"Edmundo, does Mozart know I am to be in contact with this fellow?"

"Rest assured that none of us can use a subagent or introduce him to OSS personnel without permission. Mozart has his finger in every pudding. Blum is totally reliable. Half his family have been imprisoned by the Germans. Don't worry. He will never endanger your cover."

Couples were now swarming onto the dance floor, waiters continued to pass by with glasses on silver trays. The room echoed with laughter and voices. Suddenly Edmundo put his hand on my arm. "Aline, we must dance. We absolutely must."

Whisking me onto the floor, he guided me in an elaborate tango. I did my best to follow his snaky steps; he whirled me around, lowered me in his arms, brought me to my feet, and suddenly pirouetted me. I would have felt an utter fool if not for his grace and extraordinary control. Again a pirouette, and then—thud. I had collided with another dancer, and I spun around to apologize.

Well built, sandy-haired, with his arm in a sling and a sickle-shaped scar near the left eye—I was face to face with Constantin von Weiderstock! Stunned for a moment, he nevertheless bowed.

"Entirely my fault, señorita. In my condition, I have no right to darken a dance floor." As von Weiderstock led his partner out of our path, he turned around once more to look at me. Edmundo winked and twirled me in his arms again.

"He thinks you are Spanish. He probably could have spoken much better in English. All Germans do. You look Spanish, you know. That's an advantage; you blend well into this setting. Now you have an excuse to talk to him the next time you see him, and I bet anything he'll look for the opportunity."

Had Edmundo pushed me into Canaris's godson for his own reasons? Canaris could be a key figure to Edmundo's mission. I looked toward the band. René Blum was waving his baton in sharp, animated motions, as if tempo were his only care.

As Edmundo trotted me off the floor, we approached a table where a flock of nightclubbers were demanding autographs. Juanito jumped up and although still at a distance bowed over his empty chair.

As I smiled, Edmundo murmured under his breath, *"Mi querida* Aline, you must present me to the great Belmonte." Edmundo moved me through the adoring throng until Juanito and I were face to face.

"A pleasure to see you, Aline," he said with his customary formality.

"Juan, I would like to introduce Edmundo Lassalle."

Being anxious to avoid the staring group, I added, "It's good to see you, Juan," and turned away. Too late, for of course Edmundo knew several of Belmonte's friends and engaged in a welter of hugs and kisses. Watching me, Juanito frowned, accentuating his slightly beaked nose and dark sallowness. I wondered why he was so obviously annoyed.

It didn't take long to find out. "I don't approve of your latest admirer, Aline. If he were a gentleman, he would never have brought you to a place like this."

Chapter 11

A s promised, Top Hat took me to the Marquesa of Torrejón's reception about a week later. This time he picked me up at nine-thirty. On the dusky, worn-stone Calle Ferraz, in front of a granite palace still bullet-pocked from the civil war, Edmundo energetically clapped his hands, looking up and down the street.

"Where's the *sereno*?" he asked. "He should be waiting here when such an important party is going on."

"Who's the *sereno*?" I asked.

"The guy who opens the doors of all the houses around this area. *Serenos* form an important part of the night life in this city. People are scrutinized by the *porteros* during the day, but the *serenos* protect the buildings at night." As he spoke the banging of a stick on the cement sidewalk could be heard. "Ah, here he comes," said Edmundo.

Out of the shadows appeared a figure draped in baggy pants, a knee-length jacket, a wool *bufanda* wrapped around neck and mouth, and a dirty beret slanted over his forehead. He hastened to select a huge iron key from the assortment hanging on his belt, at the same time shoving the policeman's stick under one arm and booming out, *"Buenas noches, señores."* The iron-barred door swung open.

"This is one of the few grand *palacios* to survive the siege of Madrid," Top Hat explained as we ascended the stairway. "The siege lasted almost three years." In the massive salon, faded ruby tapestries shimmied to the tread of men in evening suits and women in jewels and black Balenciagas.

"By the way, the marquesa's mother was Mexican. A compatriot," Edmundo confided.

"My *dear,*" I turned, mimicking him. "And all this time I assumed you were a Spanish grandee."

"I am a Mexican grandee," he quipped. "On my mother's side, Cortés; on my father's, Montezuma. Now you know my secret, the mystery of my wild blood—it's the Aztec in me. Remind me one day to show you my tribal tattoos.

"You're so modest."

"My dear," he retorted, "as La Rochefoucauld said, 'Humility is the worst form of conceit.' "

Every few steps Edmundo stopped to kiss a hand or pump a man on the back in an embrace, introducing me to the Duke and Duchess of Lerma, Marcela de Juan—a Chinese beauty—the French prelate Monsignor Boyer-Mas, a raspberry-red sash belting his black cassock, the glamorous Countess of Yebes. When he introduced me to the Countess of Orgaz, he paused. "El Greco's most famous painting is of this lady's sixteenth-century ancestor's funeral," he said.

"Come along," said Edmundo, conducting me through the crowded room to look at a Goya. "Observe the lady in that portrait." I did. "Now come here."

He took me to a cluster of guests seated around a woman whose identity I guessed immediately. Her resemblance to her ancestor's portrait was indisputable. "Mimosa is the slyest fox in Madrid," Edmundo confided. "Nothing that goes on in this city escapes her eyes."

"Edmundo, you *pícaro.* Where have you been hiding?" The Marquesa of Torrejón—a small, fragile creature with dyed mink-brown hair, two dollops of rouge on her cheeks, several strands of luminous pearls roped around her stick of a neck—spotted Edmundo with darting eyes as we penetrated her circle. "Blanca Velayos is furious with you for not showing up at her party." Then she appeared to see me for the first time. Kissing her extended, beringed fingers, Edmundo introduced us.

"How delightful to have an American girl in our midst. I do so like Americans. They have—how do you say it?—spunk." Her English was flawlessly British. "There are many young people here who will be delighted to meet you, my dear."

Then the marquesa introduced me to her group—the foreign minister, Lequerica, and a ravishing blond woman, the Duchess of Sueca; the Princess Agata Ratibor; the English ambassador, Sir Samuel Hoare, and his wife.

The furniture was Louis XVI interspersed with English Queen Anne. Above a mammoth unlit fireplace hung a portrait of Doña Mimosa in a floral chiffon gown, tiny satin slippers with pointed toes, at a time when her brown hair was not dyed.

Directly in front of the marquesa's banquette was an antique gilt card table, against the surface of which she fretfully tapped a small, frayed pack of cards. Now she piped, "Edmundo, it is too dreadful. Really it is. I have put my friends to sleep tonight with my readings. But I ask you. Is it my fault? I am merely the medium—the cards speak for themselves. Am I to be blamed simply because there isn't anything new to be said about anyone sitting here that the rest of us don't already know?" Mimosa's observation drew several appreciative titters. Encouraged, she continued, "It really is a shame. I would love to give you a reading, but of course it is impossible in mixed company. The cards themselves would blush." The marquesa was ebullient. The air scintillated at last.

Not to be outdone, Edmundo, preening in his element, glanced about. "My dear Mimosa, you flatter me. Surely you owe a lion's share of your delectable readings to the brilliant machinations of your own vivid imagination."

The marquesa's darting look alighted on me once again. She screwed up her bright red cheeks.

"Why, Miss Griffith," she said. "Do let me give you a reading. I have a strong feeling the cards have something special to tell you. How delightful. A total stranger." Her enthusiasm seemed to arouse supportive murmurs from her group.

Turning to me, Edmundo said aloud, "What did I tell you? Isn't she *divina*?"

I smiled but would have preferred not to be the center of attention so soon.

"Make room," the marquesa commanded. "Come sit by me. What is your name, child? Aline. Sit here." The English ambassador stood up.

The Princess Ratibor fluttered a silk fan and said as she beat the air, "Mimosa will try anything to make her parties the most amusing." Edmundo sat down beside her, resplendent in his sleek shininess.

The minister Lequerica remarked, "Be careful, señorita. The marquesa is a witch. She reads your mind as if it were her own."

I noticed others had gathered. What could I do? The anticipation was like a sudden current of air. Was I obliged to squeeze in beside the Countess of Yebes?

I had never seen such cards. They were numbered but decorated with ornate suits, designs of huge gold goblets or of men in fifteenth-century costumes on horseback. The marquesa began shuffling, flipping the cards over, one by one, faceup on the gaming table. Couples strolled by, waiters passed with trays of canapés. The sound of a piano and singing from another room.

The marquesa's eyes were brittle, glazed. "Now, you all know I have never seen this girl before. All I know about you, Aline, is that you are an acquaintance of Edmundo's and that you are American. Nothing else, is that true?"

I nodded. A couple in the room chatted between themselves, but most were engrossed with the cards on the table. The marquesa had drawn a nine, a five, a seven, and she studied them as if they revealed fathoms of information. Then she spoke. "I see that you are going to become famous in this city, my child. For one reason or another you will be in danger. Ah, and I see you will not return to your home for many years."

Even though I put no faith in fortune-telling, her delivery was so dramatic that, like the others around the table, I listened attentively.

Her eyes leaped to my own. "Shall I go on?"

I nodded. Murmurs of approval. I looked at Edmundo; his own slanted eyes were glued to the cards. The princess whispered something in his ear. The marquesa dealt three more—a six, a two, a five. "Ah, this is serious," she murmured. "The cards show you are going to be embroiled in some kind of an international plot." She looked at me. "Are you too worried for me to continue, my dear?"

"Not at all." I smiled. It occurred to me that possibly her words carried a meaning for someone else. I glanced around. Most of those around the table were watching the marquesa, but the Princess Ratibor and Edmundo were concentrating on the cards more than the others. Or could it be my imagination? But each time just three numbers! That was usually a signal in number codes. . . .

Doña Mimosa repeated her shuffling and turned over three more cards. Then she picked at her dyed hair with a bony ringed finger. "There is someone whose well-being you are worried about—and with reason. That person's life is in danger." She glanced at me again. "I'm sorry, my dear. I only interpret the cards." She dealt three more cards. I watched the numbers. Was she tapping that second card with her long nail out of nervousness, or to attract someone's attention? I knew a variety of codes which were based on numbers instead of letters. It could be possible. She flipped three more. "Adventure and intrigue."

"What kind of intrigue?" asked the English ambassador, now standing behind me. "You told me the same thing."

"And me," chimed in the Duchess of Sueca, who was leaning against the back of Edmundo's chair.

"As you all know, I am merely a medium," said the marquesa, turning. "If you wish I will give it up. The game is beginning to bore me also."

"No," said the princess. "If there is more in the cards, out with it."

This time, as she turned over the last card, the marquesa sighed. "Oh, no, I cannot go on, my child!" She touched my arm. "There must be some error in the manner in which I have handled the cards tonight. They reveal evil forces are at work around someone you are interested in, Aline." She paused. "Oh, I do hope it is not someone you care for personally." Her bony finger tapped the first card again before she picked them up and shuffled. "No, I will not do any more reading tonight. I have lost my touch."

"Not at all," said Edmundo. "This is more amusing than ever. Do continue, Mimosa."

The marquesa continued her exploit. Three more cards. She frowned, licked her little lips. Her red fingertips pecked at her pearls. "Strange," she mused. "Sometimes there is clarity so quickly. The next moment— poof—gone. The cards are muddy. I can't make them out." She frowned, confused. "What I see now has absolutely nothing to do with Aline Griffith."

"Out with it," ordered the ambassador.

"I see a bullfight," Mimosa replied. "Oh, how terrifying, all these black cards—a death by murder. She picked up the frayed cards hastily. "I'm sorry, Aline. I hope I haven't upset you with my little entertainment."

I stood up. "Why no, Marquesa, not at all. I've enjoyed it."

The Countess of Yebes intervened. "It's my turn, Mimosa. I want to hear about my future. I do hope it's more amusing than my past."

Now I was certain there had been a message in her cards. The numbers were a code. But her words about an international plot and a murder made me wonder if there was any way she could have known about my mission. Impossible, I decided. At any rate, I would question Edmundo when I could. Where was he?

I wandered through one drawing room after another, looking. He seemed to have disappeared. Then I reached the music we had heard.

A dozen young people were crowded around a piano which a pretty young girl was playing while two others sang. Their concerted efforts were charming. After some minutes, I felt a presence beside me. Edmundo stood at my shoulder. "Concentrate on those three girls. Try to make friends with them. Tell you why later. In a half hour I'll come back to take you to dinner." He slipped quietly away again.

Casually I moved toward the piano and began harmonizing softly with the girls, who were singing "Good Night, Sweetheart." They smiled, encouraging me. Their faces were pretty ovals, and if their music was not faultless, it had an unaffected naturalness. After the song, we introduced ourselves, and when Casilda, the pianist, discovered I was American, she exclaimed, "I know another American song! You must sing it with me!" Before I could protest, she launched into a slow, impassioned rendition of "It Had to Be You." I knew it, too, and did my best.

> It had to be you.
> It had to be you.
> I wandered around, and finally found somebody who,
> Could make me be true, could make me be blue . . .
> Or even be glad
> Just to be sad
> Thinking of you.

The lyrics spun out of my mouth with what I hoped was an agreeable resonance. And at the end I drew out the word *you* to a half-dozen bars.

The group loved it. Carmen, Casilda, and Nena embraced me, and when I told them I had brought a stack of American phonograph records to Spain, they invited me to come to dinner the following week.

═══

As soon as we were in a taxi, Edmundo said, "Wasn't Mimosa wonderful? I enjoyed myself thoroughly."

"Edmundo, she was passing someone a message with those numbers, I'm sure."

"Of course. She was brilliant. And very helpful."

"What do you mean?"

Edmundo's black eyes were gleeful. "The message was for me. Do you remember the numbers on the cards?"

"I didn't catch on until she was dealing for the second time. I missed the first set. But no one could decipher a code like that except the one it was meant for. You know that. How does it work?"

"The pattern of the second card was always the clue. A five, a two, and a one. Then repeated."

"So?"

Edmundo smiled shyly. "The marquesa has been doing a little work for me. A tidbit here and there. And she has uncovered a delicious piece of information." Having excited my curiosity, Edmundo gave a nonchalant yawn.

"Don't torture me. Go on."

He withdrew an envelope from the inside of his tuxedo and inserted it into my evening bag, nestling against my revolver. "Pass this on to Mozart."

"Tell me what the marquesa transmitted."

Edmundo smirked. "My dear Aline, that's what I like about you. You are as impatient as I am. Tell me, my dear, is there any Indian blood in your ancestry? I swear you have a wild streak indicative of such genealogy."

"Edmundo!" I was exasperated; his aim, exactly.

He looked at me intently. "The marquesa has discovered a rumor of an assassination plot to be made on a top official. To be executed here in Madrid."

"Do you know who?"

"Not yet! She may not know either."

"When?"

"That is what I just found out. Two. One. Five. May twenty-first." Removing a small datebook from his inside pocket, he perused it. "Oh, I see. How interesting."

"Tell me!"

"The day of the most important bullfight of the Fair of San Isidro."

I couldn't help it. I had to ask the questions racing through my head.

"Does Franco go to bullfights?" I asked.

"Ah, you have a brilliant idea—similar to my own, my child. Yes, the Generalíssimo does go to bullfights—sometimes—although he doesn't like them."

"If Mimosa Torrejón had a tip about a plot to kill Franco, why wouldn't she tell him?"

"The last thing the marquesa would do would be to warn Franco. Don't you realize that the Spanish aristocrats dislike Franco because they consider he is usurping the place of their king? They are all monarchists and would be delighted to have him out and their beloved Don Juan, who is now in exile in Lisbon, back in. Franco does not allow him to enter the country."

"But where does Mimosa get her information?"

"Maids or valets listening behind doors. Her maid, Salud, has access to every house that counts in this city. She's over eighty, and all the servants in the grand houses run to her with their gossip."

"Edmundo, why would Mimosa want to tell you especially about this if she knows it involves Franco? That's a Spanish problem, not ours."

"You're wrong," he answered. "Spain could be a last-ditch effort on Hitler's part to turn the course of this war, which is not going well for him. With Spain fighting on the side of the Germans, France could not be liberated. Why, the Allied troops couldn't even get to Italy—the whole course of the war would be changed."

"Who would Hitler get to take Franco's place?"

"Impossible to say—one of the generals from the Blue Division who favors the Nazis, or his brother-in-law, Serrano-Suñer, who is supposed to be pro-German."

The thought flashed in my mind: Jupiter, Shepardson, and Mozart have given the same mission to Edmundo as to me! For some reason, they don't trust him. Something else is going on . . . something that has been hidden from me.

Searching Edmundo's face, I said, "Can the marquesa be trusted?"

"As I've told you, I trust no one."

"Of course," I replied. "None of us is supposed to trust anyone."

We were seated in Chipén, a noisy "in" restaurant in the Calle Peligros, with walls of Arabic tiles, alcoves on the sides formed by arches, when Edmundo produced an object from his pocket. A tiny porcelain vase, embossed with hand-painted gold flowers so miniature they were scarcely larger than dots. He set the bibelot on the table.

"Where did you get that?"

"From a table in Mimosa's boudoir."

I looked at him. "I don't understand."

"My dear, Mimosa has thousands of them. She will never miss this."

"But Edmundo, did you steal it?"

"Aline, I like it. I had to have it. Don't you think it's lovely?"

Edmundo a kleptomaniac! Embarrassed, I changed the subject. "Why did you want me to meet those girls?"

"They are the kind of friends a girl your age should have in this city. The main reason I brought you here was precisely to meet them. They are always at Mimosa's parties. And after all, Mozart has given me orders to help you get into Madrid's social circles. No better way, pet."

Superbly self-satisfied, Edmundo continued to appraise the porcelain vase, probably deciding where to place it in his collection.

"Actually, I desired this 'memoir' as a memento of this evening."

"What do you mean?"

"Didn't you see how that German princess reacted? How do you Americans say it? I had her eating out of the palm of my hand."

"That's nothing unusual."

He brightened. "Do you think so? She possesses one of the most outstanding titles in Europe. I shall describe her in my next report as the latest SS agent to have arrived in Madrid."

"You don't think she is an enemy agent?"

"Oh, of course not. But it makes a good story. I've been waiting for a woman like Agata Ratibor to enter my life for years."

"What do you mean?"

"A woman with such a great title, attractive and looking for a husband. Why not me?"

"Did you know her before tonight?"

"The first time I saw the princess was two weeks ago, in Estoril."

After a waiter served our paella, I chanced, easily enough I thought, casting a line. "I understand a subagent named Socrates was murdered there."

Edmundo began to eat. After a pause he said, "He was my subagent."

"What happened?"

"The poor fellow was trading secrets about Allied munition deliveries, not only to the German legation in Lisbon, but to the Japanese as well. Now I ask you, isn't that cheek?"

"Who discovered him?"

Edmundo continued eating. "I did."

"*You* did?" A premonition dawned.

"But who else, my dear?"

"What did you do?"

Dabbing his napkin to his mouth—a sharp contrast of white damask against caramel skin—he replied, "I killed him."

"Oh, Edmundo." I half smiled, thinking it a joke.

"Remember, Aline: one life capable of betraying thousands. Think of the multiplication. What else could I do?"

Flashing in my brain was the vision of the knife jutting out of the man's black tuxedo. It was a deep, soundless moment. I stopped eating.

"You are shocked, aren't you? Well, you had better be prepared. You may have to kill someone yourself. I disliked the method, but it was silent. Think of the consequences of *in*action. Which would you prefer? The death of one double agent, or the death of ten thousand of your all-American boys?"

Chapter 12

It must have been the beginning of February about three weeks later, a Monday, at nine in the morning. I was rushing through the Palace lobby on my way to work. My attention was focused on a huge bowl of white roses adorning a commode against the wall. Paco, the elevator boy, had told me the flowers arrived daily from Alicante. As I entered the revolving doors, I was wondering if I would ever have the opportunity of visiting that city.

Then I saw him. My shock was so great I almost stumbled in the glass enclosure which was pulling me helplessly along by the momentum of the person who was entering from the opposite side. I hoped my own expression was as blank as his. Our paths crossed without so much as a nod. I dared not look back, but continued down the steps to the street, stunned.

I jumped into a cab. As soon as I entered the office, I went to the chief's room.

"Mr. Harris, coming out of the Palace lobby this morning I saw an agent I knew at the Farm by the code name of Pierre."

"Yessss." His drawl was glacial, as were his tiny brown eyes.

"Well, I thought you might want to know he is in Madrid." What I hoped was that Mozart would tell me why Pierre was here and if he would be working with us.

Shifting in his seat, all his angles rearranged, Mozart announced quietly, "Of course I know, Miss Griffith. I am aware of everything related to our activities in this country. Pierre will be in Madrid now and then. That is more than you need to know about his activities."

I remembered Edmundo had said the marquesa was the slyest fox in Madrid and that no intrigue occurred of which she was unaware. The marquesa had a rival. Mozart, the Mastermind. How I would love to see her read *his* cards. Yet I was delighted. The stiff reprimand had brought me good news. I would see Pierre again. But when?

"Now to get down to *your* business." He gave a brief cough. "I trust your first month's work has been satisfactory."

I nodded. He knew I had been working nonstop in the code room. Each cable had been an adventure, so absorbing that I felt I was fighting the war on a dozen fronts. During the evenings I had attended a variety of receptions and dinners, invited by Juanito Belmonte and also by Casilda Avila, the girl playing the piano at the marquesa's reception.

"Anything to report about your mission?"

Was challenge implicit in his tone? "I prepared a list of everyone I've met since my arrival." I handed it to him.

A wry smile settled on his angular face as he read my report.

"Good, Miss Griffith. I see you have already met some useful people." He folded the paper with precision, inserting it into a drawer. "Although an apartment practical for our work is not easy to find, you must get one as soon as possible. This will make it more difficult for others to check up on your movements. Also we urgently need a place to put up female agents coming in from France. By the way, get busy organizing your chain. You will need one to have your suspects followed."

"I wanted to talk to you about that, Mr. Harris. I'm being followed myself, right now. This started two days after I arrived."

"I'll do what I can to have one of our people protect you, but we lost two of the best men last week."

I couldn't resist. "Lost?"

"One was found dead under the bridge over the Calle de Segovia. Made to look like a suicide, but we're certain he was thrown off. The other has just disappeared."

My efforts at that moment were concentrated on maintaining an appearance of indifference equal to his. He lit a cigarette. I waited.

"Do you keep your revolver handy?"

"I most certainly do."

"Don't be afraid to use it if you're attacked. If there are no witnesses you can get away with anything here, and even if there are, in this business no one goes to the police. Neither side wants to be expelled from the country."

———

Although I didn't see Pierre again, the mere knowledge that he was near made me think about him more than ever. I dreamed of him several nights and kept my eyes alert during the day.

Finally I found an apartment on the Calle Monte Esquina, a street parallel to the Castellana and just a short walk from the office. Within the week I received the building's security clearance. The *portera,* a sort of superintendent, was considered safe because she was a member of the clandestine Communist Party, and her husband's brother had only recently been released from Portiel, the prison for subversive political activity.

I had never had a room of my own. At home I had shared one with my sister or a baby brother—or the maid when we were lucky enough to have one. At college I had had a roommate. And now a whole luxurious apartment for myself! My OSS "hazardous duty" salary was generous, and with the favorable peseta exchange almost everything I could dream of was within reach. A custom-made Balenciaga dress was two hundred dollars; my rent was fifty dollars monthly. Money ceased to be a consideration.

My *portera*'s husband was usually drunk and had a vile temper. His wife, Doña Antonia, ignored his vociferous insults and spent hours sitting on the street in front of our door, with one bared breast feeding her sturdy infant, even on the coldest mornings.

My maid, Angustias, recommended by Jeff Walters's maid and cleared by CE, was tall, bony, and black-haired and possessed two prominent gold teeth which somehow indicated her social status as above that of the *portera,* whom she treated with disdain. Her brothers had been killed during the civil war. One had been in Madrid when the war broke out and therefore had been obliged to enlist with the Republicans, who controlled the city; the other had been in Burgos and had been compelled to enlist with the Nationalists, whose headquarters were there. Angustias said she had no idea what the war had been about and had no preference for either side. When the *portera* damned Franco, Angustias responded with an assenting nod. But when our neighborhood butcher blamed the Republicans for Spain's chronic poverty, she also agreed. Angustias called Doña Antonia and her husband *rojos* who, she said, were conspiring to cause another civil war.

"I want no part of it. We suffered too much in the *guerra*. In Madrid we nearly starved—only the Russians were able to get food. They hung a poster four stories high of their Stalin on the Central Post Office, and on the Bank of Spain we had to look at a three-story-high picture of a bald ugly fellow called Lenin."

Angustias also told me, "Servants who work for *americanos* can get white flour, sugar, rice, and black beans—everything that is rationed—so the señorita will eat well as soon as I find a cook."

"Don't you know how to cook?" I asked.

"Oh, that would never do for the señorita! The señorita must have a staff of at least two servants."

Although I tried to refuse, Cecilia, the new cook, appeared with two black cloth sacks containing her belongings and with a twelve-year-old daughter. When I inquired if Cecilia's husband had been killed in the war, she replied, "No, señorita. He ran off to Uruguay with another woman, and lucky I am to have only one child. It wasn't easy—all those nights I had to spend sitting on a chair." The daughter, pale and thin, stared meekly at the ground. "Do not worry, señorita," Cecilia reassured me. "Engracia eats little and can sleep in my bed." I had been thinking how pretty the child would be once we gave her food and clothing.

Every morning my dress, stockings, handkerchiefs, shoes, and handbag were laid out in my dressing room. Angustias heated the bathroom by using a white porcelain basin filled with alcohol, which she ignited. A high orange-and-bluish flame lasted just long enough for me to bathe and dress. Her devotion even extended to ironing at midnight.

She used two bulky contrivances, the top of which lifted to enable filling with hot coals, and each had a tiny chimney for the smoke. "Look, Angustias, I appreciate your good intentions, but I can't sleep with the noise of those irons," I told her.

One morning I was awakened by a blood-curdling wail from the street below. I bolted upright in bed. "What is happening?" I yelled.

Angustias appeared with her hands on her hips, cackling heartily. "Don't tell me the señorita has never heard the bray of a burro?"

I rushed to the window. On the street, a little gray donkey reared its head, shrieking. The owner was pulling him, but the animal was determined not to budge.

I was happy in my new home, adjusting to a scale of luxury I had never known. However, I still noticed that I was followed. The faces changed; sometimes women took over when the men disappeared. I didn't like that. It showed they were pretty professional. I hoped that little by little the routine office hours I religiously kept would discourage them.

When I woke every morning, I wanted to pinch myself—to make sure this was real. The beauty of the city, the deep blue sky even on wintry days, the wide tree-lined avenues and twisting narrow streets, the politeness of the people, the beautiful children. The rhythm of the city was soothing. No one ever seemed in a hurry. Business began around ten in the morning and was relieved by long afternoon siestas. Office workers returned at five or six in the afternoon to remain until nine. There were no tourists, only Spaniards and foreign diplomatic personnel to dine on the best seafood in Europe—such delicacies as *angulas,* tiny eels caught in the freshwater estuaries on the Atlantic Coast; the *percebes,* or barnacles; and also *merluza,* a very fine white fish, called hake in English, that does not exist in North America. At night one would hear the familiar call *"Sereno!"* and then the rap-rap of a wooden stick and a long-drawn-out *"Vo-oo-oy,"* "Com-ing." The magic of the city and the people captivated me.

═══

Spain's penalty for national espionage was death. Therefore I was cautious in picking the head of my women's chain.

At the Farm I had been taught to form a chain by finding one reliable woman who would recruit another who in turn would find another, until fifteen formed the group. Some would be secretaries, others charwomen, cooks, dressmakers, laundresses. I would only know the one woman I recruited; the others would each know two, except the last woman. In this manner if one part of the chain was caught, the whole group would not be exposed at once.

Since I had been advised not to employ anyone who had fought with the Nationalists, Franco's side, I had to choose from among the Republicans. Although only about half of the Republicans had been communists or socialists at the outbreak of the war in 1936, many had switched to the Nationalist side when they realized the Republicans favored a Soviet-controlled totalitarian government. These converts had enabled Franco to win the war despite the weakness of his forces and the small amount of territory under Nationalist control at the beginning of the war. Thus those who considered themselves Republicans today were communists or socialists, and my orders had been to recruit from this group.

Neither the seamstress who was doing the curtains for the apartment nor my hairdresser, both of whom were communist "Republicans" and whom I considered for the job, was reliable. I needed someone with a higher educational background. It occurred to me to ask the *portera* to recommend a female teacher to help me improve my Castilian. She found this logical.

"A good idea, señorita. That American Spanish doesn't sound right. I know a woman who was secretary to a minister during the Republic. She is smart enough even to teach the señorita."

Pilar Hernández was plain, gray-haired, bespectacled. She always wore the same mannish suit and sturdy black shoes. From the first lesson I realized she was efficient and capable. Nevertheless, I observed her for a few weeks during our daily sessions, in some of which she expressed her political views.

"We socialists"—sometimes she referred to herself as a socialist and sometimes as a communist—"were trying to save Spain, by dividing the wealth among the people. We believe in equality, not liberty. We wanted to free the masses from the tyranny of capitalism."

No matter how I tried, I was ineffective in convincing her that democracy was the ideal way for poor people to better themselves.

"No one can change my opinions, señorita," she said. "In the three years of our war, I lost three brothers—one a year—to the fascists and Franco."

Frequently I talked about the problems the American Oil Mission had in its shipments to Spain, but I realized that if Pilar was as intelligent as she appeared, once I proposed espionage, my cover would be blown, to her at least. I proceeded with caution.

Our political points of view continued to be the main topic during our lessons, but Pilar was a firm communist and nothing I said had the slightest effect. By now I was as fond of the *"rojos"* as of the "fascists." All the Spaniards I met seemed to have the same warm personality. They also possessed an admirable respect for each other's personal dignity. My *portera* exchanged salutations daily with our neighbor the Duke of Silvela with no trace of servility or superiority on the part of one or the other, although they had been enemies only a few years before. Impeccable good manners and mutual respect existed on all levels of society.

As did good sense and courage. Two weeks later I proposed to Pilar the job of forming a women's chain and she accepted.

Chapter 13

A t eleven o'clock Horcher's restaurant was not yet full. As a waiter in tails led us to a table, I looked around at the high ceilings, the elaborate moldings, the paneled walls warm with the patina of years, the drapes of green velvet, all soft amid an amber light from silver candelabra.

As soon as I was seated, the waiter placed a pillow under my feet. "Ah, they told me at the office this is where they conceal their recorders," I confided, pumping the pillow with one foot.

Edmundo laughed. "That's ridiculous. A pillow under a lady's feet is normal procedure in elegant restaurants in Europe. This is probably the most luxurious eating place in Europe today. The owner, Otto Horcher, ran the best restaurant in Berlin and moved to Madrid when the bombing began to affect his business about a year ago."

My attention was drawn to the door, where a short, plump man of about sixty had just appeared. His hairless skull gleamed above a fringe of curly gray hair; he wore a black suit, a striped shirt, immaculate stiff arched collar. But what fascinated me was the monocle squeezed over one eye, puckering the round face. The waiters bowed as he sauntered through the room toward a door at the far end.

"Who is that?" I whispered to Edmundo.

"Hans Lazaar," Edmundo answered. "He is, among other doubtful occupations, the press attaché of the German Embassy and an important social figure in this city."

I hoped the excitement created by finally seeing one of my suspects did not show. "Does he always wear that monocle?"

"Always. I've heard it hides a glass eye. I've been introduced to him once, but I don't know him well, so I can't say for sure."

"Perhaps it's the monocle that makes him appear so evil."

"Everyone talks about it. Some say that he uses the monocle as a magnifying glass, others say he uses it to reflect light into the eyes of his victims when he interrogates them."

"What victims?"

"Oh, well, people gossip about everyone in this city. Lazaar is an obvious target, because he gives lavish parties in a palace he has rented on the Castellana. He also has a country estate outside Toledo where people say there are dungeons into which delightful spies such as you and I disappear."

Looking back at the door through which he had disappeared, I asked, "Where did he go?"

"Private dining room. Reserved for friends of the Third Reich, my dear."

Another bustle of attendants at the entrance. A ravishingly beautiful woman stalked in. Tall and sleek, perhaps thirty-five, tresses of wavy black hair, a sable cape draped from shoulder to foot, a black satin gown, and long, gleaming pearls.

"Who is *that*?"

Edmundo turned. "The one and only. The Countess von Fürstenberg." We watched her parade across the room, toward the same rear door.

"Now we know who Lazaar's dinner guest is," I commented. This was becoming the most important night of my career so far.

"There may be others in there," Edmundo said. "Perhaps important German officials."

I decided then that I had to find a way into that room.

"Edmundo, do you know her? She must be fascinating."

"Fascinating she is, but unfortunately I do not have the good fortune to know her intimately. But I know her through gossip. The Guatemalan ambassador says he saw her in a casino in Mexico at age sixteen. Her family is 'good.' Not distinguished or aristocratic or anything like that —middle-class from Guadalajara. Half and half, like me, Spanish and Indian. Who was it—I can't remember—took her to Hollywood after one look. She was in Los Angeles only long enough to meet some Dutch financier—frankly, Hollywood was too small for Gloria's ambitions— who whisked her to Europe. Then there was an Englishman, finally Fürstenberg. One night Mimosa will have to tell us the entire story. Now she may be a war widow, I don't know, and she has two small children, is totally down and out—but not for long. I hear she's seeing both the wealthy Señor March and Ahkmet Fakry, the Egyptian ambassador's son, quite a few years younger than she. She will need not only money but a new passport if the Germans lose the war."

"What do you mean *if* the Germans lose the war?" I was astounded by Edmundo's remark.

"Don't get indignant—you should realize I am teasing. Well, my dear, one thing I must say for Fürstenberg—sublime style. And a sharp wit. She's not completely accepted by all the grandes dames of Madrid. She is too much competition for the ladies." He took a long drink of red wine. "The women have every reason to be jealous of her. In Berlin she was famous; even the Führer was impressed by her, they say. Also, she's clever, because when no one could travel anyplace, she managed to go to Paris and to Rome."

"What about Lazaar? How does he fit in?"

"They're close friends. I don't know what he does for her, but you can be sure he is useful for something. In order to get a Spanish visa, she managed to have the Spanish ambassador in Berlin fall in love with her. Then she seduced General Wolff of the SS for an exit permit from Germany to Spain."

"Where does Lazaar get his money? Is he wealthy?"

"Those who knew him in Berlin say he didn't have any money to speak of." Dismissing Lazaar, Edmundo continued, "She'll do anything to support her style—why not? Hers is a rare gift. In Berlin, she palled around with all the bigwigs—Schellenberg, Goering, Himmler—all those with power, close to Hitler. I've tried to get to know her better, but there is no way she will deign even to talk to me. I'm not rich enough, nor powerful enough, nor chic enough. Alas."

Everything he said made me more determined to get into that room.

"Oh, it is so chilly here," I said to the waiter, who was filling Edmundo's wineglass. "It must be the draft from this window next to our table. Could we change to that one up there?" I pointed to an empty table in front of the door to the private dining room.

"If the señorita prefers, of course we will change the table."

Before he had finished speaking I was already on my way. Any moment, someone else might come in, and that was the only spot from which I might see into the room.

"Really, Aline. This is the worst table in the room," complained Edmundo once we were seated. "It wasn't cold at all, and at least there we could talk without being overheard."

While he was speaking a waiter opened the special door. I barely saw a small portion of a table and the countess's fur wrap on the back of a chair.

"Ah," exclaimed Top Hat. "Now I see why you wanted to change tables." He shook his head. "A wasted effort. You're not going to see anything from here. They always keep that door closed. But nothing stops you, does it, my dear? I tell you, Aline, you are the woman of my heart. If only you had a title. Tell me if you do see something, my pet, because I would have to use the mirror from your compact." He giggled. "I don't think Horcher would appreciate a man powdering his face in his restaurant."

Now another waiter was entering the room with drinks. This time I saw Lazaar only, but at least I was able to see that others were at the table. Despite the brief opening of the door, I discovered that there were two other men dining with the countess and Lazaar, but the door closed before I could see their faces. I hoped that one of the waiters would open the door wider, but little by little those inside were being served, and there was never more than one corner in my view. Unless I thought of something there was no way I could see the others at that table.

Finally, three waiters headed for the room, evidently to serve the main course. This time I was ready. Just as the first one passed through the door,

I made a generous gesture, rather as if I were showing Edmundo a new tennis swing, which knocked over the wine bucket at our side. Ice, water, and the bottle rolled in front of the now open door. The racket drew even Mr. Horcher himself to the spot. Everyone scrambled to clear the mess, which had spread over the carpet into the secluded room. Those at the table inside, startled by the confusion, turned our way, and in that moment I saw clearly face to face the man sitting in front of the German countess. There was no doubt in my mind who he was—only six yards more or less separated us.

A moment later the door was closed and calm restored.

"It will take some time before we are welcome here again, I fear." Edmundo laughed. "Was it worth the fuss, Aline?"

I buttered a piece of toast, speaking as nonchalantly as my enthusiasm permitted. "What do you think? I only saw Heinrich Himmler."

He stared at me. "You're mad, Aline. Maybe you've had too much red wine."

"I didn't drink a drop. Look, my glass is full." I was no longer a complete teetotaler, but a glass of wine would last me all night.

"You're crazy. Impossible. Himmler couldn't be in Spain. I would have heard."

"I'm telling you, I saw him," I whispered.

"Aline, Himmler hasn't been here since 1941. But we'll find out."

After dinner Edmundo ordered another cup of coffee, then another. He took his time over his cigar and cognac. The restaurant emptied out erratically, one table at a time. Finally the countess and Lazaar emerged from behind the paneled door. Constantin von Weiderstock walked out —the man I had not been able to see clearly—and no one else!

"You see, you were imagining things, my dear. No Himmler."

"Edmundo, there has to be another door going out of that room. Don't look at me as if I were crazy. That's one face I would know." By this time we were on our feet and about to leave.

"What do you intend to do?" he asked.

"What a question! To tell Mozart, naturally."

I dreaded the idea of waking Mozart at one-thirty in the morning, even if it was the usual hour dinner parties ended, but as soon as Top Hat dropped me at home I left again and ran up the deserted Calle Alcala Galiano to the office. Mozart would probably have to send a cable to Washington with my news, and it was better to use that telephone anyhow. A water line must have burst, since a gurgle of water flowing down the street was the only sound I heard.

Mozart picked up the phone himself. "Hello." His voice was curt. He had not been asleep.

"This is Aline." Just in case someone was listening, my real name was obligatory.

Pause. "What's up?"

"I was at Horcher's this evening and thought you might want to know that I saw Heinrich Himmler there in the private dining room."

Drearily, he sighed. "If that were true, I would know he was in the country. There are a hundred squat, bespectacled men in Madrid who might be mistaken for him. Is that all?"

"But I am certain I saw him."

"Can anyone else verify his presence?"

"No, not for the moment. Edmundo was with me, but he did not see him. We waited to see him leave, but he must have gone out another door."

"There is no other door to the private room. Good night, Miss Griffith."

I wandered around the empty bank of offices until I reached the code room, where a slice of light could be seen under the door. Jeff was at his desk. "Anything new?" I asked.

"Just decoding a message from tonight's drop. Ben made contact about an hour ago."

Although in Madrid the night was overcast, I remembered this was a full moon, the date scheduled for a drop in France. Our plane from Algiers would either drop an agent by parachute or land in a spot illuminated by the Maquis's flashlights and take off again without turning off the motors. A radioman always advised us in Madrid if all went well and set up the date and hour for the next radio contact.

"The news is good," said Jeff, "and a new agent code-named Pierre sent the message."

"Let me see that." I grabbed the paper from under Walters's nose. His head jerked up, surprised.

"What's up, Aline?"

I couldn't believe my eyes. Was it Pierre, my Pierre? "There was a fellow training with me by that name."

Jeff looked amused. "Well, you obviously are nuts about him."

"Not at all." I tossed the paper back onto his desk. "Just curious." I waved from the door. "See you tomorrow, Jeff."

I retraced my steps through the empty offices, thinking of what had just happened. The silence, the darkness, encouraged me to quicken my stride. As I entered my street, there was the sound of footsteps behind and no *sereno* in sight. I ran, and it seemed whoever was following did the same. When I reached my door, I slipped through the iron bars without putting the key in the lock, grateful that the glass had not been replaced since the civil war and that I was skinny, and raced up the steps.

I was discouraged that Mozart had not believed me, but at least now I knew why Pierre had been in Spain. He had been on his way to France and might come again. That made me happier. I was exhausted and fell into bed. A moment later I pulled myself out again to get my revolver from my handbag and place it under my pillow. Even though I was getting accustomed to the tension, why take chances, I thought.

I went to sleep on a good note. Finally, I was on my way to uncovering at least two of the suspects on my list.

=====

The ancient granite buildings and gray leafless tree trunks shone in the sharp sunlight as Belmonte's sleek Bugatti swept through the streets.

"Did you like the chocolates? And the carnations?" By now these deliveries had become routine.

"Yes. I like everything about Madrid."

He turned to me.

"But not Pasapoga, I hope."

"Juan, that was over two months ago. Why bring it up again? I had no idea it was not a proper place to go. Edmundo merely said we were going dancing that night."

"Dancing? Your companion looked as if he were practicing for the ring."

I smiled. "Edmundo *is* wild, but he's got a great sense of humor."

Staring straight ahead as we turned a corner, Juan said, "I don't think he's a proper friend for you. Spain *is* different from America. What is acceptable for men is not acceptable for women."

"Do you think that's fair?"

Juanito smiled. "Yes, I do."

"Well, I don't."

Perhaps he sensed my irritation, for he dropped the topic. "Well, here we are." Juan pointed to the trickling stream below. "The Manzanares. Of course, the drought has affected it somewhat, but you should see it anyway. On the Eve of St. Anthony, girls who want to find a husband within the year throw pennies into this river."

Juanito turned to me. "I hope you are not busy on the tenth of June."

"Not as far as I know." I shook my head. "It *is* a long way off."

"Good. We have a date, Aline. That night you will throw a penny in the Manzanares with me at your side—and then you will never leave Spain. St. Anthony is the patron saint of lovers."

I was stumped for a reply. Juanito's formal manner, like his stiff, measured gait, was unbelievable, but whether I liked him or not, he was useful. He knew everyone.

The scene had charm; we were sitting in an open-air café on the arid riverbank, where a few customers were enjoying the strong March sunlight. After a small glass of Tío Pepe sherry, Juan suggested going across the street to the church of San Antonio de la Florida. My eyes were temporarily blurred going from strong sunlight into the darkness when I first entered the shabby little church, and then I noticed the domed ceiling resplendent with frescoes.

"Those were painted by Goya." Juanito looked above and then said with all the seriousness of a tour guide, "The eyes in those paintings are like your own, full of smoldering fire."

I shook my head and barely stifled a laugh. He was impossible.

From there we went to the Plaza Mayor, an impressive seventeenth-century square surrounded by arches and shops in symmetrical buildings graced by numerous balconies.

"That's where the royal family and the court used to watch the bullfights," Juan explained. "When the matador was especially successful, the ladies sometimes threw pearls into the ring." He looked at me. "Like your teeth."

"My teeth?"

"Your teeth are like pearls, Aline."

And my mouth like an oyster, I thought—unable to speak. We went down stone stairs eroded by centuries—the famous Steps of Cuchilleros —and after passing through a myriad of domed chambers to a small cave of a room, entered a dungeonlike bar and feasted on crusty chunks of fresh-baked bread, *manchego* cheese, and red wine.

He lifted his glass—I should have seen it coming. "Wine as red as your lips."

I silently sipped from my glass.

"And to our future," he added. A future with Juan Belmonte? I couldn't imagine it.

"This is where the famous bandit Luis Candelas used to hide, Aline. He stole from the rich and gave to the poor—just like your Robin Hat."

"Hood," I corrected. "Robin Hood."

Shortly after that we walked through the Calle de Segovia—this was Madrid's oldest *barrio*—and then to an ancient restaurant. "The specialty of the house is roast suckling pig," said Juanito.

He looked at me a moment and started to open his mouth.

"Oh, please, Juanito, don't compare me to a roast pig."

He threw his head back, and we both roared. When we could, I told him, "Really Juan, if you keep saying such preposterous things, it will be the end of our friendship."

"What a relief," he answered. "But Spanish women expect a man to compliment them all the time."

"I'll never believe girls like the Avilas fall for that, nor the flamenco singers, either."

A burst of singing announced the entrance of a *tuna,* a group of college students bearing egg-shaped fiddles, dressed in black gowns with multicolored ribbons streaming from their shoulders. They launched into a number of ballads, after which Juan showered them with pesetas.

He made no more silly statements until I asked him if he knew the Countess von Fürstenberg.

"Of course I know her. Why do you ask?"

"Could you introduce me?"

"Certainly not. She is not the proper friend for you."

Juanito was right out of another century.

Chapter 14

I saw it in her eyes behind her glasses—Pilar was excited. Using the pretext of a lesson, she held a small blackboard on which she had chalked the conjugation of irregular verbs.

"You are right," she said quietly as soon as I sat beside her. "You are being followed at night. But we can't identify the man. He disappears on the Ribera de Curtidores in the Rastro in the old part of the city. It's a street crammed with decrepit lodgings. Many Gypsies live there—also it is filled with cheap *pensiones* where the country yokels stay when they come to Madrid. And a number of crooks and vagabonds roam that neighborhood. A difficult place to find anyone."

"Pilar, keep after him. I'm also followed by day. There is more than one person trailing me. I have other work for you, too. The Countess von Fürstenberg lives in the Palace Hotel. I want you to get as much information as possible about her."

"That's easy. We already have a maid in the hotel, one of my best."

"Pilar, I hope you have followed the system I explained to you. For your own protection, you are only supposed to know the one woman you recruited, not the others."

"Do not worry, señorita. This is exactly the work I did during the war. No one knows you, and that is what must be kept secret."

"I saw Heinrich Himmler eating in the private dining room at Horcher's, but I need proof he was there. Find out if there is a secret entrance to that room. Check the lists of Lufthansa passengers coming in and going out of Madrid—also of those taking the night train to and from Barcelona and Irún and any other routes used by officials coming in from Berlin. Do you know what Himmler looks like?"

"How does the señorita think I am not going to know that monster? If he has been in Spain, my women will find out, have no care."

———

It was in late March that the Avila sisters had invited me to dine with them at home. I was admitted to the ancient building by the *sereno,* who put on a light in the entrance and pulled the cord of a gong, announcing to those upstairs my arrival. The staircase was wide and grand, and on the landing was a carved wooden siren which had adorned the prow of a sixteenth-century ship, but the wooden steps were worn and carpetless. A white-haired servant, elegant in blue tails, vest, gilt buttons with the family crown, stood at the door and welcomed me into a high-ceilinged entrance hall, barren except for two suits of armor on small pedestals. He took my coat and led me through a vast room where an antique organ with fluted bronze spokes covered the far end. We passed English and French antique furniture, walking on a deteriorated carpet; chilly drafts came through the heavy faded blue draperies. I was reminded that these people had recently pulled themselves together after a war and realized that many old homes had been used during the siege of Madrid as military barracks. Casilda's voice called out, "Evaristo, bring the señorita in here where it is warm."

She jumped up from a round table covered by a floor-length velvet cloth to greet me. "Forgive me for not going into the other room, but we have a brazier here under the table and it is more comfortable. We are here until the small dining room gets heated. This rationing of coke and coal is terrible."

I went to embrace the two other sisters and then was introduced to the fourth girl—blond, blue-eyed, a classic beauty. "This is my best friend," said Casilda. "Carola Lilienthal." I couldn't believe my luck. This girl had to be the daughter of Prince Nikolaus Lilienthal, one of those on my list. She was outstanding enough to turn the head of anyone, even in El

Morocco. Not only that, but in a moment I realized she was extremely friendly.

"Aline, I won't pretend I don't know all about you. Casilda never stops talking about you, and I've heard from other friends. I know you were at Chipén's the other night with Juan Belmonte. You see, I know everything that goes on in this city."

We chatted at dinner as if I had known her all my life. The girls were anxious to know about American college life and clothes and also told me about their parties and pastimes, which were concerned more with getting a proper husband than working or studying. After dinner we played the American records I had brought on the phonograph—Benny Goodman's rendition of "One O'Clock Jump" became their favorite; they had never heard it before. I taught them to jitterbug, and they showed me how to dance the Spanish *chotis* and even some of the Sevillanas. In many ways it was like being back at college again; it was the only carefree moment I had enjoyed in months, and more relaxing than the large receptions where Edmundo had taken me until now.

When Carola's chauffeur came to take her home, she offered to take me also. On the way she said, "You must come for a weekend with us in the country. How about the weekend of April first? You'll love El Morisco. We will have lots of guests, and flamenco, too."

I just looked at her. This was almost too easy.

"I won't take no for an answer, Aline," she called as I got out of the car.

"Don't worry," I said. "I'll keep that weekend free."

======

It was raining. There were no taxis, and I had to go to Pilar's apartment on the Calle Conde Duque. No one had an umbrella. Angustias didn't even know of a shop that sold them.

"Who wants an umbrella, señorita? The water God sends from heaven is good for the skin, and means luck and wealth for Spain," explained Cecilia, the cook.

The narrow stairway in Pilar's old building was permeated by the odor of frying olive oil, a smell I was beginning to consider the national odor. Pilar opened the door, a finger at her lips counseling silence. She pointed to a battered radio. "La Pasionaria is speaking from Moscow—she's the woman who inspired us to fight in our war."

The strong female voice on the radio was exhorting, "Comrades, do not despair. Your brothers in southern France are grouping to retake our beloved motherland!"

The political broadcast continued, tedious and repetitive. I looked at my watch. I was anxious to receive Pilar's reports on Himmler and von Fürstenberg; and I wanted to be at the Hotel Ritz by ten o'clock, where Juanito was giving a birthday party for his fellow bullfighter Manolete.

Now a man's voice came over the radio: "Spaniards, beware of the American imperialists! When this war ends, the good Soviet people will eliminate the seat of the capitalistic system, the United States of America."

It was difficult to believe the Soviets would broadcast against us while we were allies. I asked Pilar to turn the radio off.

"You can't believe that false information about my country, Pilar."

"Do not worry, señorita. I am loyal to you now. We have a mutual enemy—Hitler. But after the war you will see how much better the Soviet system is than yours. In twenty years, Russia will be the richest country on earth!"

I shook my head in disgust. Then I looked at the barren cold room, one lone light bulb dangling from the ceiling. It was like a cell. No wonder there were communists in this country.

Pilar handed me two pieces of paper. "This is the report on the countess, but I have no solid information on Himmler. However, a man of his general appearance was in the restaurant last week. We have been able to determine that there is an invisible wall door into the private dining room. It is used frequently by certain patrons." Her news was encouraging, but I feared not definite enough to please Mozart.

Still standing in the dim light, I read the report, fastidiously typed on what must have been an antiquated machine:

COUNTESS VON FÜRSTENBERG
(week of 3/20/44)

3/20

11:00 Breakfast delivered. Telephone calls from Sra.
Stiller, wife of German Embassy official; Sr. Hans
Lazaar, Sr. Ahkmet Fakry, son of Egyptian ambassador;
and one unidentified man.

1:00 Went to Rosa Zavala hairdresser (directly in front
of Palace Hotel).

2:30 Lunch at Palace Grill with Countess Podevils.

5:00 Ana de Pombo's Salon, dressmaker, Calle Hermosilla, 14.

6:30 Returns.

10:00 Sr. Fakry, Egyptian Embassy, picks her up.

10:30 Dinner at Orcapón, Carrera San Jerónimo (with Fakry).
After dinner agent loses trail—no taxi can keep
up with a Mercedes.

4:30 Return.

3/21

1:00 Breakfast.

1:42 Telephone from Berlin—Sr. Walter Schellenberg.

3:30 Picks up children at the Colegio Alemán.

4:30 Calle Lope de Vega 12, shoemaker Francisco Franjul.

5:00 Ana de Pombo's Salon, dressmaker, Calle Hermosilla 14.

6:30 Return to hotel.

10:00 Car from German Embassy picks her up.

10:30 Dinner at Castellana 49, house of Sr. Lazaar.

2:00 Returns.

2:30 Telephone call from Berlin.

3/22

11:00 Breakfast.

12:00 Masseuse—Conchita.

1:00 Manicurist Carmen Tirano.

4:30 Phone calls, Countess Podevils, Sr. Luca de Tena,
bootmaker Sr. Alvarez, Calle Conde Duque 25

5:00   Ana de Pombo's Salon.

6:30   Return.

10:00   Car from Italian Embassy picks her up.

10:30   Dinner at Sr. and Sra. San Juste, Italian Embassy official's house.

1:00   Leaves dinner, in company of Sr. Ahkmet Fakry.

1:15   Dancing, La Reboite, Calle Prim.

5:00   Return.

I paused to look at Pilar, who peered at me with her usual primness. "This is incredible, Pilar, and very useful."

Satisfaction shone in her eyes. "In a few days I will have the names and telephone numbers in her address book. I get prompt work from my girls."

In counting out the salaries, I added five hundred pesetas. "This is for you, Pilar, so you can live more comfortably. It's freezing in here." She refused, but I insisted. I knew this was enough money for three months of coal or coke on the black market. My maid and cook made one hundred and fifty pesetas a month, which amounted to about fifteen dollars each. The Balenciaga dress which I had bought the week before had cost the exorbitant sum for Spain of two thousand pesetas, but for me it was far less than a dress at Hattie Carnegie's. I handed her the money.

She accepted. "I will recruit another chain to provide the señorita with more information."

I left, hoping I wasn't contributing to Spain's anti-American Communist Party.

Chapter 15

The war was not going as expected. Operation Overlord and Operation Anvil could not be put into action until the Italian campaign was successful, and right now that was at a stalemate. On March 15 there had been heavy Allied bombing over Cassino, destroying an ancient monastery there, which our officers had believed to be a German watchpost. They were mistaken, and now the Germans were able to move in, using the monastery and the rubble left in the town as cover for their troops. We all hoped this error had not been made because of incorrect information from OSS Italy. Also, despite the massive number of vehicles and men on the beachhead at Anzio, our troops were not advancing there either. Although our forces had destroyed the Axis advantage at sea, the failures in Italy were creating a tension which affected us all.

Mozart was especially taciturn these days, and our team was more jittery than usual. On March 27, he announced that our office would be moved immediately to new quarters. Ostensibly the excuse was that the Oil Mission needed more room, but Mozart curtly informed us, "Washington is demanding greater security for our OSS files and increased caution on the part of its agents." Code boards were concealed in file cabinets, transmitters in large boxes for office equipment. It took two days to move to the top floor of the American ambassador's residence, and during that time no messages were decoded.

Our new address, the palace of the Duke of Montellano, was surrounded by a large garden and even nearer to my apartment. When I arrived the first day, the gatekeeper opened a door adjacent to the wrought-iron portal and directed me up a gravel path to a side entrance of the house. I went immediately to Mozart's office with Pilar's report on the countess, informing him that a member of Pilar's chain had confirmed that Himmler had been in Horcher's restaurant the week before.

"I want proof, Miss Griffith," said Phillip Harris emphatically. "How reliable is this woman? Perhaps she was an uneducated charwoman? Obviously she wasn't a waiter. Did she see him personally? News as vital as Himmler's being in Madrid has to be verified by reliable informants."

"But there is a secret door in that room, and he probably used it to leave unseen."

"Ridiculous. I couldn't risk sending this shaky bit of evidence to Washington." With a nod he dismissed me.

Compliments were hard to get from the boss. I knew the others suffered the same discouraging moments, so I shrugged off my disappointment. In the new code room Walters was waiting for me.

"There you are. Now that I've done all the heavy work," Jeff teased. "We've got a stack of cables piled up, but first I want to show you the great view we now enjoy."

Streams of sunlight lit up the large corner attic room. I looked out the window at green lawns, old chestnuts, oaks, acacias, forsythia bushes in bloom. Jeff pulled me to the other window, facing the Castellana. No children were playing there yet, but a few carriages with the usual skinny nags stood waiting for customers, and a couple of automobiles passed by. Across the street was a palace similar to the one we were in.

"That's the home of the famous prime minister of the monarchy, the Count of Romanones," said Jeff as I turned away and tackled the first cable from London.

TO MOZART FROM CHESS STOP BRITISH IMPRISONED SPANIARD WORKING AS GERMAN AGENT UNDER CODE NAME GARBO STOP GARBO CHAN-NELED MESSAGES TO BERLIN THROUGH GUILLERMO IN MADRID STOP

Jeff and I amused ourselves to see who could decode faster. The next cable was typical of others we had received the week before.

FROM HOTSPOT TO MOZART STOP   REQUEST AGENTS WITH CONTACTS IN ITALY NEAR BISENTI ASSIST OUR AGENT FRITZ NEEDS EVACUATION URGENTLY STOP

Several cables later, I decoded one that I immediately tossed over to Jeff's desk. "Look at this, Jeff. It appears that the Germans' period of leniency is over."

The cable read:

HITLERS ORDERS TO WEHRMACHT AS FOLLOWS QUOTE SABOTAGE AND TERROR TROOPS WHETHER ARMED OR UNARMED IN OR OUT OF UNIFORM ARE TO BE SLAUGHTERED TO THE LAST MAN STOP   THIS INCLUDES ENEMY AGENTS IN NEUTRAL COUNTRIES STOP

After reading it, Jeff commented, "This means if we are caught or even suspected, the orders now are to kill. Do you realize this is a breach of the Geneva Convention?" He tapped the revolver in his belt. "My advice is to be damn careful no matter where you are, Tiger. Nobody will catch me taking any chances."

I stayed in during the long Spanish lunchtime and continued to work and then relaxed reading the daily newspaper. The results of Lazaar's work as German press attaché covered the front page of *Informaciones,* according to which the Germans were winning the war. Although this was propaganda, the fact that the Allies had landed in Sicily in September and were still bogged down made it easy for the Spanish press to restrict Allied victories to small notices on inside pages. And I had worried while in training that it might all end before I could get overseas.

When I went back to work, most of the cables confirmed exceptionally vital news. Another from London read:

TO MOZART FROM CHESS STOP HIMMLER PROCEEDING TO ABSORB AB-
WEHR INTELLIGENCE INTO GESTAPO AFTER REMOVAL OF CANARIS STOP
WALTER SCHELLENBERG NOW CONTROLS ALL GERMAN FOREIGN INTELLI-
GENCE STOP

It was already late in the afternoon when I tackled the last cables,
decoding mechanically:

TO MOZART FROM CHESS STOP   RELIABLE INFORMANT SAYS HIMMLER
WAS IN MADRID RECENTLY . . .

My temperature soared, and I rushed to finish it.

. . . AND BARCELONA STOP   INVESTIGATE URGENTLY STOP

This was really some day. I jumped up and rushed into Mozart's room,
hardly knocking. He was on the telephone, so I placed the message on
his table in front of his eyes and left.

While working on the last cables my mind was on Mozart's reaction.
Wasn't that proof enough that I had been right about seeing Himmler?
So absorbed was I that I didn't hear the door open. Mozart, despite his
size, also moved like a cat. Cool, impenetrable, as always.

"Miss Griffith." He beckoned to me. "Could you come to my office
for a minute?"

As soon as I was inside he asked, "Tell me, who did you see with
Himmler that night at Horcher's?"

I told him precisely what I had seen, then waited for his comments.

"Get details on Himmler's visit. Who he was with. How often he was
there. Where he stayed." Then unexpectedly he leaned back in his chair
and asked, "Tell me, Aline, what have you been doing lately? Any new
people on your list?"

I told him that I had met the daughter of Prince Nikolaus Lilienthal.

"That's excellent. How long do you think it will take for you to meet her father?"

"Carola has invited me to their country home next weekend."

"Great. We've been trying to get someone inside that place. There are a series of investigations you can accomplish while there. We'll discuss that on Saturday before you leave."

=====

Later that evening, I sat at my desk with pen in hand, stumped. Just the thought that Mozart might be the one to censor my letters inhibited every thought before I could express it. My mother had been asking in her letters who were the "young men" I worked with or went out with. So far the only person I had dared mention was Juanito, and the idea that my free time was spent with a bullfighter had not made her happy. Finally I decided, for lack of anything else with which to fill the page, to send her Cecilia's recipe for paella. Edmundo was picking me up at ten to take me to a cocktail party given by Ralph Forte, the Associated Press correspondent. Afterward we were going to a party at La Reboite, a nightclub.

I hurried into my dressing room and put on a red silk dress I had never worn before. Juanito's carnations, I noticed, had begun to wither, and as I fixed my hair, I thought how much I missed his funny compliments. As I was applying my lipstick, a strange noise shocked me out of my nostalgic mood. Someone was prying open the shutters on the balcony in the adjoining room.

My revolver was in front of me in the top drawer with my makeup. Grabbing it, I slipped through the door and hid behind the curtains.

Slowly, the glass door slid open. From where I stood I caught a glimpse of a man's hand separating the lace curtains. I thought about shooting blindly at whoever this intruder might be, but decided I should wait to see who it was. The figure emerged from behind the curtains.

"Pierre! What are you doing here?"

I stood paralyzed with my gun still raised and aimed at Pierre's chest. He strode over to me calmly and took the gun, and then, grinning, he raised my still-outstretched hand to his lips.

"How are you, Tiger? Didn't expect to see me soon, did you?" That seductive voice!

Despite the cold night, he had no coat, just a dark suit as if he were on the way to a party.

I was flustered. "How did you find out where I lived?"

"That's our business, isn't it? Come, let's sit down and talk. There is so much—"

I interrupted him. "Pierre, what are you doing here? You know, I almost shot you just now."

"I can't tell you much. You know better than anyone why. Your boss would have my hide if he knew I was visiting you now."

It pleased me that he had put himself in danger to see me. The thought that Edmundo was about to arrive was exasperating.

Pierre pulled me to the sofa, and we both sat down. Suddenly he jumped up and selected one red carnation from a bowl on the table and came back, sitting close.

"I would have liked to buy a flower lovely enough to go with a face I can't get out of my mind, but this will have to do."

He broke off the stem and slid it into my hair.

His kiss at first was gentle; then he put both arms around me and pulled me closer. I couldn't resist.

At that moment, the bell rang. Angustias's steps sounded in the corridor on her way to open the door.

"Who's that?" asked Pierre. He stood up.

"Oh, it's too terrible. That's my contact, who is picking me up to take me to a party."

We moved quietly toward the balcony.

"I can't be seen, Tiger. It's not often possible to break the rules. I doubt I'll be able to see you soon." He leaned over and kissed me quickly. "Don't forget me." Then he turned toward the open French door. The curtains swayed and he was gone.

Angustias and Edmundo were in the hall exchanging words as I looked out into the night. Not a trace of Pierre! Down below were the shadows of the interior patio. How had he gotten into my house? He must have crawled over the curved-tile rooftops, and yet his clothes were impeccable. Well, we had all learned those tricks.

The excitement of having been with Pierre probably showed in my expression when I greeted Edmundo.

"Divina, you look as if you had seen a ghost," he said.

And I thought, That's what Pierre will have to be from now on, just a ghost. But at least he was near.

———

On Saturday, a few hours before leaving for Carola's house party, Mozart gave me my instructions.

"There are a variety of reasons why Lilienthal is on top of our blacklist, Miss Griffith. Above all because our contact in Berlin suggested him as possibly being Himmler's special agent here. On our own, we have learned that top German brass have been his guests at that estate near El Escorial. We also know the place is ideal for hiding the secret radio station operating from this area to Berlin." He handed me a heavy rectangular carton about the size of a shoe box. "Here's a radio detector. You should be familiar with its use."

I opened the box and removed the small apparatus. It was one of the many sophisticated gadgets to which Whiskey had introduced us at the Farm.

"Another powerful reason," Mozart said, "is the fact that the guy stands to lose a fortune if the Germans don't win. Everything he has is tied up with them—factories in Germany, properties in Czechoslovakia. You are going to have to find out. Rifle his safe. Photograph everything you find, especially his passport with all exit and entry stamps. We will need every kind of proof against him when the day of reckoning comes."

Mozart went to a corner of the room and picked up the smallest of three black leather suitcases.

"These suitcases are for your use. They all have false bottoms, and this one"—he indicated the one in front of him—"has a variety of material you may need." He looked at his watch. "I have an appointment in five minutes with the ambassador. He never stops complaining to the White

House that this organization shows absolutely no results to warrant our continued presence here. He wants us gone, so you'd better find something incriminating this weekend."

For a moment, Mozart seemed to thaw, an unusual sight. Shaking his head, he remarked, "I'm under a lot of pressure. I keep expecting the invasion to take place, either Overlord or Anvil. Everyone, even the Germans, knows our first invasion has to take place in the spring if it is going to take advantage of maximum time before winter sets in. They're jittery, too. Keep that in mind." He gestured with a wave of his huge hand. "Oh, well. Good luck to you."

That afternoon Casilda Avila and I drove through the hills that flank the Guadarrama Mountains, weaving through groves of live oaks and umbrella pines which changed to gray jagged stone formations as we neared the town of El Escorial.

"Look, Aline." Casilda indicated the spires of four cupolas. "That's the most important royal palace in Spain, built by Philip the Second in the sixteenth century. The same architect who built the Lilienthal palace. We'll be there in twenty minutes now."

The road approaching the Lilienthal home descended a hill from where I looked down on an immense square stone building—all gleaming and sand-colored in the last rays of the afternoon sun. Dusty red clay tiles covered the roofs. The entrance doors were open, and a black Mercedes-Benz was parked there, the chauffeur unloading someone's luggage. As our car came to a stop I looked up at the carved stone escutcheon over the door, then looked around the sloping gardens, to a chapel, and back to the facade, where a row of windows covered by iron grilles crossed the building at the height of the second floor. To me the building appeared impregnable and austere, reminiscent of knights in armor and children's fairy tales.

My heels crunched on the gravel as I carried the hatbox containing the equipment Mozart had given me toward the door. Fortunately I had been able to squeeze it all in: radio detector, chemicals, wires and files, special powders, the new "spy camera." The chauffeur was unloading my red plaid suitcases, which I had used rather than those Mozart had given me. Not only would their false bottoms not have fooled a trained agent, but their masculine appearance did not seem appropriate for a young woman.

Casilda linked her arm through mine. "It's lovely, no? And you will see what a charming family."

Her words gave me a twinge. What if I discovered that Carola's father was guilty of harboring German agents or was the special contact Himmler had in Spain? Accepting a friend's hospitality in order to uncover incriminating evidence against her disgusted me. I walked into the old palace with a heavy heart.

Beyond the open double doors in the entrance hall one could see a square patio twice the size of a gymnasium surrounded by about fifty graceful granite columns and above on the second floor by a balcony corridor with a stone railing supported by more lovely columns. The entrance hall itself was barren of furniture, with the exception of a thick wooden table against the wall. The butler invited us to sign the guest book lying between two huge silver candelabra. As I picked up the pen, I observed the number of signed pages. The book would provide signatures of guests for many years back, if I could get a look later.

Male servants in livery arrived to carry our luggage, and two maids directed us up a narrow staircase. The long unheated corridors had the chill of a cathedral. Finally at the end of a hall in the back of the building my luggage was placed inside a small room with beamed ceilings, a fireplace, and whitewashed walls. Adjoining was a room with a bed framed by a red damask canopy. The maid hastened to turn on a lamp on a corner table and to draw the curtains. She turned to me, saying she would return soon to unpack my things.

A place to conceal the equipment in my hatbox had to be found quickly. The powdery chemicals were already concealed in boxes with my makeup. Only in the bathroom did I find an ideal spot. Although the large window behind the dressing table was visible from across the patio, the other part of my suite faced the opposite direction, and by standing on the toilet I could reach another window which faced a stony cliff. There was no path or garden below. The waterproof bag fit perfectly on the outside ledge and would be invisible.

A few minutes later I met Casilda in the drafty corridor. We descended to the first floor and went through several salons until we arrived at a large room with a crackling fireplace. A number of people were having tea. A tall blond man in tweed shooting clothes who was entering the room from the opposite side was commenting, "A great day's shooting, Niki. Fifty brace." Chatting while munching on small cakes were jeweled women in woolen suits, and the scent of their various perfumes reached us as we advanced. Carola leaped to her feet and ran to kiss me on the cheek.

"How happy I am to have you here, Aline. Come meet my father. My mother you will see later—she never takes tea." She led me to a group in the far corner and placed her hand on the arm of a tall, florid man. "Papi," she said, "I spoke to you about Aline Griffith, remember? I told you we imitated a singing group called . . . what are the names of those American girls, Aline?"

"The Andrews Sisters."

Prince Niki smiled. Nonetheless, he was confused. "The Andrews Sisters? They sing opera?"

Carola and I laughed. "Hardly, Papi," she corrected. "They sing jazz."

It's doubtful that the prince clearly understood, but nevertheless he continued to smile. "I must say, I once had a go at the accordion and found it quite rum." The prince's English was fluent, but with a marked German accent. "In any event, Aline, it is a pleasure to meet a friend of Carola's and to have you as our guest."

His kindness put me at ease, and I turned to meet the others. My pleasure, as I began to take note of the faces around the room, turned to astonishment. In a chair close to one of the fireplaces, the flames casting a yellow glow on his sling, was Constantin von Weiderstock. And in another circle, sipping tea, was the Countess von Fürstenberg with Hans Lazaar. As if they were not enough, I now recognized Mimosa Torrejón, the Count and Countess of Yebes, and "Ducky" Durcal, an elderly gentleman Casilda had introduced me to the week before.

Three out of four on my list in one place. Like betting all on one number and then—jackpot. At that moment I made up my mind that before the weekend was over, I would search all their rooms.

Then another familiar face, Casilda's sister Nena, strolled over to a young man seated with the Countess von Fürstenberg and Lazaar. I knew him immediately—the fellow who had approached me that first day in the lobby of the Palace Hotel and who had carried my baggage to the room. There were two empty seats in their circle, but before I could reach one, I heard:

"Aline, Aline Griffith, how are you, child?" The Marquesa of Torre-jón's brittle voice arrested me. She gave a little wave, her sharp eyes fixing me. I walked to her.

"How delighted I am to see you, my dear." The marquesa grasped my hand with excessive warmth, I thought. "It should be a lovely weekend, don't you think?"

"Oh, yes," I readily agreed. Lovely and busy.

"You will be pleased to know I left my cards at home. Don't say another word—everyone is quite plainly relieved. I would never dream of boring this charming group with another of my dreadful readings. And frankly, my dear, these days the tidings are decidedly grim. Dreadfully so. Such times we live in."

Politely I smiled at the eccentric Mimosa, excusing myself. Then I wandered over to the circle that harbored two of my quarries.

First, Nena presented me to the young man I had seen at the hotel, who was the Count of Quintanilla. "I think we have met before," he said and smiled. I was embarrassed, remembering the tip I had tried to push into his hand that first day in the hotel.

Then I was introduced to Carlos Beistegui, a sleek, gray-haired man with a paunch and sly pale eyes. And finally—finally—to Gloria von Fürstenberg and Hans Lazaar.

The countess was even more ravishing at close range, and she was simply the best-dressed woman I had ever seen. Every detail—her obviously custom-made black-and-red-checked wool suit, the diamond-and-ruby parrot on the lapel, the hand-worked leather shoes with pointed toes, the black mink-and-leather jacket slung on the arm of her chair—bespoke her good taste. Her white complexion, abundant hair, and high cheekbones made me realize I was meeting one of the beauties of my time.

"*Encantada,* Aline," she said in a low, wonderful voice.

Hans Lazaar's monocle scrutinized me. Up close he was still more bizarre—his round, ugly features made him look like the bad guy in a movie. Standing, he said in clipped, precise English, "A pleasure, Miss Griffith."

From a small marble-topped commode next to the wall, Carola poured me a cup of tea.

Lazaar's monocle was still fastened on me. "Of course. I remember perfectly." Turning to the countess seated to his left he said, "You remember, don't you, Gloria? At Horcher's? Several weeks ago?"

The countess shrugged and ran her hands through her lustrous raven tresses. "Hans, your memory staggers me. How can you remember such a detail? I can't remember a single thing I did yesterday." To the group she said, "Do you know, he has an absolutely photographic memory?"

"What a shame you recall so little of your life, my dear. You, of whom volumes could be written," said the suave Señor Beistegui.

"In that case, I am blessed to remember nothing," the countess returned. "I don't want a single word written about me—I prefer to remain a mystery."

"You? A mystery?" Beistegui smirked. "There's nothing mysterious about a beautiful woman who has always been the toast of every town she has been in. You haven't missed a party in years."

"Gloria, you were born in the wrong century," Lazaar said stiffly, though in a low key. "You would have shone at Versailles."

Thankfully the course of conversation was steered clear of Lazaar's memory, though his monocled gaze remained stubbornly trained on my face. Shortly thereafter, the gathering began to disperse.

An hour later—it must have been around seven—as I sat in front of the little fire in my room, lost in my calculations, a sweater over my shoulders to ward off the evening chill, a soft knock sounded on my door.

When I opened it, I was surprised to see Mimosa Torrejón, looking distraught.

"What is the matter?" I asked, then quickly added, "Please come in."

The small, bony woman entered and shut the door behind her. She trembled. "I am not feeling well tonight. But that's not why I took the chance of seeing you. May I sit down?"

"Of course. Forgive me."

Taking a chair before the fire, Mimosa gave me a long look. Her eyes seemed to glitter more than ever, like hard, tiny gems. I wondered if she had been crying.

"I don't know who you are, or what you do," she said at last, in her "reading" tone. "But I'm terrified, and I have no one else to talk to. I know you are a friend of Edmundo's . . . that is why I'm taking this risk. I'm frightened. I must trust somebody."

I warned myself to measure my every syllable. "I'm grateful for your confidence, Mimosa."

The marquesa fingered her pearls. "They are on to me, my child. I know it. I have been found out."

"Who is on to you? What do you mean?"

"The Germans. The Gestapo, no less."

"But why?" I held my breath.

"That's what I came to tell you." She glanced furtively toward the door, then placed a bony hand on my knee. "I have vital information for the Americans. Edmundo is out of town and I have no means of warning them, except to tell you."

She shivered and stretched her feet toward the fire. Rosettes adorned her pointed shoes. Silently she gazed at the flames. Her trembling ceased. I wondered if this was a ruse. She turned to me. Her brow and the skin around her eyes were creased in deep wrinkles. Either her anxiety was sincere or she was a great actress.

"When I read your cards I sensed I could trust you."

"Please go on," I said as soothingly as I could. "I'm a good listener."

"If they suspect I know their secret, they will kill me." She shuddered again. "And if they find out I told you, they would kill you, too. They're inexorable."

"But who are they?"

"Oh, I wouldn't dare put you in the danger of knowing their names."

Now I began to think her babble was the result of too much card reading. Nothing she said made much sense.

"My dear, you must take me seriously. The Germans are plotting to assassinate Franco. I know how this will take place and who is organizing it. They are furious with the Generalíssimo. He hasn't helped them as they counted on by handing Spain over on a platter. So they have a plan to replace him with another who will bring Spain into the war." She put her hand to her abdomen, wincing.

"Are you all right? Can I get you anything?"

"Thank you, my dear, I'll be all right once I get my news into the right hands."

"But why don't you tell General Franco about this plot?"

"My dear, I'm a monarchist. I have no use for that man, nor any influence with him either. He is usurping the place of our king, whom Franco should have brought back to Spain once the civil war was finished. Instead our king, Don Juan, is forced to live in exile in Estoril."

"But what is it you think I can do for you?"

"You can do something for yourself, my child. You can help protect your own people in this terrible war." She observed my reaction to her words. "The real problem is an Allied problem. There is someone close to the Americans involved—a traitor, someone who pretends to be working for the Americans but who is actually helping the Germans." She sat back in her chair, and her shoulders sagged. A long-drawn-out sigh made me realize that what she had just confided to me had cost her a huge effort.

I dared not speak. Her news opened frightening possibilities.

"Yes, I see you now realize this is a delicate and complex matter. I must speak to your ambassador and to no one else—immediately."

"But surely you know the ambassador and can go to him directly. Why not telephone him now?"

"There are no telephones out here in these mountains, nor in any other rural area. This is not a modern country like yours. And even if I knew your ambassador, I would not see him openly or telephone him. Then they would have no doubts about me—if they still have any, that is. No, you must contact him as soon as you get to Madrid. Arrange for him to go to the Church of San Fermín de los Navarros at eleven-fifteen the first morning possible. I know he is a religious man, and that church is close to his residence. He could easily slip in without arousing any suspicions. Likewise for me. I have been going there at that hour for over thirty years, and the church is usually empty then. No one would bother to follow me inside. Just call me, Aline, my dear, and mention the day. I have thought it all out. That's the only way I can do this."

Mimosa's reference to what amounted to a double agent was news Mozart would need urgently.

"How do you know this, Mimosa? Maybe you've made a mistake about the traitor."

She shook her head. "A mistake? Unfortunately for me it is not a mistake. I saw them—with my own eyes. And I heard every word." She shrugged her narrow shoulders. "It happened in a most accidental fashion. I was sitting in a *silla de manos*—a fifteenth-century hand chair. You know the little closed boxes on poles which were carried by four lackeys or hooked up to donkeys for traveling in those days. You must have seen many. I have two in my own house. Many friends have inherited these remnants of the past and use them for decoration." She didn't wait for an answer. "I was tired and wandered through the Duke of Medinacelli's palace looking for a quiet place to rest from the racket of all the people at a cocktail party there yesterday. Finally I found a room where there was no one and it amused me to see what it must have felt like to bounce through the country in a box with just one tiny hole for a window. No sooner had I settled myself inside than they came in. What stopped me from speaking was the shock of recognizing one who I did not even know was in Spain—someone I know too well." She paused and shook her head despairingly. "Immediately they began to go over the details of the plot. Then I dared not breathe, I was so frightened. I heard it all. Every detail. How could I help it?"

"But why are you so afraid? Did they see you?"

"No. But after they left, I opened the door of the hand chair to come out. Unfortunately, at that moment a servant who must have passed them as they walked out entered the room and looked at me astounded. Of course, it appeared to him that I had been hiding there on purpose. What could I say? Anything would have made things worse. That servant used to work in the German Embassy. I don't like him. He is always sneaking around. I wouldn't be surprised if he is paid by the Germans for every bit of news he can supply."

She stood up. "Oh, I am lost. I feel it. When I read your cards I knew something was planned against Franco. Many people expect things like that to be attempted. But now I know who is involved."

She opened the door and peeked down the hall in both directions. "I cannot stay one second longer. You must not mention to anyone that I have been here." Then she slipped out and scurried away.

<hr>

Mimosa's story made me forget everything else while I bathed and dressed for dinner. There was no way I could think of to get a message to Mozart before I returned to Madrid. At nine-thirty I joined the others in the great salon for drinks.

Gloria and Carola stood talking under the ledge of the huge fireplace, and others hovered near a table where two menservants were preparing drinks. Mimosa had not yet come down and had still not arrived when we finally passed into the dining room at ten-thirty. I dared not ask anyone about her.

Four *reposteros*—cloth hangings—over ten meters high, emblazoned with the family crest, covered the walls of the baronial room, which was a combination of rustic and baroque. There were sterling candelabra on white damask, elaborate Aubusson rugs on a broad-planked floor, lapidary vases on the bleached wood mantel of a whitewashed hearth. I immediately realized we were seated in strict protocol, the German prince with the Spanish grandee countess on his right and another titled lady whose name I had not caught on his left. The young people with titles evidently sat before older people without them. Each place was taken, so I knew Mimosa was not expected for dinner.

Princess Lilienthal was exquisite—tall, elegant, distinguished—and kept the Duke of Durcal, who was on her right, laughing all during dinner. Six servants in the family red-and-navy livery served the table of eighteen.

I sat between Luis Quintanilla and Beistegui. The latter commented that he owned a house on the Castellana which was empty because he lived in Paris and that the house had a swimming pool. When I told him I liked to swim, he said, "You are in luck. As soon as it becomes warm, around the beginning of May, I am going to have the pool filled. Please feel free to use it. You will find there is practically no other pool in the city."

After dinner we moved into a sort of ballroom where the chairs were placed in a huge circle. Already, many guests who had not been present at dinner were filling up the room. The men were being served cognac, and orange juice was offered to the women. Suddenly a troupe of Gypsies just arrived from Madrid burst in, making noisy, enthusiastic howls, stamping their feet on the ancient planked floor, testing it for its resonance, while saluting and bowing to all. Only when complete silence reigned did one scrawny man with sunken cheeks and greasy hair rest his hand on the back of the guitarist's chair and begin to wail a sad chant.

There was no other instrument, only one guitar, but the audience listened spellbound. Now and then the performance was accompanied by a mumble of *Olé* from the guests. At the end of each ballad, enthusiastic applause indicated his success. Next, a Gypsy woman stood up, kicking out the train of her highly starched white-and-red polka-dot gown, while smacking the palms of her hands in loud rhythmic beat. When she lifted her skirts to dance, her hairy legs were heavy, her shoes shabby; her hair in a knot at the back of her head was greasy. But when she began to move, she became magnetic and beautiful. The graceful movements of her body, the stance of her head, the sensuous twisting of her hands and arms, cast a spell.

The intoxicating rhythms and ballads had almost made me forget my worries about Mimosa and the work I had to do. Everyone was absorbed by the chants and the Gypsy women posturing with arched backs and twisting and stamping to the flamenco music. As nervous as I was I knew I had been trained just for moments like this.

A waiter passed by, bearing a tray with small glasses of orange juice. "Excuse me," I whispered. Beistegui looked up, Casilda and Luis Quintanilla also.

To their inquiring glances, I said quietly, "I'm going to fetch my castanets." I smiled—a question mark crossed each of their faces. It was so unexpected it let me off the hook.

I walked quietly through the dim salons. A clock someplace clanged. My watch marked one-thirty. In the entrance hall, I decided to photograph the guest book. If I could get proof Himmler had been here! A slender cigarette lighter in my bag concealed my spy camera. Page by page, I clicked the tiny instrument in the badly lit room. The film was, fortunately, very sensitive. Then I heard footsteps.

I shoved the camera into my purse.

"Aline, what on earth are you doing?" Carola's girlish voice.

"I was on my way to the ladies' room and then I became fascinated by your guest book. What an interesting life your family has had. And this beautiful house. I've never seen anything like it."

She giggled. "I never think about it—to me it's just my family and our home. Wait till tomorrow. It is lovely outdoors."

Tomorrow seemed years away at that moment. I thought it would be safe to ask Carola. "How is the marquesa? She hasn't come down this evening."

Frowning, Carola said, "Papi says she was taken ill tonight. He had her driven back to Madrid just before dinner. I was on my way to get a shawl. Will you come with me?"

Little did Carola know how much her news upset me. Did that mean Mimosa had decided to contact the ambassador herself after all? Or was she so nervous she had become really ill? Or . . .

Whatever, one thing was certain. I had to be careful.

"I'd love to, and please tell me more about the house on the way," I answered. We ambled up the stairs and down a hall to her room, chatting all the way. At one point, she stopped me, putting her hands on my shoulders. We stood face to face.

"Aline, will you tell me something honestly?"

I smiled. "Ask me."

"Constantin seems shy. He's hardly said a word to anyone. But I think he wants to talk to me."

"Well, give him the chance. He's been looking at you all evening."

Carola smiled. "Thanks for the encouragement."

Walking on, I took advantage of her company to ask who occupied the rooms we passed. Unwittingly, she was at once my guide and guardian angel. Luckily the guests I was interested in all had their rooms in my corridor.

We arrived at her room, which contained a trove of little paintings in frames and porcelain figures—Edmundo would have had a field day. Carola having covered herself with a shawl, we retraced our steps. Now it was my turn to stop her. "Would you think *me* crazy if I wandered around for a while? The paintings, the tapestries are so beautiful—I would like to browse. And I guess I do not really appreciate flamenco singing yet."

"Of course. My house is your house, as we say in Spain."

We parted at the foot of the stairs. I watched her disappear and looked at my watch. How long would the party last? Casilda had said that flamenco parties go on until dawn. I hoped she was right.

Starting at the beginning of my own corridor, I turned the first doorknob. Inside, darkness. I switched on the light. The bed was turned down, a man's flannel pajamas spread on top, a silk dressing gown on the chair. Tiptoeing to a massive armoire, I opened it inch by inch. Inside, the brown houndstooth woolen knickers identified Carlos Beistegui. In thirty seconds I was back in the hall.

I opened the next door. The perfume gave the countess away. The room was bathed in yellow glare from a table lamp, but I needed my tiny flashlight to illuminate closets and drawers. I thought I heard a noise. Holding my breath to listen, I realized it was nothing, just the wind howling around the corners of the ancient building, rattling the shutters.

On the desk was a sheet of paper. Craning for a closer look, I saw an unfinished letter, the pen lying open next to it. I bent over. It was too good to be true: *"Liebe Heinrich."* That could be Heinrich Himmler. Tilting the lampshade, I directed the gleam of my flashlight with one hand and snapped the camera with the other. If anyone opened the door right now I was a dead duck. Rapidly, I rummaged through her cosmetics and perfumes in the bathroom. I found nothing of interest until a beam of light struck shiny steel. The object on the edge of the porcelain bathtub gleamed. A small Beretta pistol glistening with beads of water. Apparently the countess bathed with soap and a revolver.

I had to leave. Time was essential. Lazaar's room smelled of talcum and shoe leather. Despite scouring every inch—checking the linings of each garment, the soles of his shoes, each compartment of his briefcase—I found only an official report on tungsten which appeared worth photographing. At this moment I ran out of film and lost precious seconds reloading. Finally I snapped off my flashlight and the wall switch and stepped into the corridor, turning the doorknob quietly behind me. Safe again. I took two steps down the carpeted hall—and froze.

He stood maybe eight yards away, leaning against a wall, as though we'd prearranged a rendezvous in this deserted wing. One arm was crossed on a black sling, which matched his dinner jacket. He hovered in my direct path—to turn around suddenly would only seal my indictment. Each footstep was an effort. As I passed Constantin von Weiderstock, I could see he was drunk. He nodded. "The *Fräulein* is missing the wonderful entertainment. Or perhaps she is enjoying her own."

Smiling, I walked by, not turning, and kept moving down the hall, down the staircase. No chance now to examine Mimosa's room. Perhaps something in there would have given a clue about her departure.

A full half hour had passed, but everyone still sat motionless as though at church. The music and dancing continued in throbbing, impassioned frenzy. Compared to my pounding heart, it might have been a waltz.

====

From my bed, bright stars were visible above the hills. My dreams had been interrupted by the memory of the terror in Mimosa's voice, her words about a traitor to the Americans. Was she imagining things? No, Edmundo had said she was the slyest fox in Madrid. My thoughts spun and collided. Listening to Mimosa hours before, I had been slightly worried. Now I was as frightened as she had been.

Suddenly I became aware of a sound. Someone was in my room. Only starlight filtered through the darkness, but I could distinguish a figure approaching my bed. The silhouette came closer until he was leaning over me. With despair I realized the Beretta was in my evening bag on the dressing table.

A man's voice whispered, "Vat vere you doing in Herr Lazaar's room?" I recognized von Weiderstock's accent. The smell of liquor was repulsive. His tone carried a note of playfulness. "Don't be afraid," he said softly. "I know all about you American girls. You give your favors easily." He tried to plant a kiss on my face but missed and fell. Then he grabbed the sheets in an attempt to get into the bed. He was dead drunk. I made a fist with both hands and smacked him.

"Get out of here."

He winced, falling to a kneeling position next to my bed. After a moment, that voice again. "I saw the way you looked at him zis afternoon. I've heard all about you American women. You are so easy." His words were slurred, his tone conciliatory.

He was harmless, like a drunken fraternity boy. When he tried to kiss me again, I grabbed his wounded arm. He groaned.

"Get away. Get out of here. Before I scream. Before I hurt you."

He laughed. "You hurt me? That's a joke." This time my sharp blow hit his wounded arm. He whined. Then staggered to his feet.

I had to act fast. His drunken condition could enable me to obtain valuable information. Snapping on the light, I slipped out of bed. I threw on my robe and pulled him over to a chair—the same one the marquesa had occupied hours before. The room now was bright.

"Sit down," I ordered, pushing him into a chair while he grunted and moaned, looking as if he might be getting sick. Taking advantage of his dazed state, I went to my makeup case and took out a small capsule. It was sodium amobarbital, what they called "truth serum" at the Farm, and it worked particularly fast on anyone who had consumed much alcohol.

"You're drunk and you'll regret your behavior in the morning. But don't worry, I understand. You've got the wrong idea about American girls. When you saw me I was lost. I, too, had had much wine. Herr Lazaar was not in his room when I stumbled in. He was downstairs with the party. I made a mistake looking for my own room, that's all."

Through the window, the sky was on the verge of paling. He nursed his head in his hands. I hastened to pour water from a pitcher on the night table into a glass, dumping in the white powder from the capsule and stirring it with my finger.

"Here, some bicarbonate of soda will make you feel better."

Holding the glass to his lips, he sipped. "Shit. Vat am I doing?" There was remorse in his tone.

"Drink it and you'll feel better. You won't remember anything in the morning." I soothed him, watched and waited, as he became groggier and groggier. The two hundred milligrams of sodium amobarbital would work quickly but briefly. In another three minutes he was like putty, although subliminally conscious. I had to support him with my hands, gripping his broad shoulders tightly. "Constantin, do you know why the Marquesa of Torrejón has left?"

"Nooo," he slurred after a moment.

"How many times have you met Prince Lilienthal?"

"Three or four," he drawled in long syllables, almost as if he were from the American South.

"Do you know Hans Lazaar well, Constantin?"

He slid a little in my arms. I had to hold him up. "Noooo."

"Why was Heinrich Himmler in Spain, Constantin? Tell me."

"I doon't knowww."

"You're lying, Constantin. You must tell me the truth."

"I don't know," he said with feeling. "He didn't tell me." It took a minute for him to expel these words.

"Why didn't he tell you?"

"He doesn't trust me."

"What do you mean?"

"None of them do. None of them trust me. Not Himmler, not Lilienthal, not Lazaar. They think I'm stupid. They don't think I know they're out for my godfather's throat. Those shitheads."

I knew I had a treasure on my hands.

"Why are they out for your godfather's throat? What do you mean?"

"Himmler hates him."

"Why?"

"He's jealous. Himmler took my godfather's job."

It took several minutes and numerous shakes of the fellow's shoulders to elicit this. My hands were numb with the cold mountain air coming in from the open window.

"What do you do for the Gestapo in Madrid, Constantin? What work precisely?"

The chemicals were abating. He was on the verge of passing out. I repeated the question three times. Finally he muttered, "I'm an office boy, pushing papers around. I'm a puppet. They got my godfather, and they're out to get me."

I had the critical question on my tongue: Who is Heinrich Himmler's secret agent in Spain? But it was too late. The next moment, von Weiderstock passed out. It seemed to take an eternity to waken him enough to get him out of my room. Fortunately, he was staying in the same wing. I watched as he stumbled down the hall, falling down at the end of the corridor. Someone would find him in time and get him to his room. At least from that spot no one could connect him with me.

After mass the next morning, while horseback riding, Carola drew her mare near mine. "Tell me, Aline, now don't you think Constantin is charming?"

"I've still never had a chance to speak to him."

She giggled. "Tell me the truth. Do you think he likes me?"

"Of course. He's continually staring at you." She chatted about Constantin all the way back to the stables.

Whenever I ran into von Weiderstock later that day he had a puzzled look, but was as distant as before. The powder had worked.

———

At the hour of the siesta, after everyone had retired, when even the groggy Beethoven on the old-fashioned gramophone ceased, I went down to the hall. The silence was complete. In a leather purse hanging from my belt was a camera and some wires for opening locks. Quietly I stalked the rooms until I reached Prince Lilienthal's private study. Carola had pointed it out to me the night before. There were no sounds. Fortunately, the servants' quarters were far away, and they seemed to take siestas, too. I checked my wristwatch and calculated I should be finished in five minutes. Turning the brass doorknobs, I went inside.

One of the doors to a balcony was ajar, a slight breeze swaying the curtains. The room contained a large desk, some chairs, a cupboard displaying rifles and shotguns, some bookcases, and a large safe. I went to the prince's table and picked the lock of the drawer. Right on top was his passport. It was from Liechtenstein, not Germany. After photographing that, I went to the safe and, kneeling on the floor, began my work. Suddenly the double doors to the hall opened with a bang accompanied by an ear-splitting barking. Four gigantic Bavarian hunting shepherds burst into the room! Their racket would wake the house. The dogs, growling and baring their teeth, barred the door. The only chance of escape was the open balcony. I leaped into the air, landing so hard I bit my tongue to cut off a scream. I was in the princess's rose garden, bruised and dirty, but at least the dogs had not followed and had stopped barking. All was silent again.

Oh, Aline, you're a fool—that was my next thought, because someone was standing in front of me with a shotgun in one hand, smiling quite amiably.

"Well, well, it seems we have an athlete here."

The flick of a cruel smile momentarily transformed the face before me. I breathed deeply and got to my feet, brushing the dirt from my skirt.

"Do you specialize in jumping out of windows, Miss Griffith?"

"I guess I do when I'm surprised out of my wits by dogs."

"What were you doing in my study?" The prince, my prime suspect, wasted no words. As he faced me so closely, I felt I was seeing him for the first time, his large teeth uneven in an otherwise strong, broad-featured face, the ruddy skin pockmarked beneath the bold blue eyes. Built like a tree trunk and barrel-chested.

"Well, I just wandered in. Carola told me it would be all right to browse through your beautiful house. Your gun collection fascinated me."

"Really, you Americans are strange. Do you just admire firearms or do you shoot, too? Why not show me?"

"I'm not an expert, but I can try."

Prince Lilienthal glanced around the garden, then handed me his shotgun. "Try a shot at one of those." I followed his outstretched finger. Atop a stone wall which bordered the rows of barren rosebushes sat a number of small red clay pots.

"Oh, I couldn't. I—"

"Go ahead, Aline. They're easily replaceable." It seemed to me his command had none of the affable charm of yesterday.

I looked at the fragile pots poised on the ledge. Lifting the gun to my shoulder, I pulled the trigger. *Screech!* The butt's recoil had thrown me off balance.

The shot went high over the pots. All remained untouched on the ledge.

The prince stood shaking his head. "Few Americans know anything about shooting. Even the women in my family know how to handle firearms." He grabbed the gun, then aimed so rapidly at the crocks he might have been in a shooting gallery. He shattered the first two, reloaded, then missed one and hit another, reloaded again, and finished off the last two in a flurry of success.

Farther down the wall was another string of the same clay pots. I couldn't resist.

"Would you mind if I tried to hit those?"

"Not at all," he said, laughing. Again he handed me the weapon. I grabbed it with two hands close to my right hip, crouching slightly. One by one the crocks crumbled. Reloading without changing position, I continued until I had destroyed twelve without a miss.

When the last shot resounded, I barely had a glimpse of the prince's astonishment, because the commotion had caused several persons to look out their windows and inquire what was going on. The prince turned to me. "The next time you wish to see my gun collection, just tell me. I would be delighted to explain it to you."

Two servants had run out to see what had happened. The Countess von Fürstenberg was crossing the gravel path, a cool vision in white silk, moving like a panther. "My dear Niki, is this how you wake your guests from their siestas? What are you doing?"

"Just showing Aline how to handle firearms."

Glancing from one of us to the other, the countess didn't know what to make of the prince's words. "I'm sure you are frightening Aline with your demonstration. Niki loves to show off for pretty young girls. As a matter of fact, Aline, it was you I was looking for."

"Me?"

"Yes. I thought we might take tea in my room and have a chat, if you have nothing else to do. Can you spare her, Niki?"

"Readily." His bearing was stiffly polite, but I sensed he distrusted me.

Following the countess into the house, still numb from the previous scene, I dared not think what I was walking into.

One of the salons we crossed was occupied. On a sofa before a fire sat Carola and Constantin quietly conversing. She looked dejected. Greeting them briefly, we walked on.

Only when we were settled in the countess's room and she had served the tea did she begin to speak. Her chin rested on the tips of two lacquered nails. "I understand you had a chat with Mimosa Torrejón yesterday."

Her words left me frozen. Although I continued to pour the cream into my tea, her huge eyes appealed for a response. Not receiving any, the countess proceeded. "She told me she liked you. Since she disappeared unexpectedly I thought you might be able to enlighten me."

"Carola said she was taken ill and went back to Madrid. You could ask the Lilienthals," I said.

Now her eyes were scoffing. "Do you think I would be asking you unless I already had? They're being so secretive about it, my curiosity is famished. Niki said she suddenly became very ill."

"Doesn't that satisfy your curiosity?"

"It doesn't."

"Why not?"

"I don't believe it." Her white silk rustled.

Neither did I. I glanced about the room, wondering if the countess's gun still lay on the edge of the bathtub. "Why don't you believe it?"

"I don't know. I just don't. I ran into Mimosa right after she saw you. She didn't look that ill to me."

"I'm sorry I can't be of much help."

"Well, perhaps you can," she said rather enigmatically.

"What do you mean?"

The countess rose and walked in her slinky gait to a bureau. From the top drawer she removed a large black velvet case. It had not been in her room last night, of that I was certain. She returned to her seat and opened it. My eyes were accosted by a blaze of jewels. "These are wonderful pieces. You might appreciate them." One by one, she held them up to the light, some studded with emeralds and others with sapphires. Never had I seen such impressive gems. She gazed at them languorously.

"Although I love beautiful things, I part with them easily. Like the marquesa, I am a medium. Things pass through me."

It occurred to me she was suggesting a bribe of some sort. Then we were interrupted by a terse staccato knock. Before answering it, she jammed the glittering pieces into the case and concealed it behind the pillow of her chair.

"Come in, Hans. I have a visitor you'll be delighted to see."

Stiff, erect, gruesome, Lazaar entered the room. Curtly he bowed to me. For a moment, they both stood watching me. It was hair-raising, not because of what their eyes expressed, but because of what they didn't. They were inscrutable. "Please, don't let me interrupt."

The countess quickly explained how she had came upon me and in what strange circumstances, concluding with a frank account of our conservation. I wondered at her need to explain. I also couldn't wait to get out of there.

She then drew up a chair for Lazaar. His monocle focused on me as he said, "Wherever you hide your jewels, be careful, Gloria. I'm sure I can be frank in front of Miss Griffith. Someone was in my room last night. In fact, someone searched my room."

"What *are* you talking about, Hans? Why would anyone want to rummage through your room? And how do you know?"

A terrible little smile—it made him uglier, if possible—distorted his chubby face. He raised a fat finger as well. "A telltale sign, dear Gloria."

Another knock on the door. "Oh, I love small parties. Don't you, Aline?" When she opened it, in stepped Niki Lilienthal.

It was a conspiracy! How could I have been so blind? How would they get rid of me? As swiftly as the Marquesa de Torrejón!

"I had no idea you were so popular, Aline. Everyone seems to have taken a liking to you. You're like an old friend of the family already."

For a moment, I wondered if Gloria had poisoned the tea—I felt drained. Forcing a smile, I said, "I have had a wonderful weekend, although too short, but I must go to my room to pack. Luis Quintanilla is driving Casilda, Nena, and me back to Madrid in an hour. I have to be at the office early tomorrow morning."

As soon as I got to my room, I rushed to investigate the canvas bag outside the bathroom window. There was no sign anyone had disturbed it. However, the threads in my bedroom drawers and closets had moved. What better explanation for the tea in Gloria's room? Just enough time for someone to inspect my own.

Before I left, Carola came in. After one look, I said, "What's the matter?"

Bleakly she returned my gaze. "He's leaving Spain tomorrow."

"Who is?"

"Who do you think? Constantin."

"Leaving for where?"

"Berlin."

"Why?"

"If I tell you, will you promise not to breathe a word? Not to anyone?"

"I promise."

"He says something terrible is brewing in Madrid. He wouldn't tell me what it was, but he said he wanted to get as far away as possible."

"I hope for your sake he's not sent back to the front."

"He's frightened," Carola said. "His godfather no longer has Hitler's confidence. And they may ship Constantin to the Russian front."

Slowly I said, "Then why does he want to go back to Berlin?"

"He says at the front he knows how to take care of himself—but here he is surrounded by enemies."

I remained silent.

"Oh, Aline, I'm so sorry. I've been terrible company this weekend, thinking only of myself, my foolish fantasies. Promise me you'll come back soon."

Impulsively, I hugged her. "Don't be silly. I've had a wonderful time. I'll come back as soon as you see fit to ask me."

I had to come back—I had not accomplished my primary task. The radio detector lay untouched.

Chapter 16

Although it was late when I arrived home Sunday night, preoccupied by the urgency of the Marquesa de Torrejón's information, I called Mozart. He was out. Early the next morning when I recounted all that had happened in detail, the boss showed no reaction. Not even the blink of an eye. By now I had learned that this was often his attitude when major crises occurred.

His first comment when I finished was "Don't mention to anyone the marquesa's reference to a traitor. Is that clear?"

"Yes."

He continued, "Lilienthal's Liechtenstein passport is a perfect protection and cover at the same time. He's number one on our blacklist and could be Himmler's man here, but, Miss Griffith, we need cold proof." He pointed to the detector I had just laid down on his desk. "You will have to get invited back again to search for that secret radio station."

He asked me to wait while he contacted the ambassador and then suggested I call the marquesa to confirm the meeting for the following day.

Answering the phone herself, as if she had been awaiting my call, Mimosa sighed with relief when I said, "Tomorrow, Tuesday." Her only response was "Thank you, my dear child. May the good God reward you."

He listened while I played back the call, but he already knew both sides of it. "Very well, Tiger." Mozart sounded relieved. "When the film is developed I'll let you know if there is anything that might affect your mission."

═══

Late that night, just as I was going to sleep, Edmundo called.

"Are you sitting down?" His voice quickly alerted me. What now? Another crooked agent in Lisbon, where he had just been?

"I'm practically on the floor. I'm in bed. What is it?"

"Mimosa is dead. A heart attack, I'm told."

For a second I couldn't say a word. Edmundo's voice came through. "Are you there?" Then, mumbling, "This damn line is cut again."

"No, I'm here. It's just that your news is such a shock. I was speaking to her this morning, and she was at the Lilienthal country home this weekend, where I was, too. I can't believe it."

"What I can't believe is that she died of a heart attack. She was one of the most energetic, healthy persons I know—never even complained of a headache."

Flashing through my brain was the mental image of Mimosa wincing and touching her lower abdomen. The impression I had had at that moment was that her nervousness was giving her a slight attack of diarrhea. Mimosa had said, "They are on to me." She had been terrified. My intuition told me someone had poisoned her. Her warning resounded in my ears: "If they find out I told you, they'll kill you, too."

"Aline, are you there?" Edmundo's voice sounded exasperated.

"Yes, forgive me. I'm remembering things she said. She was most anxious to talk to you."

"No sense getting out of bed at this hour. She's already dead—what can we do? But I want to hear every detail about the weekend and what Mimosa said to you about me."

"I don't mind getting up at all. It's important we talk as soon as possible."

"How about tomorrow morning?"

"Whenever you say." My head pounded. "When is her funeral?"

"The burial and *pésame*, the offering of condolences, take place tomorrow. You should go with me."

"Of course I'll go. I liked her very much."

"I adored her. She was my most loyal friend."

"Will many people go?"

"Nobody would dare not to. It will be her last great splash."

"When did it happen?"

"Just a few hours ago, I guess. I called her as soon as my train got in, and to my astonishment they told me she was dead. Naturally, I went there immediately. There was a crowd of distant relatives streaming into the house. She wasn't even laid out yet. Poor Mimosa. All the relatives are thinking about is who will get her money. Her closest relations live in France, I understand, so there will be a squabble among a lot of people who did not care for her at all."

"What time will you come to pick me up?"

"Tomorrow morning, about eleven-thirty. Since people are not embalmed in this country, the law obliges all to be buried within twenty-four hours. She'll be interred about one o'clock. The funeral services may not take place for a week."

When I awoke Mozart with the news, he grunted. "A great loss." I knew what he meant. He had just lost, by only hours, the magnetic needle that would have pointed to a traitor among his agents. Not a minor death for him.

When Edmundo arrived the next morning, he was more distressed than I had ever seen him. "How about giving me a cup of coffee and then telling me all about the weekend before we face the crowd over there."

I recounted Mimosa's words, with the exception of her reference to a traitor. He listened but made no comment. We were both depressed. Finally Edmundo broke the silence.

"Do you suppose one of those Germans at El Morisco did away with my dear friend? You know, Lilienthal is a strange bird. His friendship with important Nazis is public. Even so, is he capable of such an atrocity? It's still more my hunch, after what you told me, that it wasn't a heart attack that finished her off." Then he stood up. "Come on, let's find out."

As we rode in the taxi, he explained the protocol. "In Spanish burials only the men go to the cemetery. The ladies stay at the home of the deceased to comfort the women of the family while the body is taken to be interred. The procession to the burial place today is bound to be impressive. Probably a huge open black hearse drawn by at least four shiny black horses with enormous black plumes. Mimosa would never want me to miss it." He sighed. "At least it's not hot weather. We men have to walk behind the hearse for almost ten blocks before it's considered proper to get into the automobiles to continue on to the cemetery."

When we got down in front of the ancient building on the Calle Ferraz, we had to wait until a picturesque procession went by, several black-frocked priests with white cotton tunics fringed in wide bands of lace and carrying tall crucifixes, followed by twenty young boys dressed in black robes, each bearing a candle. One swung a small bell which tolled in rhythmic cadence. The passersby stopped in their tracks, crossing themselves, until the robed figures had passed on down the street.

"The visit of the parochial priests to bequeath the last rites," explained Edmundo. "In this case, since she died suddenly, they have just made a visit to bless the dead one in order not to miss their fee."

Inside the dim entrance hall, Mimosa's *mayordomo,* whom I recognized from the reception, stood stiffly in a black morning coat and black tie next to a table where people were waiting to sign a paper. Edmundo whispered, "This custom enables the family to know who attended the *pésame,* and more important still, who did not. If someone did away with our friend, you can bet his name will be there. What better way to appear innocent than to mix with the mourners? He—or she—may be upstairs right now. Keep your eyes open."

At the top of the grand staircase in front of the main salon, priests were receiving the visitors. Beyond milled and buzzed a heterogeneous mass: elegantly dressed socialites, ill-at-ease shepherds and their wives. "Probably employees on some of the marquesa's country farms and ranches," explained Edmundo.

Nuns moved about in winglike coifs that looked like giant white butterflies floating above the crowd. Up and down the corridor ambled the marquesa's female servants, their black uniforms wrinkled from a night without sleep, sobbing and providing the only note of tragedy. The main portion of visitors chatted and laughed freely as if attending a cocktail party.

"Look who's here," Edmundo said, nudging me. In a group of Axis ambassadors and other men and women I had never seen before stood Gloria von Fürstenberg, Hans Lazaar, and Prince Lilienthal. "The Traitorous Trio."

"Please, Edmundo. Someone may hear you."

"My dear," he whispered huskily, "I'm doing it on purpose. Mimosa would definitely approve. My wit is sharpened for this occasion. After all, there is a chance one of that lovely threesome finished off our late friend." He pushed me on. "Let's take a look at the old girl."

Edmundo pushed me into the next salon, where a candle in a gigantic bronze candelabrum flickered at each corner of the coffin in the center of the almost empty room. Only two nuns knelt there deep in prayer, their fingers rubbing each bead of their rosaries as they mumbled a litany in unison.

Quietly we approached and knelt on the other side of the ornately carved black wooden box. "Jesus," said Edmundo irreverently under his breath. "She looks like Minnie Mouse dressed as a nun."

I couldn't believe my eyes. Mimosa was garbed in the same black habit as the nuns praying at her side, her bony fragile fingers intertwined over her chest clasping a large wooden cross and a rosary.

Edmundo could not keep still. "They should have buried her with her cards, too."

She did look smaller than I remembered—no dabs of rouge lightened the haggard gray cheeks; a white starched band encased her head. The nun's habit seemed to exaggerate the narrowness of her body. I glanced questioningly at Edmundo. He understood immediately, mumbling in English with his head bent as if in prayer, "This is the usual attire for the dead in Spain." Suddenly he bent over the casket as if to kiss the puckered lips. Instead, he made the sign of the cross over her face with one hand and with the other went for Mimosa's neck like a cobra. In one second he flipped open the starched surplice around the scrawny throat—and then we saw them, for one split second: the *welts*. His gestures had been so deft I thought the nuns, whose litany never ceased and whose heads remained bent, had not noticed. Those kleptomaniacal fingers again! This time instead of serving to lift one of Mimosa's bibelots, they disclosed a dreadful truth. She had been strangled.

"Well, well," murmured Edmundo, rising. "Now we know."

My legs were trembling as I got up.

When we joined the mass of friends in the large room, the Trio were seated and regarding us with considerable interest. Fürstenberg, Lazaar, and Lilienthal nodded to me in a chorus. Although in a daze, I felt obliged to go over and say hello and to introduce Edmundo.

"Please, do sit down," suggested the countess from under her netted veil.

I took the chair next to her, Edmundo the one next to me. "What a terrible shock," said Gloria von Fürstenberg to both of us as she leaned over to kiss my cheek. "Obviously Mimosa was more ill than we realized this weekend."

"I had no idea when she complained of chest pains that she was having the first of several heart attacks," Lilienthal commented. "I wanted her to stay, but she insisted on being driven back to Madrid. She must have known she was critically ill. Fortunately Hans was able to spare his driver."

Edmundo kicked me. Our minds were evidently one. So Lazaar was responsible for her trip back.

Now Lazaar shook his head. "When Pedro returned he said the marquesa seemed to be feeling better." His monocle caught the glow of a light in its disk. "So you see, Miss Griffith, one never knows when one's turn is next."

Was he trying to frighten me or warn me?

"Mimosa was in Aline's room just before she was taken ill on Saturday," Gloria announced to the small group. "What did she talk about, Aline?" Her gaze went from sultry to icy in a split second, or so it seemed to me. Perhaps it was the tension that her words had created, or more likely, she was frightened, too, I thought. She knew as well as I did that Mimosa had been murdered. Or had she done it?

"We didn't chat at all," I answered. "She was looking for some aspirin or medicine to calm her stomach. I had neither."

A scrawny old woman in a black maid's uniform crossed in front of us at that moment, distracting the Traitorous Trio and Edmundo as well. I stood up.

"I must get back to work." The two men stood as Edmundo and I left. When we were at a slight distance, I asked him, "Who was that maid you were looking at?"

"Mimosa's personal maid. She's been in the house as long as Mimosa has. Probably born there. She has to know the truth about her mistress's death, since she is the one who would have bathed and dressed the old girl."

"But why does she not say that Mimosa was strangled, then?"

"That is the mystery. She must have a reason. She may be too frightened to say anything. The fact that the Trio observed the old maid so closely may indicate they do not believe in the heart attack, either."

He walked with me down to the street. "Mimosa was about to solve my mission for me. She must have had a tip about who is masterminding the plot against Franco. Just my bad luck! And I fear without wanting to, she has embroiled you in this murky affair. The Gestapo has a gigantic network, and Lazaar could be connected to it." Edmundo hailed a taxi for us. "I'll have to stay to accompany the procession. Tell Mozart immediately that she has been assassinated and ask him to give both of us some protection. We're going to need it. But don't think he gives a damn what happens to us."

All the way to the office I tried to figure out why Edmundo seemed to hate the boss so much. I now knew Edmundo's mission involved discovering who was masterminding the plot against Franco. Could it be the same person I was looking for? Glancing back, I saw a black Mercedes, and behind that a black Renault. The Renault had been trailing me for weeks, but the Mercedes was new.

Then it occurred to me! Why had Edmundo gone straight for Mimosa's neck to discover if and how she had been killed? Strangling was only one of many methods. Why would he not have considered a knife wound in the heart, or a bullet or poison or smothering or any other means, none of which would have been revealed precisely at the neck?

Chapter 17

P rotection! You tell Top Hat to be damned. He hasn't resolved his mission yet. You haven't either, Tiger. You both have chains of subagents whom you can order to protect yourselves. We are understaffed. I can't fulfill the requests from Washington, London, and Algiers as it is. We are in a war. Think of the guys in the front lines. They take their chances, and you have to also. Isn't that what you signed up for?" It was the first time I had seen Mozart lose his calm. Something had happened. Nevertheless I asked him about the film which I knew had been developed and about the photographs of the guest book also.

"Just a lot of fancy names, most of them unintelligible. No Himmler. No important German officials at all." He almost spat the words out.

"What about Lazaar's report on tungsten?"

Mozart smiled without amusement. "Nothing you couldn't get by walking into the German Embassy and picking it up on the counter."

"And Gloria von Fürstenberg's letter?" I was crestfallen.

The chief opened the top drawer and removed a paper. In his lethal monotone he read: " 'Dear Heinrich, I am writing you a hello. I arrived at El Morisco for the weekend with Hans Lazaar and several other guests. The weather is perfect. Blue skies, chilly days, rolling fields, mountains like gray steel.

" 'How does the weather fare in Berlin, my dear Heinrich? I worry about you, the way things are going. I miss our nights in Berlin. They were good ones. I'm afraid it will be a dreary weekend. Do you know the Marquesa de Torrejón? She is here and rattles on until you would like to choke her. The Avila sisters, two fools if I ever met any, arrived this afternoon with an American girl whom I don't trust. And guess who little Carola Lilienthal is playing up to? Your favorite—Constantin von Weiderstock. Tell that to his godfather. Really I am bored to tears. Only Lazaar amuses me with his grotesque perversity. Lilienthal is as falsely gallant as usual—how can his gorgeous wife stand him?' The letter stops here," he said. "We have tested the paper for invisible ink. None of our formulas show anything. Of course, the words could contain a code. But this kind, as you know, would be unbreakable. However, there are a few points to consider." His tiny eyes fixed my own.

"Although there are many Heinrichs in Germany, it is just possible that this letter *was* directed to Himmler. Which intensifies interest in the beautiful countess as a prime suspect."

======

The following Thursday, April 6, Angustias awoke me as usual with breakfast in bed. She drew back the white cotton curtains and unclamped the weighty wooden shutters, letting in a burst of sunlight which pinpointed the bowl of glistening red Málaga cherries on my tray. From my bed I gazed at the rectangle of pure azure sky visible through the window. Another perfect day! Then I heard the doorbell. Angustias went to answer it and returned a few moments later.

"Two women are waiting in the salon for the señorita."

I had been expecting only one. Twice during the past month I had put up a woman agent from France bringing military information which was relayed on to London, where plans for Overlord and Anvil were being worked out. There were twenty Allied combat divisions in Italy, but obviously that was not enough to enable our forces to gain territory. Nevertheless, plans for Operation Anvil were being made in southern France. These women brought us maps with the location of coastal fortifications, traps, roadblocks, the number of German troops, and other information necessary for the generals who were preparing the invasion.

"The women look awful," Angustias said, wrinkling her nose. "And they smell worse."

Hastily I threw on a robe and went to the front room. Two disheveled women leaped to their feet as I came in. One's hand was wrapped in a dirty bandage; her cheek was scarred as if a knife had slashed it. Angustias was right about the smell.

I pulled a smile. "Welcome. I'm relieved you've arrived safely. What have you brought?"

The wounded one plunged a hand under her shirt and produced a stained packet. "I am Marta. Madeleine, my companion, does not speak Spanish, but she is the one who obtained this information. I guided her across the Pyrenees and to Madrid. Since we have no identity cards we will have to wait here for a ride back to the frontier. We dare not use the trains or buses. The fish truck that brought us will make another trip back next Monday. Will the señorita allow us to stay until then?"

"Of course. One of you will have to use my room, but that is not an inconvenience, since I will be away for the weekend."

It was Holy Thursday, the beginning of the most important holiday of the year. Stores, theaters, and movies were all closed—even restaurants. Pointing to her hand, I asked, "Do you want us to get you a doctor?"

"Oh, no thank you, señorita. We don't want to be seen. We won't go out of the house, and we need a rest. The climb across the mountains was strenuous and dangerous. All the routes are infested not only with German spies but with Franco's as well. We have to move like foxes. This will be my last trip. I've already killed two fascist Civil Guards, and if they catch me, I'll be shot without trial."

While I was dressing I marveled at the courage and stamina of the Basque women. They were becoming better couriers than the men, and they were fearless.

A few hours later a chauffeur from the office picked me up to take me to the Avilas' palace in Toledo, where I had been invited for the Holy Week processions. We managed to ditch the old Renault shadowing us in the narrow streets near the Puerta del Sol. As we passed through the city, many women were entering or coming out of the churches dressed in black and wearing high combs and lace mantillas. Paco, the driver, told me, "On Holy Thursday it is customary for women to visit seven churches and to wear mantillas."

For the rest of the forty-five-minute ride to Toledo he described the processions in Sevilla, Granada, and many small villages. He was proud of his country's traditions, and like most Spaniards he loved to talk.

As we approached Toledo the sun was shining on the thick stone walls, bringing into relief the massive arches and crenellated walls. The fortified medieval city was perched high on a mountain of rock, surrounded by the Tagus River, which was spanned by several ancient ornate bridges. The narrow cobblestone road passed through a gigantic stone arch with a round turret on either side, then wound up a steep hill. Donkeys, carts, chickens, children, and beggars had to move aside to allow our car to pass until we arrived at the Plaza de Zocodover, where a policeman told us to proceed on foot, since the streets were closed for the night's procession.

"Many of these buildings were built before the twelfth century," explained Paco, who carried my two suitcases as we walked through the narrow streets, lined by ancient granite palaces, each with a family crest carved on its facade. Many buildings possessed turrets, all had intricate iron grilles over the windows. The open double doors of the Avila palace revealed a patio encircled by graceful granite columns, and in the center two maids were dusting long-leaved green plants. At the top of the wide stone staircase Casilda and her sisters greeted me. They were excited.

"What do you think? You are going to meet General Franco. Papa has invited him here to see the procession tonight."

"I thought you aristocrats were monarchists and didn't like Franco," I said, surprised.

"That's more or less true. But when the chief of state makes an official visit to Toledo, he comes to this house, because the kings did also whenever they came to the city."

We commented on Mimosa's death, and I noticed that none of them doubted that she had died of natural causes.

"She was such fun," said one of the girls. "And we will all miss her parties. After all, we have her to thank for our meeting you, Aline."

After tea, Casilda took me to her room. "You should wear a mantilla for the evening's procession. We do, and if Mrs. Franco comes she most certainly will put one on. I have a beautiful high comb and mantilla prepared for you, and María will place it on you. Nobody places a mantilla as well."

The hairdresser was waiting with large pieces of black lace about two yards wide and three yards long. I sat at the dressing table while she combed my hair back into a large Spanish knot. Then she slid the high pronged comb underneath the chignon, hooking it solidly so it wouldn't move. The lace was draped over the comb, then pinned on each shoulder so I could turn my head from side to side without pulling the mantilla from the comb. After that the scalloped border of lace mantilla was pinned to my hair in front, so that it framed my forehead and face. When I stood up the lace reached from the hem of my skirt to about six inches above my head. The girls laughed.

"You look more Spanish than I!" exclaimed Casilda, delighted.

The others then took turns while Carmen placed their mantillas. Just as she was finishing, a racket from the street below announced the arrival of the Generalíssimo. We ran to the balcony. There were three Mercedes-Benzes below. As Franco stepped out, I remembered Mimosa's warning and thought, What an easy shot from any balcony nearby!

A few seconds later we went to the top of the wide staircase, where the Count of Avila, surrounded by guests and the servants of the house, awaited.

I'd never seen Franco before and studied him as I waited in line to shake his hand. He wore a white military jacket with a mass of decorations and a red beret. He was shorter than I had supposed, plumper also, with a large nose, good smooth reddish skin, a pleasant expression. Close up he was neither the monster described by Pilar nor charismatic, either. He would have passed unnoticed in any group of Spaniards if one did not know he was the great Caudillo. His wife was taller than he, slim and distinguished. After an almost wordless series of handshakes, they both passed on to one of the salons with the count and the other guests. The commotion the Caudillo's presence created was the only indication of the power he wielded; few officers accompanied him. I was about to follow when Casilda grabbed me.

"Come to the balcony. You must see every minute of the procession."

I wanted to learn something about those who accompanied Franco—it would be the least Mozart would expect. But I could not refuse my friend's insistence.

Gradually the streets became dark. Then the somber slow beating of a drum in the distance seemed to impose silence. From afar a line of hooded figures, like a black-garbed Ku Klux Klan, appeared, each carrying a flickering candle. Behind them was a float ablaze with hundreds of candles illuminating a statue, which swayed as it moved in our direction. Some of the hooded figures were marching barefoot on the cobblestones; their long black robes could easily conceal any weapon. A perfect disguise, I thought. Suddenly from a balcony in front a voice sang out, the eerie, beautiful voice of a woman. The huge float supported on the shoulders of about twenty men paused. When the song ended, the bearers lifted the float again, dipping it first in the direction of the singer and then toward us, giving the effect of a bow from the statue. Only then did I realize that the Generalísimo was standing directly behind me. I turned and tried to move, but he stopped me.

"I have seen these processions all my life, señorita. You probably have not."

"Oh, your excellency," I replied. "I did not know you were there. I would have moved."

"And I did not know an American girl was hiding under that mantilla." The Generalísimo smiled. His high-pitched voice surprised me. His air was friendly and unpretentious. I was about to tell him Mimosa's message when one of his aides appeared.

"Your excellency," he murmured, "it would be convenient to change balconies."

The Generalísimo turned to me. "Sorry. I would have enjoyed explaining the ceremony to an American." He was well aware of the threats to his life.

===

Entering my apartment in Madrid early Monday morning, so early that my servants were not yet awake, I went straight to my bedroom. When

I saw someone sleeping there, I turned to leave. One of the Basque women, I supposed. They probably had not yet left. At that moment the sound of a shutter creaking in the wind made me turn around. Surprised that the shutters were open, I approached to close them. I glanced down at the bed as I tiptoed by, and instinctively my hand covered my mouth to muffle a scream. The pillow and sheet were covered with blood! The body in the bed was a woman with long, black hair, a horrendous hole through the temple. Little cords of dark blood lined the cheek. Next to her hand was a revolver.

I could hear my own deep breathing. For a moment I was too shocked to react. Then I gingerly picked up the phone and dialed Mozart's number. When I gave him the code phrase for an emergency, he wasted no words. "Do nothing until I arrive."

When I walked out of the room, Cecilia was just beginning to light the coal stove in the kitchen.

"Señorita, you look so, so—pale. Is something the matter?"

"No. Please don't disturb the woman in my room."

She was startled by my firmness and the lack of the usual early-morning pleasantries, especially after an absence of some days.

"I will call Angustias to help the señorita," offered Cecilia.

"No, no. Please." Just the thought of Angustias screaming and wailing as she was apt to do at any slight provocation made me weak. What a fuss she would create if she knew a woman had shot herself in the house!

I took the key from the inside of my bedroom door, locked it from the outside, and went into the front room to await the boss.

Running up the steps had given his inexpressive countenance a deep red tone.

"One of the Basque women is dead. I think she shot herself. I just arrived from my weekend at the Avilas' and found her in my bed with a hole through the head."

The chief's eyes darted back and forth. He frowned, but his tone was calm. "Who knows about this?"

"No one that I know of."

"What about your maids?"

"So far, I have only spoken to the cook. I presume the other Basque woman is still asleep, and Angustias also."

"Which one is dead?" The chief exhaled audibly.

"I don't know. The hole in her head, the blood, the long black hair —I couldn't tell. Come, look for yourself."

Mozart followed. The sound of his large feet was certainly going to awaken whoever might still be asleep. Angustias, disheveled, appeared at the end of the hall—she ran away when she saw the boss.

The sight was more macabre than before. Now sunlight was entering the half-open window, and blood could be seen splattered over the upper part of the bed.

"Would you identify her?" the chief asked. "I've never seen either woman."

We barely fitted into the small room. Leaning over the body, lifting a strand of black hair from the face, I recognized the Spanish woman, Marta.

Mozart was visibly irritated. "Why does it have to be just the one who can create the most trouble? If we are caught harboring a Spanish communist, our whole operation can be expelled from the country. We have to remove the body without anyone, including the servants, becoming aware." He took a closer look at the woman.

"I had heard she was emotional, unbalanced. Probably it's a suicide."

The gun was lying next to her right hand. Then I saw the bandage enclosed the fingers in such a way that it would have been impossible even to clasp the weapon. "That hand . . ." I mumbled.

"What's the matter?" Mozart said.

"Look." I pointed to the Colt .45 and the bulky bandaged fist.

The chief picked up the phone. "Jeff, get Ronny and come by Tiger's apartment immediately with a large car. Be quick. Try not to attract attention, and don't bring the chauffeur." When he hung up, he asked for a blanket to wrap up the body. "A sheet is too obvious. Bring a scarf to tie around her head.

"Perhaps I've been too hasty with my calculations," he said, his eyes straying around the room. "This woman did not pull that trigger. Nevertheless, we must get her out of here. We can investigate later."

He took the blanket, pulled down the covers, and rolled the woman into it, removing the weapon and placing it in his pocket. The bloody pillow and sheet were also wrapped in another blanket by the time Jeff and Ronny appeared. Rapidly they carried her out of the room and down to the car.

Meanwhile in the kitchen, Engracia was about to leave for school. The two maids and Madeleine were having their *bollos* and coffee. All knew something was wrong.

Madeleine spoke first. "Is Marta sick, señorita? Is that tall man the doctor?"

"Yes. He would like to know if she was ill yesterday. Did she complain during the night?" I asked. Madeleine shrugged her shoulders.

"No, not especially. She never speaks except to complain, but she was not sick yesterday nor during the night either, that I know of."

Angustias and Cecilia also said they had not noticed anything unusual. I asked them to stay in the kitchen until the doctor had left.

The chief was pacing back and forth in the salon when I returned. "We have other agents who can take the French woman back across the mountains, and she can be driven to the frontier by my driver. That is no problem. It's fortunate this Spanish woman has no family. Send the French woman in so I can take care of this. Meanwhile, question your servants to find out if they heard anything unusual last night."

"I already have. They sleep soundly. No one seems to have heard anything. They think Marta is ill."

"Say she has been taken to a hospital."

"That's easy, but Angustias will miss the pillow, the blanket, and the sheets."

"Let her, but be certain she keeps it to herself." He pointed to the sofa. "Sit down, Tiger."

I did, but he continued to pace the floor. Two steps to the left, two to the right.

"The assassin was not after Marta. He was after you. Few people knew you were out of your house. She was shot in your bed, at night, in the dark, at close range.

"The murderer came in through the window. He did not know someone else was in your bed, but when he finds out, he may be back. The least you can do is to change your room."

He turned back just as he was about to leave. "I have to go to Algiers this morning for a few days. Go to the office as usual this morning and say nothing about this affair to anyone. When I return I'll take care of that protection you asked for. In the meantime, be careful!"

Chapter 18

A couple of weeks later on the first day of May, Edmundo called to say he was picking me up at ten that night to take me to Pasapoga. There was a crucial reason, though he declined to tell me what it was. When he rang the bell, I opened the door myself.

"Divina," he said, appraising my dress. Then he looked up. "But you are so pale."

"I can't imagine why," I replied dryly. "I live such a boring life." I couldn't explain to him that I'd been sleeping badly—on a cot for the past two weeks.

He helped me on with my coat and we left. In the taxi, Edmundo confided: "René called this morning. He said to bring you and to meet him at Pasapoga. He has two bombs to drop but dared not tell me on the phone."

I would have liked to ask his opinion about Marta's murder, but did not. He handed me an envelope which I recognized as one of those destined for Mozart.

"No luck tracking my marquesa's assassin. Even her old maid has disappeared. So I concocted a spy story, which you can read before passing it on to Mozart. Can't let one's reputation fall, you know."

I put the letter in my pocket, looking forward to the moment I could read it and not mentioning my apprehensions about his false reports to the boss.

In Pasapoga, René was nowhere to be found. When the owner complained that he hadn't shown up nor telephoned, Edmundo became visibly agitated. He grabbed my arm and pulled me out to the street.

To the taxi driver, he said, "La Calle Rivera de Curtidores. *Pronto.*" Mexican expressions always slipped into his speech when he was excited.

"Where are we going now?"

"Blum's apartment. Something's wrong."

In fifteen minutes we jumped out on a shabby street. In front of the large double doors of a peeling facade, Edmundo clapped for the *sereno*. No one appeared. He clapped again. Then he tried the *portero*'s bell. No answer. "I'll do the honors," he said. From the inner pockets of his gray jacket he withdrew a wafer-thin file. Kneeling down, he inserted it into the lock and gently twisted until the spring was caught and released. He opened the door and with a sweep of a lean arm invited me in. We walked through a short tunnel into an open courtyard, then up an iron staircase which like a fire escape circled the courtyard. Obviously, Edmundo had been here before.

On the third landing he again deftly picked the lock of Blum's flat. Turning the doorknob slowly, he opened it. A cringing hiss—from the dark. I pulled my revolver out so fast I tore my beaded evening bag. *"Relax!"* ordered Edmundo. "It's just his cat. What's the matter with you tonight, Aline?" He switched on his tiny pocket flashlight. Looking down at the beam of light, I saw Edmundo had drawn his own instrument— a stiletto as thin as an icepick.

Suddenly I remembered the stabbed corpse in Estoril. At first it was the tenseness of the moment—then I recalled Edmundo's cool expression when he told me that first night in the little German restaurant that he had killed the man. I let out a gasp.

"Have you gone mad?" Edmundo's whisper was vehement. We stepped into the apartment. I took a look back. Overhead, clusters of stars glittered. Not a sound out of any apartment off the courtyard; we might have been in a vacant building. Closing the door behind us, Edmundo turned on lamps and pocketed his flashlight. His knife gleamed as he prowled the living room. Blum's cat was nowhere to be seen. I put the revolver back in my torn bag. The place was empty.

The apartment belied the rundown building in which Blum lived. It was attractive, full of antiques, a mammoth grand piano dominating one far corner. "You take this one and the dining room. I'll take the bedroom."

I scoured the place. Something nestling between two floral silk cushions on the sofa sparkled and caught my eye.

Holding the brooch in the palm of my hand, I recognized the same ruby-and-diamond pin—a parrot—I had seen on Gloria von Fürstenberg at El Morisco. I ran to find Edmundo.

"Put it in your purse, for Mozart. There's no sign of Blum. Come on, we've got to find him."

It was a side of Madrid I hadn't yet seen, and one that Edmundo knew as well as the choicest drawing rooms. The streets were narrow, and now, after midnight, extremely noisy. We went from bar to bar—*antros*, Edmundo called them, "dives." Smoky rooms filled with Gypsies and the sound of guitars and the clacking of castanets. Everywhere we went, Edmundo found someone to ask about René Blum. He was more serious than I had ever known him before.

Finally we were in the Calle Núñez de Arce, in the Plaza Santa Ana, entering a bar whose facade was covered with blue-and-white tiles of flowery design on which rounded spidery letters spelled out *Villa Rosa*. It was two o'clock in the morning. The front room was like all the other bars we had visited. Behind that were several small rooms, in two of which clients were enjoying private flamenco parties. The wailing of the voices and the stomping of feet was deafening.

We wove our way to a table in the corner, where I recognized the flamenco dancer I'd seen on New Year's Eve—Lola Flores. Then I did a double-take. Sitting next to her was Juanito Belmonte! Fresh carnations had arrived yesterday, and I had refused dinner with him twice last week and tonight also. When he saw Edmundo, he glowered.

"Juanito, what a surprise," I said.

Lola's eyes flashed. "Edmundo! Where have you been?"

There were three more at their table—a woman and two men. One of the men stood up and fetched two chairs. Everyone squeezing together,

Edmundo and I sat down. At once he and Lola began talking confidentially. Across from me, Juanito wouldn't speak. I fidgeted. Then Edmundo laid his hand on my arm. "Don't look now, but we have a strange bedfellow among us."

I had no time to look. Juanito stood beside me, asking me to dance. An *organillo* had started to play a *pasodoble,* and a few couples moved toward the tiny space between the bar and the tables. The little room resounded with the movement of feet. Rising, I followed Juanito. On my way I saw the unexpected visitor Edmundo had spotted.

The door to one of the rooms in the back was ajar, and I could just see beyond the figure of a twisting Gypsy dancer the man whose home I had visited a month ago. His rugged features were compressed in a tight grin, oblivious to everything except the young girl's movements. Obviously Niki Lilienthal liked flamenco.

Belmonte held my right hand aloft, his right hand tightly around my waist. We began to glide across the floor to the peppy rhythm of the *pasodoble.* In my ear he whispered, "What is that man to you?"

"Edmundo? He's a good friend."

"Nonsense."

"I'm telling you the truth, Juanito." I kept trying to distinguish who the other people were in the room with Lilienthal, but the door was only slightly ajar.

"I have a rival, it seems," Belmonte scoffed.

I laughed. "Are all Spanish men jealous?"

"You tell me you are busy when I call, yet you have time for him."

"Oh, don't exaggerate. I have seen you almost every week since I met you. I can't go out all the time. I am a working girl and have a lot to do."

"I don't see how you can always be so busy if your Oil Mission is not delivering any petroleum these days." He was right. The American ambassador had stopped deliveries in order to encourage the Spanish government not to sell any more tungsten to the Germans.

At that moment, Edmundo jumped up and grabbed the arm of a man passing by. The fellow started to run for the door. In a flash, Edmundo was at my side, my coat and bag in his hand. "Come on, Aline. That guy knows something about Blum." To Belmonte, Edmundo growled with all his feline charm, "Sorry to end the evening so abruptly."

I thought Belmonte would punch him. Juanito regarded me indignantly. "Juan, *adiós*. Call me tomorrow before your bullfight," I shouted.

We charged out after the man, who was running down the street. "That fellow knows I'm looking for Blum, and he's trying to get away. I bet he knows something. Hurry," urged Edmundo. Bending over, I yanked off my spike-heeled red pumps and ran down the hill, trying to keep up as best I could. The man ahead lunged for a taxi; we jumped into another. "Follow him!" Edmundo cried, handing a wad of pesetas to the driver. The ancient car screeched into motion.

The two vehicles careened up the tortuous street, one behind the other. Edmundo steadied me in the backseat as the driver lurched to turn a corner to the right, then the left. We stayed right behind the cab, never losing it. Suddenly the car in front seemed to stall—our driver jammed on his brakes. Edmundo grabbed me. "Duck!" he screamed and with his hand slammed my head to the seat. The shatter of glass was terrific. The aim had been fortunate. The bullet entered the windshield dead center. The car rocked and spun. The vehicle ahead tore off.

Edmundo sat up. I leaped up, too. The driver was thrashing his arms and crying; he shook his head slowly back and forth, in total shock. Several windows on the street opened; lights came on.

Edmundo sputtered. "That shot could have killed one of us, but it was probably intended just to get us off his trail." By now he was helping the driver out of the car. A crowd had begun to form, and it was impossible to leave until we had assured the driver that he was all right and Edmundo had paid for the broken window. We spent about ten minutes sitting with him as he downed a bottle of red wine and regained his composure. The crowd in the street had grown considerably, but nevertheless Edmundo managed to propel me out the door and through the mass of people.

Finally we found another taxi, and Edmundo gave Blum's address.

We looked at each other in the dark, lights flying by. Finally he said, "That gunman was one of the guitarists at the prince's party. He knows plenty or he wouldn't have risked a shot like that."

"What makes you think René will be at home now?" I asked.

"It's the obvious place at this time in the morning, unless . . ."

We had reached Blum's building. Again Blum didn't answer the bell, but the lock yielded to the pick as swiftly as before. This time we didn't hear the cat. In fact, everything was different. The apartment was a shambles. A table was broken in the middle of the room, two chairs were overturned, the sofa was spotted with pieces of a broken porcelain lamp and on it was a painting which had fallen from the wall above. Edmundo rushed to turn the lights on in the bedroom.

"Nothing out of order in here," he called.

In the living room, glasses and bottles from the bar were strewn across the floor. Some had broken, and the contents were still running in rivulets soaking into the carpet. Edmundo bent down and poured himself a glass of sherry from a decanter which was, miraculously, intact.

Strolling over to the piano, an impressive Steinway, I sat down. I don't know why. With my fingers I depressed a key—middle C. Instead of melodious sound, there was a dull thud. My two hands struck a chord —*thud*. I stood up and peered behind the heavy raised top. I gasped. Edmundo ran over.

Blum's small, thin body was lying crumpled up on the piano strings. Edmundo and I stared. His white shirt was torn and bloody, disclosing pink flesh. A stream of blood crossed the forehead and face. Then I saw the marks around the neck—rough strong hands had left red imprints. Mimosa's welts had been dark blue, but otherwise the same. René had been strangled too.

"He's dead, and Blum knew whoever killed him," Edmundo declared at last. "No one broke in here to do it. He's not been dead for long. There's no time to lose. We may catch the damn assassin yet."

My mind was computing the events of the last weeks. Mimosa, Marta, now René Blum. Were they connected—by their killer?

As I ran after Edmundo down the wooden steps, I went over my suspects. Lilienthal, Gloria von Fürstenberg, Hans Lazaar—they were all friends. And Serrano-Suñer, whom I had not met—maybe he was connected to them in some way. When we arrived at the quiet street, I asked Edmundo, "Do you think somebody connected with Lilienthal or Fürstenberg shot at us?"

"You read my mind better than Mimosa," he replied. "What a pity I can't have a session with her. Come on, let's get back to those flamenco joints. I have a feeling the murderer followed Blum from one of them. Someone may have seen René tonight."

Although we went from one place to another, no one remembered having seen René Blum. Edmundo finally left me at home around three in the morning.

I watched the night pale and become morning, pacing my room, struggling to remember the details of the past hours. I couldn't ask the boss; he was in Algiers. Could Lilienthal and Lazaar be working in tandem under Himmler's command? Certainly Gloria wasn't strong enough to turn Rene's apartment upside down or throw him into the piano. Despite my training, I knew I couldn't do it, either. But she could have hired assassins. "Only five hundred pesetas a job," Edmundo had said.

If I could speak to Pierre, he might have some advice. It seemed ironic to be working for the same cause and not be able to collaborate with each other.

Then I remembered Gloria's parrot pin in my bag. It was lying on my bed, and I sifted through it. The pin was gone! Oh, no . . . it must have fallen out at some point during the frantic night. I was additionally distraught, for it would have served as a clue.

As I hung up my coat, I happened to reach in the pocket. Only then did I realize that before leaving, Edmundo had given me his latest report.

Deciding to forgo the cot for something better, I went back to my bedroom, and propped against my bed, dawn making the room go violet, my eyelids drooping from exhaustion, I read:

My very dear friend Mozart,

I am seeing Princess Ratibor whenever possible and can truly say I have won her affection. To be quite frank, it was only in the middle of our last romantic meeting in Lisbon that I was able to extract the confession that yes, she was being paid by the Gestapo in Madrid—to be exact, Karl Wizner is the chief—to collect whatever information she might. Well, there was only one thing to do. In order to please me and to satisfy her personal desires, she will have to provide the SS with a delicious array of false information. Well, my dear fellow, I have Ratibor on the spot, so to speak. What else can she do but comply? I feel it safe to say we can count on the princess's assistance from now on, though of course the price will be my attentions, and she is most demanding. Fortunately, it is one thing I do take great pleasure in. I will keep you up to date on the latest developments as always. And send me as much disinformation as convenient.

Top Hat

Edmundo was an incredible liar. Not only had he told me the letter was a concocted spy story, but he was offering to pass on false information to the Axis through a German agent that did not exist. And he was proud enough of his duplicity to invite me to be aware of it.

Closing my eyes, I dozed, then fell asleep, even as I remembered that it was probably I, not Marta, who had been marked for death in this bed.

=====

The next day was May 2, a holiday commemorating the day the Spaniards had rebelled against French troops occupying their territory and against Napoleon's brother, who had been imposed upon them as king. I awoke late. When I rang, Angustias entered the room.

"Don Juan Belmonte has called twice, señorita, and is on the phone again."

Juanito's voice was agitated. "You raced out of Villa Rosa last night before I could ask you who was going with you to see me fight today. I hope not your friend Edmundo."

"Not at all. I am going with Carola and the two Avila girls."

"Good. Be sure you're not late. I hope the fight will be good, especially since it's your first. You know, one can never tell how a fight is going to turn out." Juan's voice revealed an unusual nervousness. "Success sometimes depends upon the bulls more than on the matador. If the bulls are not brave, if they do not attack, there is no way the bullfighter can do a good *faena*. You must understand that."

I didn't care at all. I was still so preoccupied with the happenings of the previous night that seeing Juanito fight did not interest me. However, I tried to sound properly excited. "I'll be thrilled just to see you in that ring and to learn what goes on. Don't worry."

"You'll see Manolete, too. He's a friend of mine, and it's always a challenge to be in the same ring with him. I hope my bulls are as good as his. You must go to the bullring at least fifteen minutes ahead. This is the only occurrence which takes place on time in Spain."

Our seats, according to Casilda, were sensational. *"Barreras de sombra,* ring seats in the shade, difficult to get and very expensive."

"Look," said Carola, waving to Gloria von Fürstenberg, a few seats farther down. "What a hat. I bet she got it in Paris."

The countess was exquisite in a navy suit piped in red, her shiny jet-black hair in a tight chignon under the bright red wide-brimmed hat. I wondered if she had missed her parrot pin. The women in the lower seats were all well dressed, many wore hats, some black lace mantillas draped over high combs. Lola Flores was resplendent in a white lace mantilla over an especially high comb, a mass of red carnations behind her left ear.

"Gloria makes a point of dressing to attract attention," added Nena. "And that is not elegant."

"Who are the men with her?" I asked.

Carola knew all the answers. "One is the German ambassador—don't you already know him, Aline? The other is Walter Schellenberg. He's an important Nazi—what a pity, he's so handsome."

So the new head of the Gestapo's foreign department was only a few seats from me. I took another look. Yes, I knew so much about him that it was easy to hate him. That pleased me. I was afraid I was becoming too soft on the enemy. I could not help liking Carola no matter what her father turned out to be.

"Who's that incredible-looking woman in the big hat with the feathers and frizzy orange hair?" I asked.

They laughed. "That's Ana de Pombo," Casilda said. "She's a strange woman—she worked with one of the top dress houses in Paris and has just returned from several years in France. The cellar of her apartment in Madrid is decorated in black, and she dances flamenco while her guests are served tea in the middle of the afternoon. Can you imagine? Flamenco in the middle of the afternoon!"

"She has an Argentine lover twenty years younger than herself. There he is with her." Nena pointed to a man at her side. Then Casilda waved to the pretty blond daughter of the Duke of Alba and her aunt, the Duchess of Santoña.

A general murmur made us look behind just in time to see Franco enter the royal box far above our heads. He and his wife and entourage were barely seated when the blaring of trumpets announced the fight was about to begin. I remembered Edmundo's interpretation of Mimosa's card reading. An assassination at a bullfight. Franco!

Everyone sat down, and the band struck a *pasodoble,* the doors on the opposite side of the arena opened, and the parade of bullfighters, *picadores, banderilleros,* and *peones*—all dressed in shiny satin, beads, sequins—began. Casilda pulled my arm. "Look at Juanito! Maybe he will place his cape on our railing."

I had to pull my gaze away from Gloria von Fürstenberg, who seemed to be entertaining Schellenberg with her conversation.

Juanito was front-line, next to Manolete and another matador. His heavily embroidered cape over one shoulder sparkled brightly in the sun, the exotic black matador's *montera,* hat, was straight over his black eyebrows, the face was dead serious. They stepped forward across the golden sand in unison, shocking-pink stockings moving in time to the music, walking straight to the president's box just above us, next to Franco's. Juan bowed deeply, saluting the president of the ring, bowing with hat in hand, as did the others. Then he turned to one of his *peones,* handing him his glittering green cape, and nodded in our direction. In a minute, the cape was spread out in front of our seats. The girls were ecstatic.

The matadors executed a few test swirls with their yellow-and-red capes, the trumpets announced the first bull was to be released, and then I saw talking to Schellenberg a familiar profile. I was frozen, staring.

"Aline, what's the matter with you? You're going to miss Manolete." Carola was incredulous. I was trembling. The man talking to Schellenberg was the fellow who had run out of Villa Rosa last night. The one who had shot at our taxi.

I didn't want Carola to notice and looked back to the ring.

The great Manolete was slim, haggard, gray-faced, and he did not impress me with his first bull. In fact, I decided bullfights were cruel and disagreeable. I would never go again. Casilda explained that the bull had been bad. Manolete had had to kill quickly, which did not allow time for passes which would show his skill and courage. We stood up, as did most of the crowd, while the carcass of the dead bull was dragged out of the ring by two horses urged on by red-bloused men snapping long whips, the *monosabios*—"wise monkeys." "Wise enough not to fight a bull," explained Casilda. I looked around the ring. The man had disappeared. Schellenberg and Gloria still appeared to be sharing a joke. Who would dream there was a war going on?

Then the trumpets again. A gigantic black-and-white bull roared into the ring. I could hear him snort like a locomotive as he stormed past our seats. Only the empty arena and that wild, ferocious beast racing around looking for a victim. Then dramatically Juanito appeared from behind a small enclosure, lifting his bright red cape high in the air, swaying it to attract the bull and yelling, *"Eh, toro, toro."* The crowd was like one person—breathless with anticipation. Now the bull attacked. The bull was easily four times the size and ten times the weight of my friend.

I held my breath, horrified, not knowing what to expect. It appeared that the animal would plow right into Juanito. It was headed straight for him, alone in the huge ring. Then, *swish*—the bull raced through the cape, raising it in the air as if it were chiffon. In one split second, the animal whipped around and was after his victim again, more ferocious, more determined to tear him to bits. I forgot Schellenberg, the war, my mission. Here was excitement as I had never imagined it: intense, compelling, hypnotizing—a death struggle enacted before my eyes. And the certain victim was a friend! How long would it take? Again the bull lurched for the man. This time he was certain to rip him to pieces. Juanito pulled the cape closer to his body, and just as the beast reached the heavy cloth, Juan twisted, wrapping the cape around his body, leaving the animal plunging into open air. The crowd roared in one voice, *"Olé!"* I relaxed. But only for a second. Juan bluffed the bull several times, the horns just grazing his body, all the weight stabbing and thundering into the cape harmlessly, Juanito moving gracefully, with ease, as in slow motion, moving at just the perfect moment to avoid the sharp needle points of the huge ivory-colored horns.

Then the inevitable happened. The bull as he passed the matador hooked with one horn, just slightly, but Juanito was thrown into the air. The *peones* rushed into the ring, three of them at once, waving and tossing their capes. Juan lay inert on the ground. I was sure he was dead. My hands clenched the iron rail. Men groaned; women screamed. The strength of the bull was such that one flick of his left horn had thrown Juan like a rag doll. One of Juanito's black bullfighter's slippers was lying on the sand.

Then, to my amazement, Juanito jumped to his feet. A trickle of blood ran down his embroidered green satin pants, an open tear split his sparkling jacket. But he was running toward the bull again with the red cape in hand as if nothing had happened, with more determination than before. With a gesture of insolence and indignation, he taunted the bull while directing the *peones* to disappear. This time when the bull attacked, Juan was ready. He knew now that the animal hooked on his left side, so Juanito pulled him close, very close, to the right. The crowd rolled out an agonizing *Aaa-ahhhh,* until the animal had stormed through the cape, then they let loose, screaming, jumping to their feet in a delirium of joy. I remained seated, exhausted. What I had witnessed was unbelievable. I had even forgotten that last night's thug was somewhere in this plaza.

The *picadores* on their padded horses entered the ring. Juan's man of swords, the one who had appeared at my door that first day, rushed to his side to investigate the cut under the jacket. Juan brushed him away and entered the ring. After the bull had been picked, and had thrown down two horses and their riders, and the *banderilleros* had plunged three pairs of spiked sticks decorated in colorful crepe paper into the beast's neck, Juan took the red woolen cape and approached the animal for the important part of the *faena*.

Again he drew the bull close to his body, in a circle so small that the animal was almost bent in half, drawn around the man's waist like a towel, the horns no more than an inch away. Every movement was a delight of elegance, lightness, precision. Now and then, Juan directed the animal with a swing of the cape away from his body, and then stalked toward the audience, his back to the bull in an arrogant display of fearless disdain. Each time the mass roared their delight. Then he killed the animal with one stab of the long silvery sword.

After Juan paraded around the ring, his *peones* behind throwing back the flowers, hats, cigars which the enthusiastic public tossed at him, he stopped in front of us to throw me the ear he had been given as his prize. His gesture was so unexpected I almost missed catching the horrible thing.

"What luck, Aline—to have a famous bullfighter throw you an ear at your first bullfight."

I looked at the ghastly prize in my hand, amused. Yes, I was lucky. I had always been lucky.

Then I remembered the possible assassin. No sign of him. Schellenberg was talking to the wife of the ambassador. I looked above me. To my surprise, Edmundo was there, accompanied by two men I had never seen. He must feel terrible, I thought, to have to go to a bullfight when his friend has just died. He saw me and gestured across toward Franco's box. It was filled with Civil Guards and police milling around, but there was no sign of Franco. I looked back at Edmundo, who was glancing from one side to the other. I didn't understand. Then I saw two Civil Guards running through the rows below Franco's box. Policemen were rushing through the rows below those, also. I could hear people mumbling all around us. I asked Casilda what they were saying.

"My heavens," she said. "Somebody tried to kill Franco."

"Is he dead?" I asked.

"Evidently whoever tried to shoot him missed. They say Franco walked out."

"Franco está a salvo," was the murmur that ran through the crowd—
"Franco is unharmed."

The trumpets sounded again, and the people turned toward the ring.
In a minute, the incident seemed forgotten, and the audience's attention
was concentrated on the activities below. Confused by so many emotions,
I hardly saw the next fight.

At the end, it was the general opinion that Belmonte had been the hero
of the day. And I was impressed. He had to be some man to be able to
face death almost daily, without showing a sign of fear, of nervousness.
To be able to laugh with me the day before, and the day after, never
commenting on the danger.

———

I called Edmundo as soon as I got home. He was not in, so I left a message
for him to call. When he did, our conversation was brief.

"Yes, Franco was not touched. They're looking for the man."

"How did it happen?"

"A shot during the fight when the crowd was roaring for Belmonte's
big pass . . . naturally, so no one could hear anything. Now what do you
think of my *divina* Mimosa and her readings?"

Edmundo's call had come just in time. I had promised Juanito I would
dine with him if the fight had been good, and he was already waiting
below. Perhaps I had become a fan. Juan noticed the difference when he
opened the car door for me. When he leaned over to lock my door, I
noticed for the first time his strong thin brown fingers. Driving down
Monte Esquina, we didn't exchange a word. Then I turned to him.

"What can I say? I've been trying to think of some completely original
compliment, something you haven't heard. I can't come up with a thing.
Juanito, you're extraordinary!"

He smiled briefly. "Thank you, Aline. Coming from an American, that
is original. Few of your compatriots understand the art of the bullfight."

"Your *faena* was incredible. But the bull doesn't have enough of a
chance."

He stiffened. "Now you sound very American. Don't you think the bullring a more glorious end than a slaughterhouse in Chicago? Here the bull has as much chance as the matador—several *toreros* are killed or maimed each season. These bulls are bred for that fight and crave it. They'll attack anything that moves—not just a red cape and a matador, but even a moving car."

The new respect I had for him made me more easily influenced. Yesterday, I wouldn't have believed a word of it.

"You know, Aline, in order to understand Spain you're going to have to shed your foreign ideas. You can't judge other countries as you would your own. Each country has its own customs, which have developed because of its climate or geography or necessities. This skill was invented by our ancestors to defend themselves against the attack of wild bulls who always existed here. Today the *corrida* celebrates the courage of man and beast alike. If executed with grace, it is an incomparable experience."

"It is," I agreed wholeheartedly. As soon as we reached Guria, a *tasca* —tavern—known for its Basque cuisine, Juanito was besieged by fans, but finally we faced each other in a cozy corner over two sizzling bowls of *angulas,* tiny eels fried in bubbling oil. "Juanito, Edmundo says a novel has been published about your life."

One look told me that Edmundo was the wrong name to mention. "I think your friend is a . . . a . . . fop."

I smiled. "That's because you don't know him. Edmundo is a character, I admit, but a good friend."

Juanito frowned, his large nose wrinkling. "I have something to confess, Aline. I am a very jealous man."

I laughed. "Why, I had no idea. Tell me about that novel."

"My story isn't a happy one. My mother was born in a poor family in Sevilla; my father also. They fell in love, and then he became the world's greatest bullfighter. They intended to marry when he returned from his winter fights in South America. Just after he left Spain, my mother discovered she was pregnant. Her father put her out of his house, and she supported herself by sewing—until my father returned. But my father had married a rich Peruvian girl and when he returned refused to see my mother or me. It was only when I was ten years old that he recognized me legally. He had no choice, because I looked so much like him that people stopped me on the street to say, 'You must be the son of the great Belmonte!'

"I became a bullfighter, not because I liked it—to be honest with you, I don't, Aline—but because it was the only way I could become rich enough to repay my mother for all she had sacrificed for me. I know I'll never be as great a matador as my father, but at least today I can give my mother any luxury she desires. So let them write about me any way they want. I've accomplished what I care about most." He smiled simply. "Can you understand that?"

"Yes, I understand." Juanito was improving in my eyes by the minute.

Chapter 19

When Mozart returned from Algiers, I told him about René Blum's murder and the attempt to assassinate Franco. No mention of either had appeared in the censored Spanish press or radio.

Mozart drummed his fingers on the barren desk during my lengthy explanations.

"Maybe the marquesa was a more reliable source of information than we thought," he admitted grudgingly. He started to speak again, then stopped. Evidently he was undecided about something. His decision made, he leaned down to a lower drawer and pulled out a metal container, which he unlocked with a key from his right-hand pocket. He held up a small black pillbox. "It's my duty to give you this." He tossed the shiny container from one palm to the other, then handed it to me.

I didn't need to open it to know what was inside. The lethal "L pill." Just a quick bite between the teeth—we had been told to use the molars preferably—and one was dead on the spot.

"My advice is to be on guard," said Mozart. "We'll protect you as much as possible. Just realize most of our agents already have a similar box."

Once back in the code room I had to face the fact of my fear. There was more to Marta's and Mimosa's and Blum's deaths than Mozart wanted to tell. The main reason for the L pill was to enable an agent to avoid divulging vital information and blowing the cover of colleagues under interrogation and torture.

Immersed in my worries, gazing out the window, I realized I was peering down into Carlos Beistegui's garden. I remembered his invitation and decided a swim might improve my spirits. Cecilia brought me a picnic lunch—some fried fish, tortilla of eggs and onions, and a few apricots. An hour later I knocked on the garden door on the Calle Fortuny. I explained who I was. The guard led me in through a garden of chestnut trees and pink oleanders to a small rectangular pool, at one end of which a man about forty-five, thin and distinguished, was having a picnic lunch. When he saw me, he stood up and bowed politely. The guard indicated a room to change. I made an effort in the space available not to disturb the bathers' clothes, put on my suit, and came out, taking a place at the opposite end of the pool. The gentleman again stood until I was seated, but did not pronounce a word. He continued to read papers from a thick briefcase, and I stretched out to take the sun.

My silent companion slipped into the pool and swam back and forth a few times. When he came out, I waited a few minutes and did the same. For the remainder of our two hours together, we both tried not to get into each other's way. I was grateful I could sun and read without having to make conversation. How wonderfully discreet these Spaniards were.

My hair was still wet when I returned home to find Edmundo slouched in a chair, sipping a whiskey and soda. He had disappeared from my life since Juanito's fight. Not even the maid had answered when I called.

To my expression of surprise, he answered, "Just one of my black moods." I sympathized with him. Naturally he was depressed about the death of his friend. So was I. Only a week had gone by and there wasn't a day I didn't wonder who had done it.

"You won't be so cool when I tell you my reasons." He sat up and put his glasses down. "René has had no funeral."

"What do you mean?"

"When I called his maid the day after he was murdered to ask the hour of the burial, she was horrified. She didn't know where he was and told me the house was a wreck and that someone had stolen the piano. She's a loyal servant—if she knew he's dead, she would tell me. So there you are. Somebody has done away with the body and the piano under my very nose, so to speak. I'm a lousy spy. For one whole week I've been looking for clues."

I sat down. What would happen next? "How could anything as gigantic as that grand piano disappear without everybody in the building being aware?"

"Don't think I haven't questioned his maid, the *portero* of his building, and the people who lived above him. There was only an empty apartment below. They've either been paid off or they're frightened for their lives. I suspect the *portero* knows more than he pretends to. Someone is putting the pressure on him."

"It seems to me Lilienthal could be involved," I suggested. "He was in Villa Rosa in the same group with that thug, and Gloria could be in on it, too. Remember her pin was in René's apartment."

"I've come to the same conclusion myself. That's why I'm here. You can help, because you know them better than I do and have access through your young girlfriends. But I believe it is only one, working alone. Why, you ask? First of all, Himmler is too paranoid to put his trust in more than one chef—you know the old adage, too many cooks spoil the broth. Second, don't be so naive as to think one of the Traitorous Trio trusts the others for a minute.

"Now, I've learned absolutely nothing more about Blum's death than we already know. It seems quite logical to presume that thug we chased and the guy who chased us—I'll never forgive him for that nasty unnecessary shot—is mixed up in all of it. My guess is, a thug does the dirty work. But for which one of them? That's the question we have to answer."

"Mozart told me he wants cold hard proof. Which reminds me, guess what I lost besides sleep the other night. Fürstenberg's diamond-and-ruby parrot pin."

Edmundo smiled and said with tender consolation, "Well, what could you expect the way we were dashing around? Nobody's perfect."

"Well, I'm still a working girl and must keep up appearances. I have to get back to the office."

We went down to the street, and I hailed a taxi. It was already five o'clock. When I walked in Jeff said, "Mozart is looking for you. He's been here a dozen times asking when you'd be back."

When I reached Mozart's office, I knocked. "Come in," he said.

"Any news about Blum?" His greeting was curt and to the point.

I told him everything Edmundo had found out. He shook his head pessimistically for a few seconds. Then he said, "Take a seat, Tiger."

Obeying, I watched him. Hunched over the enormous desk, which except for a telephone and blotter was as usual devoid of any object, its surface blank and smooth. I wondered if he cleared it of papers and pens before every meeting. He always seemed so perfectly controlled, yet the strange thing was that his eyes, cut brown beads absurd in so gigantic a frame, would often timidly avoid mine. Maybe it was just women who caused him to act shy. How should I know? I had seen the chief outside this office only that one time in my apartment, so I still found him an anomaly: bulky, fastidious, and—something else. What was it? I couldn't tell. In dim light he was less florid, less jagged; three wan lamps burned around the spare mausoleum of a room. Sealed shutters barred the waning daylight and the noise from the street of Eduardo Dato and the Castellana.

"We have something for you," he went on quietly. "It seems nobody with more experience can travel today." I thought he sighed; was it disappointment? "You're leaving tonight, you see. On the ten-o'clock train to Málaga."

I swallowed.

The chief paused, perhaps expecting a response; but Edmundo had warned me a long time ago, "Keep your mouth shut with him. He does everything his own way." A thrill of anticipation ran up my spine. Silently, however, without expression, I kept watching.

"Your friend Edmundo calls you our 'fashionable front.' Well, I hope that's to my advantage. Ostensibly you are taking advantage of a weekend off to see something more of this extraordinary country. You're a frivolous American girl out for some sightseeing. It might be healthy to get you out of Madrid for a few days anyway."

No inflection betrayed his voice, his intent. He sounded like a mortician, or a surgeon.

Opening a drawer, he extracted something wound taut inside a transparent envelope. He held it up; it was shiny, even in the dimness. "You've heard of microfilm, no doubt." The word was exotic, a recent technological breakthrough. "In this strip are the names and addresses of Spaniards ready to hide—and aid—our agents on the underground route from

Málaga to the Pyrenees. The culmination of, oh, I'd say about a year and a half of 'research'—very tedious research, as I'm sure you know. The compilation of four colleagues' efforts. I must get it to Blacky *now*—he's your contact in Málaga—just arrived there from Algiers by way of a PT boat and then a rowboat to come ashore. Blacky and those who came with him need safe houses immediately."

He removed the coil of tape from its packet and displayed it between two fingers. "All this on a tiny piece of film—ingenious, no? You don't say a word to Blacky when you meet him." He shook his head, ever unsmiling. "What one of Franco's secret police would give to get a crack at this . . . I dare hardly imagine. Stand up."

I flinched involuntarily. Then I stood up.

Then the chief lumbered over to me—we suddenly faced each other. I took a step backward. I could smell cigar fumes on his breath. Edgy, self-conscious, I remained stiff, still.

"This is how you wear it," he explained. "Only inside your dress." He reached out and began to wind the ribbon of microfilm around my waist. Strangely, the hands of this looming, ungainly man, in the drab American box suit, were nimble as they skirted and circled my body.

"You have to use adhesive tape. It won't be comfortable, I promise you." After unrolling the film he rewound it into a tight cylinder and inserted it into the cellophane envelope, which he placed on a corner of the bare desk. He signaled me over to a table against the shuttered window. There was a single lamp on it, and a new valise.

"We've prepared this suitcase for you." He opened it.

At the bottom was a sizable briefcase. "There's a transmitter inside." Using both hands, he worked the valise until he scooped a part out—it was a false front. My eyes widened. Under it gleamed a lightweight Colt automatic, like a flat shiny fish. "A present for Blacky," he said nonchalantly. "It goes into the briefcase when you get to your hotel. At the last possible moment before contact, you'll have to maneuver the film from your waist and plant it in the briefcase also. That's an added precaution, you see. If for any reason—for any particular reason—something were to happen to the suitcase, the incriminating information wouldn't be found—unless they got to you, of course." His eyebrows lifted.

"Are you trying to frighten me?" I asked and then regretted it. We stood in absolute silence, in the dim vast office.

No shadow, no change of expression crossed his face. He didn't look at me. "Now for your safe drops," he continued coolly. "Tomorrow, at two-thirty P.M., in the back bench of the cathedral in the center of Málaga, Blacky will be seated with a white scarf around his neck. Kneel in the same pew for a few minutes. Pass him the briefcase and microfilm, if you are unobserved. Otherwise leave both when you get up to go. If that meeting fails—somehow—drop two is six-thirty P.M., same place, same day. Drop three is two-thirty the next day. Churches are always open in Spain. If any problem or emergency occurs, call me. If being overheard endangers your mission, use your personal code. Which one is it?"

"Shakespeare's twenty-fourth," I answered.

"What lines—tell me."

I looked at him. " 'For through the painter must you see his skill/To find where your true image pictured lies.' "

I swear he nearly smiled, or came as close as his features would allow. "I like that one," he said, almost with enthusiasm. "I do indeed." He thought a moment. Then, swinging a forefinger, he added, "Remember, Tiger: 'Yet eyes this cunning want to grace their art;/They draw but what they see, know not the heart.' " With that he turned and padded back to his desk.

How amazing! He liked my favorite sonnet! I didn't move. The table divided us, but we were closer than before.

He pulled out a drawer. "Here's your ticket to Málaga. There may be trouble on the train. A new stipulation requires travelers to carry travel permits. The Germans received theirs a week ago; we're still waiting. You will probably get by without it—your age and all. Even if I had a man available I couldn't send him. If they do pick you up, find a way to destroy the microfilm, above all."

He was silent; there was an awkward moment. The sound of someone walking down the hall.

Suddenly, he looked me full in the face. A change—I couldn't decipher it, for it was subtle—lit up his own. "It might interest you to know that my intention is not to frighten you. I don't like sending you—or anybody, I don't care who—into danger. It's just an unfortunate part of the job. I do it the best I can." Then, simply, slowly, he said, "I didn't ask to be an executioner." He paused. "I do have feelings, you know. That may come as a shock to you." The next instant he lowered his tiny eyes, himself again, closed, mute.

Chapter 20

While I was packing the phone rang.

"Hello, stranger. I've called you many times but you are impossible to reach."

"Oh, Juanito, I'm so glad you called. I've been wanting to see you."

"Good. How about dinner tonight?"

"I'd love to—but I can't. I'm leaving for a few days. Oh, and by the way, thank you for the new carnations." Juanito's continuous flower baskets had transformed my apartment into a permanent nursery.

His voice cooled. "Where are you going?"

"Málaga."

"Whom are you going with?"

"I'm going alone."

"Why are you so mysterious about everything you do, Aline?" Though he was trying to be pleasant, Juanito's patience was clearly wearing thin.

"There's no mystery. My boss told me to take a few days off. Málaga's a place I'd dreamed of seeing years before I ever knew I would come to Spain. I've been working hard and need to relax."

"I have a great idea. How about my going along to show you the city? I have a friend there who's the greatest Gypsy singer in Spain. He'll arrange a flamenco in your honor."

"Thank you, Juan, but no," I answered quickly. "If you were to come with me, everyone would think I was your *novia,* your fiancée. You know that. Besides, don't you have a fight on Monday in Barcelona? If you came to Málaga, how could you get there in time?"

"What do you think we bullfighters do at the height of the season?" he scoffed. "We travel all night by car with our *cuadrillas* following in another. Often we arrive just in time for the fight. I do that almost every day in July and August."

"If you arrived in Barcelona so tired you were caught by a bull, I'd feel responsible."

"If only you cared that much, it might be worth it," he replied. My simulated concern hadn't fooled him.

"Juan, let's have dinner next week."

He sighed. "Bulls I understand; women, never. I look forward to next week and hope you have a relaxing trip, if that's what you wish." He paused. "Aline."

"Yes."

"*Cuidado!*" Be careful!

"*Prometo.*" I promise. As I hung up, I regretted that it was never Pierre when the phone rang. Since he did not call, I assumed he was probably in France blowing up bridges and railroads, the most dangerous job in the OSS.

===

A freak windstorm hit Madrid that night, combined with an abrupt drop in temperature. The battered cab rattled along the Castellana; a broken window mended with black electrical tape quaked with each gust as though it would shatter. A few figures scurried along the street, scarves draped over their mouths flying like kite tails behind them. "One must cover the mouth in the night wind—it carries germs," Angustias had informed me often.

The golden dome of Atocha Station came into view. Even before the taxi screeched to a stop, ragged urchins were banging on the door, their small palms out for a peseta.

The yellow glow from sputtering gaslights illuminated the bustle inside, people, packages, boxes, trunks passing by in all directions. As I plowed my way to track number four, two plump women in black head scarves and dresses passed in front of me carrying their belongings in dusty cloth sacks. Young soldiers in shabby khaki uniforms sauntered back and forth. A raggedy old man behind a makeshift counter tried to encourage me to buy thin sticks of fried dough wrapped in oily paper cones. At the end of a line waiting for tickets a pregnant woman rocked a wailing baby in her arms, while another child slept huddled at her feet.

When I arrived at the steps of sleeper number two, the conductor checked my name from the list on his clipboard. Before entering the coach, I scanned the passengers. Fortunately. Climbing the steps two cars down was a plump man in a homburg and long overcoat with a wide velvet collar—and wearing a monocle. Lazaar. His valet followed, bearing small pillows and what appeared to be bed linen. What was *Lazaar* doing here? Quickly I jumped into the coach.

The compartment was luxurious and old-fashioned. Thick burgundy velveteen drapes, white lace window curtains, a red plush sofa, a polished mahogany corner table, shiny brass doorknobs. Through a door the toilet with marble washstand and a Victorian cut-glass mirror. What a pity I couldn't make this trip in peace.

The whistle blew; we were ready to leave. From the window I watched an army officer spring up the steps. Then another man caught my eye. There was something familiar about the short, stocky frame, the sloppy suit, and an air not that of the usual first-class passenger. I opened my door just a crack as he came down the narrow corridor. He stopped to converse with the conductor, to whom he gave a pack of pesetas. Was I imagining things, or had I seen that fellow several times on the corner of my street?

I sat down, hardly daring to move. Lazaar was on the train. The roguish-looking fellow could be a thug he had paid, or he could be just another passenger, paying for his ticket. Lazaar, I hoped, was not aware I was on board.

I patted the suitcase containing the transmitter and the pistol, rubbed my hand over the band of microfilm. After all, it was only a matter of hours. By tomorrow at two thirty-five, it would be over.

A knock on the door made me jump. I was more jittery still than I had realized. "Who is it?"

"*Policía, señorita.*"

I slid back the chain lock cautiously and inched open the door.

In the passageway stood a man with a shiny badge on his uniform. His expression was noncommittal. "Your passport please, señorita."

I unchained the door and handed it to him.

"Now your travel permit, please."

"Travel permit? What do you mean?"

"Señorita," said the policeman, "you should be aware this is a new regulation for foreigners. You cannot leave Madrid without it. Surely you know this."

I feigned dismay. "No. I did not. I'm terribly sorry."

"In that case, in the morning I will have to take the señorita to the *comisaria* in Málaga." Shaking his head, he moved on to the next compartment despite my effort to plead with him to reconsider.

I was angry with myself for not having handled this problem better. Covering my shoulders with my jacket, I curled up in a corner next to the window; outside was blackness, not even the outline of a tree or the warmth of a light. The wind groaned pitilessly. My sentiments exactly. Going to the police station could be a serious complication, especially if the police opened my luggage. I had no intention of getting undressed and into my berth.

Eventually, the train rocked and cradled me into a half-dream. Although I tried to remain awake, the light on, facing the door, I slept soundly until daylight when the train was winding through the mountains outside Málaga. This was the bandit-infested country described by Prosper Mérimée and by Théophile Gautier a century before. And it was still just as breathtaking: green fields of sugarcane, graceful palms, patches of wildflowers like vivid multicolored carpets. How could there be a war going on anyplace? Surely not here; no danger could lurk in this paradise.

When I stepped out into the corridor, the policeman was waiting, prepared. So was I with a wad of *pesetas* in my hand. Mustering my most innocent smile, I said, "I'd be so grateful if you would allow me to go directly to my hotel. I have only two days to see this beautiful city."

The officer looked at me severely. "Marcelo Domínguez does not accept bribes, señorita. We will leave for police headquarters right away." By this time, the train had pulled into the station. He picked up my incriminating suitcases and indicated I should follow him down the steps. We passed groups of Gypsy women in long skirts with babies in their arms, small stands with fat red cherries in wicker baskets, sweet-smelling carnations, gardenias, roses. I kept an eye out for Lazaar and for the shabby passenger, but saw neither.

We arrived at a plaza where some children played in the dirt under date palms. In the center was a fountain where women were filling red clay jugs. Some carried them on their hips, others balanced them on a round pad on their heads. I was aware of the salty perfume of the Mediterranean, but too worried to enjoy it.

The *comisaria* of Málaga occupied a stately whitewashed building graced by an interior patio of leafy plants and red geraniums. However, the room we entered was dismal and barren. Adjacent were three empty iron-barred cells.

An unshaven policeman slouching near the door jumped up. Above his head on the wall was a discolored cloth emblem of the Falange, six arrows crisscrossed, superimposed on a huge eagle; just inside the door on an otherwise barren wall was a photograph of Franco.

"Ramiro," said my companion, cheerfully giving the fellow a slap on the back. "Go tell Don José I have to see him."

The fellow stretched to his full height of about five feet five, favoring us with a toothless grin of childlike innocence. "Impossible. Don José is in Ronda at the bullfight."

Don Marcelo pushed his cap back and sat down, placing my suitcase on the floor at his side.

"Who's fighting today?"

"It's a *mano a mano* between Domingo Ortega and Gitanillo de Triana. You know Don José would not want to miss that one."

"Yes, yes. I know, and if it's a good fight he will celebrate. Both you and I know how much red wine Don José can consume." He shook his head again. "Well, it's hopeless. He won't be back until tomorrow, at least." He stood up and went to the back of the room, where a bushy black head was sunk on crossed arms on a tabletop.

He tapped the man's shoulders. "Wake up, Damian." The sleeping man didn't move. He nudged him harder and raised his voice. "Come, Damian. You have a prisoner."

The man lifted his head, peering through bloodshot eyes. For a few seconds, he remained motionless, then he jumped up, knocking over his wooden armchair. The crash echoed throughout the room.

Don Marcelo explained, "This young lady is *americana,* do you hear me?" He waited to see if his words had sunk in. "She came from Madrid on the night express and has no travel permit."

Damian continued to look at me. "What can I do, Don Marcelo?"

"A fine answer for a policeman. What can you do!" Don Marcelo was losing his patience. "She's your prisoner. She cannot leave here or speak to anyone until she has Don José's permission."

I interrupted. "Please let me telephone the American consul in Málaga. This matter could be cleared up immediately."

Don Marcelo was quick to answer, "Nothing of the kind, señorita." Victoriously he looked at the two men awaiting his decision, then at me. "You are a prisoner of Spain. This is not America. Here it is Spanish law that will determine what is to be done with you."

My impulse was to become indignant, but I remembered the microfilm around my waist, the gun and transmitter in the suitcase. "Then I am under arrest with no possibility of defending myself?"

"Señorita, there is no need to defend yourself." He lowered his voice. "We will take good care of you. Our jail is clean and has all modern conveniences." I realized that I was in luck; he meant it had a toilet. "Only Don José can decide what should be done."

There was nothing to do except follow the officer into the barred cell. Don Marcelo placed my suitcase on the bench next to me.

"I trust the señorita will not be uncomfortable." He bowed and left.

Each passing minute was torture. Twelve. Twelve-thirty. One. I couldn't believe my bad luck. When Ramiro returned to his chair by the door and dropped his head on his chest once more, and when Damian was also asleep on his desk, I reached my hand into my blouse and began to untape the microfilm. Slowly, cautiously, I fished out the ribbon of film, wound it back into a taut small spool, and pocketed it in my skirt.

The afternoon wore on. Two-thirty had come and gone. A bedraggled Gypsy appeared at the door. Without speaking, he cast an importunate glance at Ramiro, whose head listed when the door opened as if on cue. Ramiro waved him away, and he retreated with a hound-dog gaze. Bushy-haired Don Damian never stirred. I stretched out on the hard wooden bench.

By six-thirty, the hour for my second contact, I was desperate. Somehow I had to escape. Calling out to the dozing policeman, I begged him to let me walk around the room. "This small cell is making me nervous. I need more space."

Opening my mouth wide as if to scream, I shook the bars until they rattled.

"No, no." His voice was imploring. "Have patience, señorita." Ramiro grunted as he shuffled across tiled floor while fumbling with a huge round key ring. "It is against orders, señorita. But I can't stand a woman screaming." As the door swung open he rushed to lock the front entrance. Meanwhile the other fellow with a wide gesture of his arm indicated that I was free to walk around the not very spacious room. At first I took large steps and circled quickly while trying to observe every possibility. But there was no exit available. The windows had bars. A door which was ajar and from which wafted a repulsive odor was the "modern convenience" proudly referred to earlier. When I peered inside, there was only a small slit near the ceiling where a bit of light and air came in. My two captors were taking no chances. They had become alert and were watching my every move.

As I circled Damian's desk at the back of the room, my eyes focused on the only piece of paper on its surface. I paused to look at it. Damian, noticing my glance, lifted up the yellow sheet.

"Here, señorita, read the important matters we transact in this *comisaria*. We work hard, you can see." He continued to shake the paper. As soon as I had put it in my hands I recognized the address of the German Embassy at the top. It was an invoice listing articles to be shipped on the

Cabo de Buena Esperanza from Málaga to Buenos Aires on June 10 to Sr. Don Hans Schumacher, German Embassy, Buenos Aires. The sender was a Karl Wizner, German Embassy, Madrid. My eyes raced over the items mentioned. Was this shipment the reason Lazaar had come to Malaga?

12	paintings entered at Bilbao on the *Monte Ayala* from Amsterdam, arrival March 23, 1944
6	paintings Cezanne
2	paintings Van Dyck
3	paintings Rubens
1	18th-century anonymous
1	Steinway piano, crate no. 5788.

When I read the last entry, I remembered seeing "Steinway" over the keyboard that fateful night. Could that be the piano? Could René Blum's body be in that crate? I memorized the list. My thoughts turned again to Lazaar. He was capable of anything. Shipping a body in a piano crate would certainly not faze him, but wouldn't the odor attract attention?

My responsibilities seemed to be multiplying. I would have to find out what was in that crate. How was I going to do that when I did not even have a way of getting out of this police station? And still the most important problem at hand was that the transmitter, the gun, the roll of microfilm might be discovered and lead to the capture of dozens of Spaniards loyal to our cause. I decided to flush the film down the toilet if I was still here at the time of my third and last contact with Blacky tomorrow at two-thirty even though that would mean total failure.

My spirits hit rock bottom. The hours that followed seemed the longest night of my life. Eventually a new pair of *policías* came on duty, but they were as impossible to bribe as the others. My only hope was that Don José would arrive soon and that no one would search me.

The next morning, Damian and Ramiro returned, greeting me cheerfully and offering horrible thick black coffee. Minute by minute, the morning waned, and no sign of Don José. I would miss my final letter drop.

About twelve-thirty, the door opened, a florid man walked in, and the two policemen jumped to attention. "Don José!" they exclaimed in one voice.

"How are things, my boys?" He ambled into the middle of the room, and before either of the men could speak again he exclaimed, "What a fight! Ortega was *una maravilla.*" The police chief took the stance of a matador, an imaginary muleta in his hand, imitating the passes of the day before. Don José's fat, protruding abdomen hardly resembled a *torero*'s silhouette, but he did have a certain grace and style while executing the classic passes. He swung the imaginary cape around his body, turned with it, and then saw me. His *manoletina* was cut short. "What's this?" He walked toward me to take a better look. I forced a smile.

"This is *una americana,*" answered Damian as proudly as if he had caught a white shark in the blue Mediterranean.

"But what a way to treat a beautiful señorita, Damian." Don José stretched his hand through the bars to shake mine. "Welcome to Málaga, señorita. Do not worry. Whatever your problem is, I will solve it. Damian, unlock this door."

He took a chair from behind a table, dusted it with his hand, and offered it to me. It was already one o'clock. "Please sit down. Now what can I do for you?"

When I finished my story, the commissioner took a key out of his pocket and proceeded to open the desk drawer, scattering pens, papers, stamps.

"We'll settle this right away," Don José replied. "Just need to stamp your passport and sign it."

More than twenty-four hours in jail for this! He took a pen from his pocket and signed in a dramatic flourish of zigzag scratches. Then he picked up the rubber stamp, squashed it into the ink pad, and, with a resounding smack, pounded my passport. The page was as spotless as before; the ink pad was dry. Shaking his head, Don José ordered Ramiro to go out and buy some ink—a procedure which seemed to take years. Finally the official mark graced the proper page. Then he proudly handed me the document. By this time, my watch marked one-twenty and I was frantic.

"The señorita is free to go." Lifting his hand, he reconsidered a moment. "No, it will be necessary for someone to identify you. Only formalities, of course. I shall call the American consul. Although it is Sunday, I know his home telephone number. We are good friends."

Fifteen minutes later, the American consul, tall, young, and handsome, limped in.

Don José pounded him on the back in the affectionate Spanish style.

"You won't mind this duty, my boy," declared the chief. "You have to identify the passport of a pretty compatriot." Then Don José turned to me. "This is Barnaby Conrad, and a damn good bullfighter. That bad leg was a gift from a Romero bull in Mexico."

We shook hands; the consul declared my passport in order. Don José carried my incriminating suitcase to the car, placing it on the backseat of Conrad's green convertible.

It was two-twenty when we left the *comisaria*.

"How about lunching with me and going to the bullfight afterward?" Conrad asked as he drove. "You'll never eat better seafood than in Málaga."

I hesitated. I knew I didn't have time to check into the Miramar, get rid of Conrad, and reach the cathedral by two-thirty for Blacky's pickup. Conrad sensed my reluctance.

"I'm sorry. You have plans to meet someone here? A friend, perhaps?"

"Not at all. It's just that I have an important errand. I promised Sister Catherine back in New York that I would deliver a box of candles made by her own hand to a priest in the Catedral de Santa María as soon as I arrived in Málaga. Since this is my first opportunity, I would like to deliver the candles right away and get that off my mind."

Conrad smiled. "That's easy. The cathedral's on our way."

While he parked in front of the church, I turned around in my seat and took Mozart's specially prepared valise out of my suitcase. I jumped out quickly to avoid giving the consul time to accompany me.

"Back in a minute," I called from the wide stone steps.

Opening a small wooden door next to the entrance, I stepped into the musty shadows. It took a minute for my eyes to adjust to the dimness. A gilt-embossed triptych adorned the candlelit altar, at the foot of which knelt a few parishioners. Pale streams of light filtered through the high Gothic stained-glass windows, illuminating those bent in prayer in the front of the church. But nobody was in the last pew, nobody in the back of the church at all.

My heart sank. I looked at my watch and hoped Blacky would not be too late and that the consul would not come to investigate. Silently I took a seat on the far side of the appointed row. As the minutes passed, I wondered what the nuns at Mount St. Vincent would think if they could see me in a church with a gun and a valise of incriminating material waiting for a communist agent. I surmised Blacky was communist, like most of the Spaniards working with the Maquis.

A man entered the pew and knelt a short distance from me. He had a dirty white scarf around his neck. It all took place in a few moments. Without turning my head, I slid the gun wrapped in my silk scarf over the wooden bench. A hand reached out. A second later, my empty scarf was replaced. Then I pushed over the case containing the transmitter. Then I stretched out my upturned hand with the roll of microfilm in my open palm. I didn't even feel his touch as he removed it.

Barnaby Conrad was reading the Sunday paper when I returned. While waiting, he had rolled back the soft top of his convertible. We drove off. The spring breeze made my hair blow in every direction—and I took the silk scarf still in my hand to tie around my head. For the first time in forty-eight hours, I relaxed. Now I could enjoy the city! Conrad drove down the Alameda through the center of Málaga toward a beach restaurant. We feasted on *chanquetes,* a delicious minute fish fried crisp, and after that crayfish and *boquerones,* baby sardines. By four-thirty, we were on our way to the bullfight.

Afterward, the charming consul strolled with me through the beautiful marble streets around the Calle Larios and showed me the city's luxuriant gardens and parks, as well as the view from the Nautical Club. Everything had worked out better than planned.

The Hotel Miramar looked out to sea. Only a narrow railroad track separated its gardens from the low rumble of the waves beyond. My room was magnificent, with a huge four-poster mahogany bed and balcony windows gazing out toward Africa, only about twelve miles away. As I lay musing in the great porcelain tub, thinking how I would recount my experiences to Mozart tomorrow, someone entered my room. I called out to the maid: "Would you please close the door. I'm in the tub." The door was closed softly, and I continued to relax. A hot bath seemed better than ever after a night and day on a hard wooden bench.

After washing my hair and donning the hotel's large terry-cloth robe, I opened the door into my bedroom.

The spectacle that greeted me took my breath away. The place was a shambles. Someone had taken my clothes from the mahogany cupboard and thrown them helter-skelter around the room. All the drawers and closet doors were opened. A lipstick was still rolling across the carpet. Pillows had even been pulled off the bed. There was one thought that cheered me: the briefcase and microfilm had already been delivered. I went through everything, but nothing seemed to be missing, not the money, not even my revolver. So it was fortunate after all that the policeman had taken me to the *comisaria*. If I had gone directly from the train to the hotel, all the equipment and the list of names on the tape might have been stolen. I remembered the Spanish proverb Juanito repeated so often: *No hay mal que por bien no venga*— "There is nothing bad that does not bring some good."

Could Lazaar be responsible? Had he seen me after all? Nobody else knew I was in Málaga—only Mozart and Belmonte. I rang for the maid.

"Señorita! Señorita!" the horrified woman exclaimed when she saw the room. "The director must come immediately," and she ran out. When the hotel manager appeared he threw his hands in the air.

"Oh, I am *sorry,* señorita! Someone must have been looking for the señorita's jewels. Oh, it is dangerous to travel with jewels," he admonished.

"I have no jewels," I said. "And nothing has been stolen, but I would like to know how people are able to enter my room without my permission."

The manager was speechless. His eyebrows lifted as if in despair. His hands went back into the air indicating his helplessness, and he bowed silently out of the room.

"A robbery, a robbery," repeated the maid.

And so it was listed. What could be better? I did not insist any longer that I had not been robbed, and I certainly could not tell anyone that whoever had broken into my room had been searching for something far more valuable than jewels.

Chapter 21

Strolling home a few evenings later, I was about to turn the corner of Monte Esquina when a robed figure in a hooded cassock passed by —one of the many monks seen everywhere on the streets. This monk, however, not only caught sight of me but grasped my arm and stared boldly at me, full in the face.

For a moment I was stunned—then I nearly exploded with laughter. Preening under his coarse cotton hood, Edmundo stroked his mustache with ecstasy. *"Divino,* no? Felisa at Balenciaga had it made for me."

I rolled my eyes. "Edmundo, don't tell me you were at my house dressed like that!"

"Angustias and Cecilia nearly prostrated themselves at my feet. Of course, that's nothing new. I assured them I wasn't there to deliver your last rites."

"At least not yet."

"Don't talk that way. God knows there's been enough of those lately."

"Come back to my house. I'm dying to talk to you."

"No, I'm in a terrible rush."

"On your way to join an order?"

My friend's bronze face was rapturous. "Only the Order of St. Mimosa, my dear." Edmundo crossed himself. "I give you fair warning, Aline, I intend to crack a few mysteries soon. I'm on the warpath. Positively. My Aztec blood must avenge Mimosa—and René Blum! What more ingenious way to investigate these mysteries? In this costume,

I can get into almost any place in this country. I've been talking at length with the old maid who washed and dressed Mimosa's body. She admitted seeing the marks on the neck, but she insisted she did not want to talk about it. It would bring an investigation and create a scandal for the family. She knows something she is afraid to tell. Tell me, what have you been up to?"

Rapidly, I told him I had been in Málaga and discovered that the German Embassy was shipping masterpieces and a Steinway piano out of the country.

"Do you suppose it could be René's piano with him in it? Mozart says I am mad to even think of such a thing."

Edmundo lifted his head so suddenly that the monk's hood nearly slipped off. "I follow you too well. Why didn't you tell me this sooner?"

"I called you a hundred times. You didn't answer. Where have you been?"

Edmundo indicated his draped habit. "Where else? Working, my pet. Tell me, do you know when that ship is leaving?"

"There's still plenty of time to do something. It doesn't leave until June tenth."

"Well, *you* certainly cannot go back there again."

"Edmundo, then you will have to go."

"Málaga? Are you mad? What would the monastery say?"

"Don't make jokes at a time like this. Who can go, then?"

"Ask your bullfighter to help. He wouldn't be suspicious. Belmonte knows you're American and that you would want to help your own side in this war. All the clues seem to lead to the flamenco spots where René spent his free time. Juanito knows the Gypsies better than anyone. You've got to do all you can. If we trace René and find his body, we may uncover the guy who has done all the dirty business. And think of Mimosa! The same could happen to you or to me." He readjusted his hood, which had come awry during his animated talk. "Tell me, Aline, apart from discovering wayward pianos, what else did you do in Málaga?"

"Nothing much. I saw Lazaar on the train, spent the night in jail—and oh, yes, my room was ransacked while I was in my bathtub."

"Oh, your humor is simply too delicious for words."

"Unfortunately, I'm serious."

Edmundo's eyes bulged from behind his hood. "Aline, how do you do it? You're delectable. Well, don't torture me, as you say. Who done it?"

"Who do you think?"

"Lazaar!"

"That's what I think."

Edmundo quickly crossed himself.

"Mozart doesn't share the same opinion," I added.

"My dear, who is Mozart, compared to Mimosa's *pícaro*? My detective work with the princess continues. She's very demanding, but I have the patience of a king. Perhaps I should hold out longer—surely a deposed queen will float into Madrid any day now. Anyway, I'm suddenly very depressed."

"Why?"

"Because your trips sound more juicy than mine. I guess I shall have to spice up my report, that's all."

"That shouldn't be hard. You're the Mata Hari of literature."

"And you, my love, are my favorite protégée."

"You know, Edmundo, your devotion to Mimosa is hard to believe. Once when I asked you if you trusted her, you said, 'Implicitly not.'"

"My pupil, that was when she was alive." He smoothed his hood. "Don't trust a *living* soul, my sister, not in our profession, at least. But now that my dear Mimosa is no longer with us, I tell you, I trust her. And I vow that the one who murdered her shall have his or her neck wrung very soon."

"Please, Edmundo, remember your holy vocation."

"Oh, but I do, I do. Edmundo Lassalle's vows are not to poverty or chastity—never! I am consecrated only to the vows of espionage."

"And above all, nobility."

"Don't be profane, sweet. You're talking to a monk."

"You mean a wolf in monk's clothing."

"You're sinfully delicious. As soon as I've said my prayers, I'll come by to teach you a helpful proverb or two. Like 'The Lord never sleeps.

He dances until dawn, just like us.' " My monk bowed to kiss my hand and scurried off into the early evening.

Ten minutes later, the phone rang. It was Belmonte.

"*Guapa,* how was your trip? Did you get to see as much of Málaga as you had hoped?"

"In a manner of speaking, yes."

"You're having dinner with me. I'm holding you to your promise."

I had forgotten completely, but the date couldn't have been more timely, if I wanted Juanito to help me find out what was inside that piano crate.

Juanito said he was going to ask his friends the Alvarez-Pickmans to join us for dinner. I told him I preferred to be alone to discuss important confidential matters. He was delighted. At ten he picked me up as planned. "We are dining at L'Hardy in a private dining room, so we will be alone."

A narrow stairway led to a tiny room. Candles flickered on the white damask cloth; thick red plush curtains covering the entrance were closed gently so that we were completely isolated. I looked surprised. Juan laughed.

"These salons were designed for secret love affairs and confidential conversations. Respectable ladies did not go to public restaurants before the civil war." He gestured around. "These same walls have witnessed many secrets, even conspiracies against the government."

"Then I'm in an appropriate place."

"I am all ears, Aline." Juanito's small olive face was ardent.

"Where do I begin? Last weekend in Málaga, I was in jail." I waited for the shock to hit him.

"I know that." He smiled pleasantly.

No way I could mask surprise.

"Do not find that unusual, Aline. I have friends all over Spain."

"But how? How do you know? Who told you?" His answer was vital.

"Shall we say, someone who knows I admire you. Aline, what are you doing? Don't tell me you are a conspirator in a coup d'état."

I had to trust him. "No. But I am conspiring against the Germans, and I need your help."

Juanito's gaze was full of childish wonder. "Ahh . . . so that explains everything." He nodded to himself. "How can I help?"

I went to it. "While I was in that dirty cell, I saw an official report from the German Embassy requesting an exit permit for a piano to be shipped to Buenos Aires."

"What is so unusual about shipping a piano to Argentina?"

"Don't be impatient and you'll find out. The night you saw me run out of Villa Rosa with Edmundo, we were chasing a criminal. We followed him in a taxi and he took a shot at us."

"But what does that have to do with a piano?"

"Everything," I continued. "Edmundo thinks that fellow knows René Blum and knew René had important information for us and that we were looking for René."

"I still don't see any connection." Juanito looked sincerely confused. He grabbed my hand. "Please, try to get to the point."

Removing my hand, I explained, "When we got to Blum's apartment . . . I saw him."

"Well, I am glad. What did René have to say about the fellow who shot at you? Did he know him?"

"Juanito, René was there—huddled inside his grand piano. Dead. Someone had strangled him."

Juan said nothing. But his look was skeptical.

I continued, "The next day, René's body had disappeared—and the piano was gone, too."

Juan's gaze was befuddled, and undoubtedly he thought I was mad.

"You do believe me, don't you?"

"I don't understand anything. First of all, why would anyone want to kill René Blum? He's so kind to everyone." Juan looked sincerely distressed.

"He was helping to get Jews—especially children—out of France into Spain. You can be sure the Germans were not overly fond of him."

"René had information for your friend Lassalle?" Juan's brow was furrowed in deep wrinkles. "And you help him?"

I smiled and nodded my head. I could see he was catching on.

"Then Edmundo is a . . . sort of . . ."

"Business associate." My smile was very sweet now. After all, I was blowing my cover—and Edmundo's as well. But there was no choice if I wanted his assistance.

"Ah, he's not my rival then?"

"Of course not. And you must help me. You are the only one I trust. Realize my country is at war and I must do all I can to help—as you did in your war."

He put his hand on my arm. "Of course. Don't worry. I'll do whatever I can."

"Can you find a Gypsy who is capable of maintaining silence, who knows René and the flamenco joints he used to frequent? Please, can't you think of someone like that who could work for us?"

For a moment he shook his head. "No, I don't think . . ."

Then his face brightened. "Perhaps I know just the person. A friend of mine who hates the Germans, which would make him thoroughly reliable for this kind of a job. His daughter was raped by a German just a few weeks ago, and he is determined to take revenge. In the world of the Gypsies this means that no Gypsy would marry his daughter." He was speaking more enthusiastically now. "Of course—José Heredia is your man."

"Can I rely on him—really?"

"No one is more perfect for this delicate task. And I've known him all my life. He lived near us in Triana and he taught me how to fight the bulls. He's the only person I would trust to do such an important job for you. Remember, your problems are my problems, Aline."

═══

Belmonte was fighting almost every day that month all over Spain—Valencia, Palma de Mallorca, Alicante, and in the northern province of Guipúzcoa. Not until the end of May did he have time to introduce me to José Heredia.

Parking his Bugatti convertible on the highway a half hour southwest of Madrid, Juanito pointed over rolling fields carpeted with crimson poppies. In the distance was a Gypsy encampment of canvas-covered wagons and makeshift tentlike shacks partly obscured by the smoke of scattered bonfires.

"These Gypsies live in covered wagons like nomads traveling from one country fair to another, buying and selling horses. The women are as proud and fierce as the men and work harder—and believe me, the women are just as skillful with a knife. You can bet every woman will have a knife, probably hidden under the elastic band of her stocking. Gypsies are so expert at stealing—though many don't—that farmers and ranchers board up their chickens and donkeys the minute they spot one. On the other hand, they can be the most devoted, loyal friends."

The camp was a bustle of men in dark corduroy trousers and cheerful cotton shirts, women in long multicolored flounced skirts, noisy children, horses, donkeys, and pigs.

As soon as we entered, Belmonte was surrounded. Then a man made his way to Juanito—and I knew at once this was José Heredia. He was rugged yet fine-looking, with a broad smile and graying black hair. Juanito hugged the Gypsy and slapped him on the back as though they hadn't seen one another in years. Then he introduced me.

We followed José to a shack and took seats on some three-legged wooden stools, and José waited for Belmonte to explain our visit.

"I need your help, José. I would like you to do something for my friend here—but think of it as a personal favor for me. It's important, secret, and possibly dangerous. Something right up your sleeve, hah, José?" Juan smiled affectionately.

Glancing back and forth at us, José waited.

"My friend is looking for someone who she believes was killed by a German."

I watched Jose's reaction—he didn't flinch. Then I explained only what was necessary for him to know about the disappearance of René Blum and the piano crate in Málaga.

"What do you think?" Juan asked José.

The Gypsy had a rasping voice, as if he had sung too many flamenco songs the night before—or maybe he was a chain smoker. "That is like a chance to go back into the ring, Don Juan. I'm ready. You know what I think of the Germans. When do I start?"

"Now," I answered. Then I asked, "What do you mean, a chance to go back into the ring?"

Belmonte started to answer for him, but José said, "As Don Juan will tell you, I was not a bad *novillero* and hoped to become a matador. But I was injured by a bull in Caceres and . . . I chose not to fight again. Sometimes I am sorry for my decision. Now I have another chance. Does that answer your question, señorita?"

Unsure, I nodded anyway. It was only after we left the Gypsy in his tent that I asked Juanito about José Heredia.

"José is too modest. He was compared to such great Gypsy matadors as El Albaicín and Gitanillo de Triana—everyone thought he had a spectacular future. But after Caceres, José was plagued by fear. It happens to many; the real test of a matador is his first brutal goring."

"Have you ever been badly gored, Juan?"

He sighed. "Oh, yes, many times."

"How is it you're not afraid?" We were walking back to the car.

"I'm scared to death every time I enter the arena, Aline."

The endless shimmering of crimson poppies seemed to bob in agreement.

Weaving across the fields, I watched the back of the proud bullfighter in front of me—and suddenly thought of Pierre. How different these two men were!

Chapter 22

On June 4, news arrived that our troops had taken Rome. On June 6, the long-awaited D-Day finally took place.

We expected the invasion in southern France to occur about a week later, but our troops were bogged down fighting in Normandy. There was no telling how long we would have to wait for Operation Anvil. The invasion in Normandy had stunned the Axis and most of the world with its undetected location and its colossal scale—a landmark in military history. No one had any doubt our boys would win, but the Germans were resisting and the loss of lives on both sides was enormous. We all hoped that our work in Madrid could help avoid the same when Anvil took place. Complete secrecy was being maintained about the place of Anvil's embarkment. We spent much of our time in the office betting on where it might be. Some put their money on the border between France and Italy, others on the Marseilles area.

About a week later the next piece of good news arrived. A cable, from Jupiter to Mozart. Jeff, who had started to decode it, handed the paper to me.

"This concerns you, Aline, from the big boss in Washington. Must be important."

Decoding the letters, I read:

SENDING PIERRE ON SPECIAL ASSIGNMENT TO MADRID STOP   USE TIGER AS HIS CONTACT STOP

This was the best news since the Overlord landing. Just knowing Pierre would be nearby relieved me. When I took the cable to Mozart he was uncommunicative.

"We will have to work out some way for you to meet Pierre publicly. Something like what was done with Top Hat. I'll let you know about that."

As I walked back into my office, the telephone rang.

"Aline, can you meet me right away at the Prado? It's rather urgent."

Now that surprises were second nature for me, I responded easily, "Why yes, Prince Lilienthal, of course."

"Good. I'll be just inside the entrance opposite the back door of the Ritz."

On my way out, I stopped by Mozart's office to inform him of my unusual appointment.

"Beware of that guy, and let me know what he has to tell you."

═══

I had visited the Prado several times during the last months, and it never failed to awe me—one of the world's great treasure houses of Western art. No one seemed to be following me as I walked up the steps and into the museum. By now I was taking no chances, and on the way to the Prado I had used all the tricks I'd learned at the Farm to lose a fellow I had spotted the moment I walked out the gates of the ambassador's residence. Lilienthal was waiting for me, and we began to walk along the wide center hall and then to the left into a room dedicated to El Greco. It was obviously not Lilienthal's intention to look at the immense gilt-framed masterworks.

After a few minutes he began, "Carola has no idea I have asked you here—nor anyone else, for that matter. I would like to keep it that way. Quite frankly, Aline, can I trust you?"

"Of course." We kept walking around the empty room. My handbag with the Beretta was under my arm. Even a museum might be considered the proper place for murder by my unknown stalker.

"You know, in a general sense I have always thought myself a good German. I say that because at various times in history my lands and the lands of my ancestors have been occupied by an enemy. When Hitler first came to power in 1933 it appeared that he was going to do great things in the country. Then his manner changed. I was privately alarmed but publicly adopted a wait-and-see attitude, not unlike many of my friends. It soon became apparent what was in store for us, although even then I was inclined to give Hitler the benefit of the doubt. After all, Germany was a shambles, and I had to admire his sheer tenacity in putting the pieces back together—or pulling them together, really, for the first time. I hope I'm not boring you, Aline."

"Boring me? Not at all. Please go on. I'm a good listener."

"Yes, so Mimosa told me. The last time I saw her alive. That Saturday at El Morisco. Well, as I was saying, Hitler was the man to bring Germany into the twentieth century and to make her a first-rate world power. No doubt about that, whatever happens. It's hard not to get swept up in all that, you know. And of course everyone thinks, Maybe he'll leave *me* alone. I thought that—before some of my properties and holdings were controlled by the Nazis. Then I saw Hitler become mad with power. Fortunately, my wife is Spanish, and so we have lived much of the time here. Most of my children have been born here, in fact. But my holdings and business are in Central Europe. Today, all that is in the hands of the Nazis. I don't have a penny to my name. That's unimportant, however. At least my wife and children are safe."

Should I believe him? I couldn't imagine the florid prince such a facile actor. But then, I couldn't imagine this robust, distinguished, beautifully dressed man penniless, either. Why was he telling me all this?

"Now I'm going to surprise you further. If it were the money alone, I probably wouldn't act as I'm about to. I can live without my money —I don't like it, but I can. My wife has enough for us to live as we do here in Spain, and though my pride might be wounded, my conscience would survive. In other words, Aline, it isn't money that is the motive for my actions at this moment. It's precisely my conscience."

"What do you mean?"

"Lately the Gestapo in Madrid is putting a lot of pressure on me. They want me to let them operate a radio station out of El Morisco, with which they can receive reports from German agents in southern France." His remark reminded me that since I had not yet been invited back to El Morisco, I had not been able to pursue my investigation about a radio station. Was he telling me the truth? He went on: "With which they can intercept Allied communications transmitted to Madrid. With which they can communicate directly with Berlin. That's why young von Weiderstock was there at El Morisco that weekend—to approach me on the subject. Of course, I know he is their errand boy and that his godfather is in deep trouble back in Berlin. When I told him no, he went away quite upset."

I listened, not daring to say a word.

He stopped me—we were in the middle of the room. "I think I've had it."

"What do you mean?"

"Until now, the horror of Russia's communist system taking over Central Europe with its bloodbaths and scourges has kept me from helping the Allies. But today Hitler has become a madman and will destroy us all." He stopped, as if considering what he was going to say next. "Yesterday, a strategic piece of information was passed on to me —so important to the Allies' success that my conscience leads me to convey it, no matter what the consequences. That is why I have asked you to meet me here."

"Why are you telling this to me, Prince Lilienthal, instead of to someone more important?"

He chose his words carefully. "I am on the American blacklist. I know no Americans. If I were to be seen by anyone in conversation with any high American official, I might end up like our dear late friend Mimosa. Also, the Germans would take reprisals on my relatives inside the Reich. You are the only American I could talk to without arousing the suspicions of the Germans." He smiled for a second. "Have you met the American ambassador in Madrid?"

"No, or rather, yes. I have met him, but I have no contact with him."

"No matter. It is easy for you to speak with him. I would like you to transmit a most delicate message. Mention it to no one else. Do you understand?"

I nodded. His eyes fixed on me. "Don't you see? You're absolutely above suspicion. No one would suspect that you would be the go–between for important intelligence information."

Was he trying to let me know that he knew I was involved in intelligence? I still felt he had suspected me ever since he saw me jump out of his study window.

I answered as calmly as I could, "I will do my best. What is the message?"

"A relative of mine, a member of the Italian royal family working in the office of General Karl Wolff, the Gestapo chief in Italy, overheard a telephone conversation between Wolff and Himmler."

The prince looked at me. Then he looked around to make certain no one was nearby. El Greco's long thin faces, the wild dark eyes, looked down on us as if they, too, were waiting for the prince's vital piece of information.

He turned to observe me when he finally began to speak again. He spoke slowly, enunciating each word in that clipped German-British English. "Himmler clearly informed Wolff that he has a Gestapo agent working inside—and I repeat, inside—the American intelligence group in Spain."

His words were like an electric shock. I tried to conceal my agitation. He must not see any reaction other than a minor glance of surprise. The cold fear which was penetrating my brain must remain completely concealed. But his news was chilling!

"Would you like me to repeat the message?" Lilienthal asked.

"No, thank you. It is quite simple. I thank you for the confidence you have shown in me, and I will try to get this information to the ambassador as soon as possible."

I was thinking—that meant Himmler's special man could be one of our own group. Maybe even Edmundo—oh, God—maybe Mozart himself.

＝＝

I almost stumbled out of the museum, confused, frightened, trying to calculate the implications. If the message was true, any colleague could be the guilty agent. Not only the four suspects on my list were dangerous, but any one of my group could be a traitor. We were so few. Jeff Walters, Larry Mellon, the others in the office—oh, if it was Mozart! Or Edmundo!

Suddenly I felt alone, trapped. Without Mozart's permission I couldn't do anything. He would be the ideal person for Himmler to plant inside our group. He was, after all, the one who knew all the operations, all the reports from the agents and subagents. But I already knew Edmundo was unscrupulous. The only consolation was that soon I would be in contact with Pierre. Would it be soon enough?

＝＝

When I got to the office, Mozart was out and was not to return until the next day. That was luck and gave me time to decide what to do.

The entire afternoon was a trial. Jeff noticed it. "What's the matter, Aline? You look as if you had lost your last friend."

"Maybe I have." I observed him for the first time suspiciously. Where did he go when he was out of the office? He was strangely mysterious about his movements, yet he always questioned me about mine. Oh, it was impossible. I suspected everyone. There was only one person I could pass Lilienthal's information on to. That was Jupiter. But he was far away in Washington.

Since I was on call for the code room that night, I appeared at the gate around midnight, as I had done many times before to decode a top-secret message, different from the usual ones in that the urgency required immediate action and relay to the chief. A sleepy guard let me in.

"Anybody working tonight? I asked.

"No one is up there, señorita. Your countrymen are still celebrating the invasion. They all seem pretty happy."

I had almost forgotten D-Day. Waiting for that moment so long, and then the pressures had made it pass practically unnoticed.

Once in the code room, I went to work fast. Anyone could appear. Often Ronnie would come during the night to listen to one of our radio stations in France.

FROM TIGER TO JUPITER STOP   LILIENTHAL TODAY INFORMED ME A SOURCE RELATED TO ITALIAN ROYAL FAMILY WORKING IN GESTAPO OFFICE ITALY OVERHEARD TELEPHONE CONVERSATION BETWEEN GENERAL WOLFF AND HIMMLER INDICATING HIMMLER HAS AGENT OPERATING INSIDE REPEAT INSIDE AMERICAN INTELLIGENCE SPAIN STOP   ADVISE IF I SHOULD COMMUNICATE SAME TO MOZART STOP   TIGER TO JUPITER

I picked up the telephone and, as was customary, transmitted the coded message through the Spanish telegraph service. There was no other way to get the message to Jupiter, since the Spanish government permitted only certain telephones to telegraph coded messages out of the country.

Slipping out of the garden into the street, I walked briskly back to my apartment, enjoying the agreeable fresh night air.

Gradually I became aware of steps behind me. I continued at the same pace and turned my head, but could see no one in the low glimmer of the gaslights on the street. Perhaps it was the *sereno* doing his rounds. Perhaps not. I put my hand on the small revolver in my bag.

I turned from the Calle Fortuny to the Calle Marqués de Riscal, the same soft thumping of feet hitting the cement behind. This time I saw a shadow when I looked back, about fifty meters away. As I walked more quickly, the feet following quickened their pace, too. Fortunately, I was wearing saddle shoes and my skirt was wide. Sprinting to my door and without taking out my key—there was no time—I turned sideways and slid between the iron bars. Once inside, I ran to my second-floor apartment, locked the door, and rushed to the window to look down into the street. Vaguely I could distinguish the figure of a man walking toward the next corner, where he disappeared into the shadows.

I wondered how long it would take to receive an answer to my cable. There was no time to lose. Operation Anvil might take place at any moment. Heredia should be contacting me soon, and Pierre would certainly be put in touch with me. If Lilienthal's tip was correct, not only were we all in danger, but the landing in southern France, which involved thousands of Americans, could be a failure.

=====

The next day the Gypsy's voice on the phone was difficult to hear. There was not only static on the line but also noise in the background.

"Señorita, I have completed the job you gave me."

"Did you find the piano crate?" I screamed.

"*Sí*, señorita, but it is a complicated story."

"Was Don René in it?"

"Señorita, I will have to see you. I cannot go to your house. Could the señorita come to the theater?"

"Theater?" I thought I had misunderstood.

"*Sí*, señorita, the Teatro Maravillas, where my daughter works."

I had never heard that his daughter worked in a theater, but I knew with the bad connection I would never get any more information.

"Very well, but it will have to be right away."

"That is fine, señorita. The best arrangement would be that the señorita buy a ticket and sit in the last row of the theater, where we can talk without being observed."

"Please be prompt, José. I will leave right now."

Madrid theaters have two shows daily: a matinee at seven and one at eleven. It was already seven-thirty. And I had to go to the Rumanian Embassy reception at nine. I called Edmundo and told him to meet me in the last row of the Teatro Maravillas. Whether he turned out to be a mole or not, René was his subagent. Between José Heredia and my revolver, I figured I would have protection.

The old theater on Calle Malasana was half empty. I stood for a moment in the darkness before I was able to distinguish Edmundo in the middle of the back row. Taking the seat next to him, I leaned over to speak. He silenced me putting a finger to my lips. "Shush—listen to that song. It's my favorite of all the Spanish *zarzuelas*."

The last thing I cared about was a song at that moment, but I had no choice except to listen. At center stage a man singing walked slowly across the platform with two girls dressed in long, flouncy polka-dot dresses, white kerchiefs tied around their heads. Despite my agitated state, I was captivated before long by the lilting tune, the spirit and tempo of the music. *"Una morena y una rubia,"* repeated the singer, looking first at one girl and then at the other. As the song finished to hearty applause from the audience, Heredia appeared at my side. I introduced him to Edmundo and asked, "Well, what did you find, José?"

"I found piano crate number five seven eight eight, señorita."

My pulse quickened. "Did you find Blum's body?"

He paused uncertainly. "Uh, no."

I let out a sigh of relief.

"I found two bodies."

"What?"

"I found two bodies in the crate. A man and a woman. But no Don René Blum."

Even Edmundo was at a loss for words.

"The man was in a German army uniform but had no identification," he continued.

"What did you do, José?"

The Gypsy flashed a keen smile. His teeth gleamed despite the dimness. "Well, señorita, I saw the address from which the piano was shipped stamped on the side of the crate. It read: 'German Embassy, Castellana, Madrid.' The official on the pier was grateful to me for discovering bodies being shipped out of the country, and agreed with me that they should be shipped back to the sender and the authorities duly informed."

Edmundo slapped him on the back. "Bravo, José."

I wondered if Lazaar's monocle would fall out of place when he heard of the delivery.

"José, you acted brilliantly." I congratulated him. "Are you willing to continue to help us?"

"Yes, señorita, I certainly am."

"Do you know Villa Rosa?"

"No one knows it better, señorita."

"You might discover there when René was last seen and with whom.

It is urgent we discover who killed him and how his body was disposed of."

"Señorita, I will go to all the cafés Señor Blum frequented. I know them well. I want to help you. For reasons of my own. By the way, the girl on the stage now—the thin dark one—is my daughter."

We stopped talking to look at the beautiful Gypsy girl twisting and bending to the flamenco song. No wonder José Heredia wanted to find the man who had attacked such a young and beautiful girl.

Chapter 23

W hat did your friend Lilienthal have to say, Tiger?"
I was looking at Mozart in a new way—as a suspect. I had never considered the day would come when I would have to lie to him. "A false alarm. It seems Carola's despondent about Constantin von Weiderstock's leaving Madrid so suddenly. Lilienthal thinks I have some influence over his daughter and asked if I would discourage her interest in that young man."

Mozart grunted, coughed. Did he detect duplicity in my answer?

He stood up and walked to the window, lifting the shutter to peer into the street below. "Anything turned up on René Blum or his piano?"

I told him the news the Gypsy had given me the night before. In his presence, I felt more than ever that Mozart could be the mole. My discomfort must have been obvious, because he said, "You seem unusually quiet. Where's your enthusiasm? That's important information. Can cause a lot of trouble for those Germans. Just what we want. Are you tired?"

"Not at all, thanks. It must be the unusual heat today."

"Probably. By the way, there's a ball at the Country Club Puerta de Hierro on the twenty-third. It would be convenient if you could manage to be invited." As I was walking out of the room, he had an afterthought: "Take the afternoon off, Tiger, and relax."

=====

It occurred to me I could take advantage of Mozart's suggestion and buy some clothes. Ever since Pilar's report on Gloria von Fürstenberg, I had wanted to visit Ana de Pombo's shop. If the countess bought her clothes there, the collection had to be the best in town.

The sky was its usual deep blue, and a slight dry breeze ruffled the branches of the trees along the Castellana. The facade of number 14 on Calle Hermosilla was not unlike Hattie Carnegie's, except for a wide carriage entrance in the center of the building flanked by two flights of marble stairs. Another exception was the shabbily dressed maid who let me in. Arched doors in the foyer opened onto a spacious, eccentrically furnished salon—pieces of Louise XVI mixed with Art Deco—where to my surprise I was entirely alone in an extremely silent atmosphere.

After some minutes, the frizzy-orange-haired woman I had seen at the bullfight entered the room. Up close, Ana de Pombo looked older; it wasn't easy to imagine her dancing flamenco or having a young lover.

"You want something?" she asked in perfect English, which let me know she knew who I was.

"Yes, I wanted to order some clothes. Have I come too late? Or too early?" She didn't offer me a seat.

"Yes—oh—yes." We stood awkwardly facing each other. "Of course, just a moment."

Indicating a blue velvet sofa, she excused herself. For another ten minutes I regarded myself, reflected on the mirrored wall; or looked toward the French doors opening onto a balcony; or admired the carved molding around the high ceiling. Finally the bizarre couturier returned with a stack of drawings. "I'm afraid everything from my collection is gone. I have only sketches left. Would you like to see some?"

As I studied the sketches—which did not resemble even slightly the clothes I had seen on Gloria—my astonishment grew. They appeared to be at least two seasons behind the style.

"Maybe you should try Pedro Rodríguez or Flora Villareal," she suggested. "They'll have some things that I'm sure you can use." Ana de Pombo forced a smile.

"No, I like these designs—I do not mind ordering without seeing the finished models. May I see some fabrics?"

Another awkward silence. Only the muffled sounds from the Calle

Hermosilla. As eccentric as Ana de Pombo appeared, I detected an equally surprising shrewdness. She answered, "Just a moment, please."

I waited again, but when the door opened it was not Ana de Pombo who entered.

"Why, Aline. Ana told me you were here. What a wonderful surprise!" The Countess von Fürstenberg stalked toward me. "How did you find this place? I thought I had it all to myself. It's my secret, you know. Ana dresses me and only a few others—how did you hear of her?"

"I can't remember offhand. It may have been one of the Avilas."

"Really? How odd. I wouldn't think the Avilas dressed here." Gloria sat down next to me. "I'm here to be fitted for a dress I intend to wear to the big dinner dance coming up at the Country Club Puerta de Hierro. Are you going?"

"Not that I know of. I'd love to see the dress."

The countess sat down beside me. "I'd much rather surprise you. You'll certainly be invited. Everyone will be there."

"Well, I'm waiting to see some fabrics."

"Ana is unique, a bohemian. She keeps nothing here. She draws her ideas, discusses them with the customer, and only then orders the materials. There is no other designer quite like her. Her taste is flawless. And frightfully expensive. Take a tip from me and go somewhere else. She takes ages to finish anything." Her large gorgeous eyes were intense, searching for my reaction.

I would have liked to confront her on the spot and ask some questions. But instead, I stood up. "You're right. I'm a working girl, and I have no time to wait." But I fully intended to have Pilar make certain Ana de Pombo's establishment was watched twenty-four hours a day. For if I had found out nothing else, I had made one peculiar discovery—Ana de Pombo ran no dress house. Her salon was a fake.

=====

Pilar failed to show up at my house for a "lesson" the following week. Not only would her information on the countess now be more useful than ever, but I wanted her to place a woman in the fake dress salon. Finally, in my growing concern, I asked Doña Antonia if she had heard from Pilar. The *portera* said she hadn't, but would try to find her.

The next day when I came home from work, Doña Antonia greeted me from her chair on the doorstep. "Guess where our friend is," she said with a shrug of disdain.

"Where?"

"In jail. Damn those fascists!"

"But why?" I asked, trying to swallow my panic.

"Damned if I know. Excuse me, señorita, but I would like to wring their necks."

Once upstairs in my apartment, I considered the implications, which were terrifying. Picking up the telephone, I dialed a man I had met with Juanito, Paco Aylagas, the chief of prisons. I explained that a woman who gave me Spanish lessons had been imprisoned for reasons unknown to me, and asked if he would try to get her released. I said she seemed an honest, good person, and I would like to help her. He told me he would check her out and was delighted to do me the favor.

The wait was agonizing. How many of the chain had been picked up as well? I advised Mozart and sat next to the phone for twenty-four hours. Aylagas finally called. His voice sounded preoccupied. "Do you know why Pilar Hernández is in jail, Aline?"

I feigned nonchalance. "No. Is it bad?"

"Is it bad?" the chief repeated. "It couldn't be worse. There's no way I can release her."

"But what has she done?" I tried not to sound overly concerned.

"You'll never believe it." Aylagas sounded thoroughly amazed. I waited for him to explain. "She is the leader of the women in the Communist Party in Spain."

Relief may have shown in my voice, although I tried to control it. "But can't you get her out anyhow?" I asked.

He laughed. "Aline, you Americans are indeed strange. If this woman was just any communist, perhaps I could oblige you. But you obviously don't realize that she is a dangerous political enemy of the government. She takes orders from Moscow. *Moscow!* Don't you know the Soviets are also working against the Americans right now, even though they pretend to be your allies? Soviet intelligence has infiltrated every democratic government in Europe. Pilar Hernández is as much an enemy of America as she is of Spain. I'm rather surprised to find her in your employ."

His voice was modulated, without overt insinuation.

"Why, I had no idea, Paco. Pilar has never once discussed her political views with me."

"Yes, well, I suggest you find yourself a more suitable tutor. One who isn't plotting to overthrow our government. Sorry I can't be of more help."

As soon as he hung up, I pondered my next move. I would have to create a new chain.

I called José Heredia. We met in the Puerta del Sol, as if by accident, in the middle of the noonday traffic. As we crossed the street together I explained what was expected of him and asked him to begin by following Lazaar and Countess von Fürstenberg. Although I had not been able to talk to Edmundo, I told him to use Edmundo as an alternative contact when he could not reach me. In a few minutes he grasped the details, and we went our separate ways. After purchasing some stockings and trinkets, I rushed to the office.

As if my worries about Pilar were not enough, a week passed and Operation Anvil did not take place and Pierre did not appear in Madrid. I was still being followed, and I was jittery. Angustias's daily warnings did not help.

"That woman Marta from France went to bed hale and hearty, señorita. Cecilia fed her the best Madrid could offer. She ate more than three men. She wasn't sick. I know the señorita is hiding something from me, but the señorita must be careful. Cecilia and I see someone lurking on the corner almost every night watching this house. Who else would be important enough to watch in this building? Certainly not Antonia's drunken husband, nor the family on the first floor."

As Mozart had hoped and Gloria had foreseen, Casilda invited me to the party. "It's the last event of the season, Aline, before everybody goes north for the summer. You must come to the San Juan dinner dance at Puerta de Hierro tomorrow. Carola, my sisters, Luis, whom you met at El Morisco, and a group of friends are all going." Casilda was enthusiastic.

"What else are you going to do? Your bullfighter friend will be fighting in Granada, and you haven't come to any of our parties for two weeks."

Her invitation delighted me. Unfortunately, Mozart had just left for Lisbon and wouldn't be back until the next night, too late to find out what he had wanted me to accomplish there. But I was tired of waiting for Pierre to appear, for Operation Anvil to occur, for Heredia to give me news about poor René Blum, and anxious to enjoy myself a little.

"Thank you, Casilda. I'd love to. Why don't you all come here before for cocktails?"

"Thanks. I'm sure we'd love to."

Months before, I had converted one of my small salons into an American-style bar with a Spanish flavor. *Banderillas,* bullfighting posters, and Juan's matador cape, which I had finally accepted, adorned the walls, and the long bar was stocked with hard-to-get scotch and almost unobtainable American cigarettes.

The gramophone was playing Sinatra's "Melancholy Baby" when at nine o'clock the Avila girls and their guests arrived. Carola came with Pucho Gamazo; then a young Portuguese artist, Pedro Leitao, arrived, and Luis Quintanilla, the Spaniard whom I had met at Morisco. When Edmundo showed up, he pulled me out of the bar into the hall, where he presented me with a tiny gift-wrapped box.

"This is a memento of my special affection for you, a fellow soldier and comrade-in-arms. My own protégée. To La Divina!" he whispered.

When I opened it, I saw on a bed of cotton inside the little beribboned box Gloria von Fürstenberg's diamond-and-ruby parrot pin! I looked at his shining face for an explanation.

"Now, don't scold me. I returned it, didn't I? It wasn't easy, I must confess. But in the end, you deserve it, Aline. Think of it as your Distinguished Service Cross."

I laughed. "You've had it all this time. You lifted it from my purse!" Again it struck me that Edmundo's character might make it easy for him to be the mole.

Edmundo glowed. "Now, consider my point of view as a patron of beauty—it was simply irresistible. I had to have it, for my collection. But after D-Day I decided that my duty as a fellow spy came before my prized possessions. It is with love and gratitude that I give it back to you. Now let's say no more about it, my delicious accomplice."

"Edmundo, I *can't* keep this."

"Well, at least keep it until you can put it to good use and find out how it came to be at René Blum's apartment. Think how our poor friend looked crumpled up in that piano. And don't diminish the importance of my gifts. Edmundo Lassalle is a modern Medici, guardian of clues for espionage activities. I am a Renaissance man and you are my Mona Lisa."

I couldn't help laughing at his wild remarks.

"You're in fantastic spirits tonight, Edmundo."

"And why not, love? Our boys are winning in Normandy. And tonight is the finale of the social season. Oh, Aline, let my epitaph read: 'Edmundo Lassalle. The party never ended.' Shall we go back to your own, my dear?"

They all seemed to be enjoying themselves, chatting loudly and snapping their fingers to the lively rhythm of "Let's Fall in Love." Carola and the Avilas started dancing—it seemed the former had survived her recent unrequited crush. I hurriedly placed the pin in my purse.

When it was time to leave, several of us piled into Luis Quintanilla's low sleek Cord convertible. Things were warming up, some literally. The heat of the motor nearly destroyed my silk stockings as we roared out of Madrid on the barren road to the country club.

Chapter 24

P uerta de Hierro was a modern brick chalet on a high hill in the outskirts of the city surrounded by a golf course. Its circular drive bustled with the arrival of ancient Rolls-Royces, some equally old Hispano-Suizas, Peugeots, Citroëns. Luis, at my side, explained that no new cars had been imported since 1936 before the civil war had begun. Doormen in navy-and-yellow uniforms stood at the entrance.

The first person I bumped into going up the steps was Gloria von Fürstenberg, with Hans Lazaar.

"Oh, I'm so glad to see you, Aline," she exclaimed. "I want you to be the first to see the dress you were so curious about."

By now we were standing in front of the cloakroom. She peeled off her floor-length red silk evening cape, revealing one of the most astonishing gowns I had ever seen. It exposed Gloria for the divided soul she was. The pure white silk shoulderless tube of a dress was embroidered with tiny blue stars mixed with black geometric patterns that almost suggested— I swear—little swastikas. She was courageous—of that I never had a doubt. I had to admire the irony of her humor as well.

The dress's effect was not lost on Lazaar. His raised eyebrows seemed to indicate his thoughts. Aloud he said, "A smart dress, Gloria." And then added a smile. "A smart girl, too. You're bound to be a winner in that outfit."

"Why shouldn't I pick a winner, Hans?" she said in her husky musical voice. "I love winners. Everybody loves a winner."

I took off my wrap and handed it to the girl. Gloria took a step back to survey my appearance. She gasped.

"You've outdone me!"

"What do you mean?"

"Why, you're practically nude!"

Hardly. I was wearing a long red cotton Hattie Carnegie (as usual) from last summer's custom-made collection, its only dramatic feature a triangular cutout above the waist, revealing a minuscule bare midriff. The last reason I had chosen it was for shock.

"I adore it," said Gloria next. "I love your daring. It's so refreshing."

=====

The room was crowded with people I had never seen before, but I saw the man from Beistegui's pool.

I waved at him. He waved back and smiled in a surprisingly friendly manner, I thought, considering his usual reticence.

"How in the world do you know Serrano-Suñer?" asked Edmundo, who was at my side.

"Serrano-Suñer?" I asked. "Is that man Serrano-Suñer?"

"None other."

"Well, I've been lunching alone with him for the past eight weeks at least."

"Aline, you must be in love. How could you not have told me you were on intimate terms with such an important man?"

"Nothing intimate about it. We never spoke."

"But why didn't you take advantage of—"

I interrupted. "Edmundo, I had no idea who he was." The pictures Mozart had of Serrano-Suñer showed a tall man in an elaborate diplomat's uniform with a high hat full of plumes, and another dressed in the uniform of the Falange. Neither had any similarity to this gray-haired man seen in bathing trunks. After all these months of looking for him! A fine spy you are, Aline, I thought.

Inside, waiters were already serving dinner, five to each table of twenty guests, and there was the soft glow from countless silver candelabra and salmon roses against white damask.

"The way this crowd is dressed, you'd think it was the Countess of Elda's grand ball." Edmundo was enchanted, and so was I. "Now, if you really are the trouper I think you are, you'll attach my gift to your bosom and tear the place apart."

"Oh, no, Edmundo." I shook my head. "I intend to return it to its rightful owner. At the proper time."

"Promise I can watch."

At that moment, I recognized someone who distracted my attention from everything. Mingling in the crowd. Fortunately, Edmundo did not notice my excitement.

"Well, well," he quipped. "It appears to me we are at the same table with the Traitorous Trio."

He saw us just as Edmundo was leading me to the table Casilda indicated. Pierre gazed steadily with no sign of recognition, then turned away.

Lilienthal, Fürstenberg, Lazaar, Carola and Nena Avila, and several young men were already seated when we arrived. Had Mozart arranged for Pierre to meet me here? I sat down and tried to take part in the conversation. In a far corner, the tuxedoed members of a band began to tune their instruments.

Nena Avila pointed a finger at Pierre. "Look, Casilda, isn't that the good-looking fellow we met at the fair in Sevilla year before last?"

"Yes, of course. It was at the birthday party Papa gave for me."

"His name is Francisco something-or-other. He flirted with you, remember?"

"How could I forget? He's so *guapo* !"

It might have been the most triumphant moment of my career in self-control. Finally I knew his real name. Francisco. I wanted to ask Casilda to tell me all she knew about him. Instead, I said quite casually, "Who are you talking about?"

"The fellow who just came in," answered Casilda. "Nena fell in love with him on first sight."

"Is he an old friend?" I asked.

"Not at all. Papa didn't like him—said he was a fortune hunter and a phony. But he is good-looking, don't you think?"

"What nationality is he?"

"French, but he speaks excellent Spanish. Look, he's coming to our table!"

I watched every face. Who among them knew Pierre? Not Fürstenberg. As he came up, she simply looked at him with unfamiliar curiosity. Not Lazaar. He didn't take any notice at all. Not Edmundo either. Pierre stretched his hand out to Casilda.

"Hello, Francisco. What a surprise to see you in Madrid." She beamed at him.

He took the hand of each of her sisters. Then Casilda said, "I want to introduce you to Aline Griffith."

He touched my hand, murmuring a few words while glancing at the others. Then he leaned on Casilda's chair chatting for a few moments. I tried to begin a conversation with someone, but he turned to me. "What did Casilda say your name was?"

"Aline. Aline Griffith."

"I'll remember that." Then he asked Casilda to dance.

During the short interchange of words, Luis had been standing at my side waiting to dance. Now he whirled me around the floor. Undoubtedly he was a wonderful dancer, but I was so perturbed by Pierre's presence that I paid scant attention to my partner, who danced me directly to the table where Serrano-Suñer and others were seated.

"Aline, I would like to introduce you to my mother and father." The Countess of Velayos was a strikingly beautiful woman and as distinguished as his father. When the countess saw that Serrano-Suñer already knew me, she inquired, "Ramón, how is it you know this young girl?"

"We're old friends," he said, laughing.

Had he known all along whom he was sharing the pool with? There was no time to find out, because Luis whirled me away again. I made an effort to keep up a conversation, while attempting to watch Pierre. "Tell me, are your ancestors Spanish?"

"For hundreds of years. Why do you ask?"

"You don't look Spanish. I thought all Spaniards had dark hair and eyes."

He smiled. "Not at all. As you see, in my family we're blond."

"Forgive my asking, but why is your name Quintanilla and your father's Velayos?"

"Quintanilla is not my name nor Velayos my father's. Those are our titles. Our name is Figueroa. My grandfather's title is Romanones, but of course his *name* is also Figueroa. Only one person uses a title at a time. The next in line cannot use it until the current holder has died. When my grandfather dies, my father will be the Romanones, because he's the eldest. If there were only daughters, the eldest girl would inherit all the titles." He sighed.

My question probably bored him, so I changed the subject. "Do you know the man who just came to our table?"

"Only slightly. I think I should warn you, though, he has a way with women. Be careful."

About one hour later, Pierre appeared again, taking an empty seat at our table and eventually turning to me. "May I have this dance?"

I glanced at Nena, trying to indicate surprise, and followed him onto the floor. My last impression was of Luis regarding Pierre and me intently. Gloria von Fürstenberg seemed to be concentrating on us also.

In the center of the crowded floor, Pierre tightened his hold. "So, Tiger, we have another dance at long last."

"What are you doing here? And be careful to call me Aline."

"I came to find you, to warn you. You're in danger."

"Of what? From whom?"

"I don't know all the answers—but be careful. Are you glad to see me?"

"This is too good to be true. It isn't real."

As we danced, I saw that everyone at our table was watching. Pierre seemed unperturbed. "I want to ask you a question. I wanted to ask you the night I surprised you in your home."

"What are you getting at?"

"Don't be so impatient, Tiger. That seems to be your only fault."

I was aware of his manly grip.

"It's a simple question. And yet it holds the key for us."

"What is it?"

He leaned closer to my ear, his face grazing my cheek. "Do you trust me?"

"Shouldn't I?"

"You're not answering my question."

Past us danced Edmundo and Princess Agata Ratibor. We brushed the Avilas at the edge of the floor. "How am I going to explain your attentions to them?"

"Tell them anything—tell them I'm drunk. It's not often I can hold you in my arms." He tried his mischievous smile on me.

"Don't overdo it, Pierre. I don't even know your last name."

The music broke at that moment, and Pierre led me off the floor to the terrace outside. A small crowd had gathered around a bonfire in the starlit night. He explained this was the ritual to commemorate St. John, the saint walking on hot coals. We watched a young couple race through the flames, squealing in fear, thrilled. A minute later, another couple burst with loud cries through the dancing circle of flame.

"You still haven't answered my question," Pierre said, his hand conducting me to the rim of the blazing fire. The scorching wood perfumed the air, heating our faces. I looked at him. His face was coppery.

"How can I *not* trust you, Pierre? We trained together. We're comrades, you and I."

"Trust me!" he whispered and seized my hand. Before I could react, he pulled me toward the fire. I couldn't loosen his grip in time—and then held on to it for dear life. Starting through the wavy, hazy flames, Pierre tugged me after him. Suddenly, I was running faster than ever in my life. Racing through the bonfire hand in hand, our bodies locked in a kind of dance, I couldn't help but scream; it was like running through a broiler with flames roasting my cheeks. Panting wildly, the growing crowd cheering us on, we lunged out of the fire on the other side. Sparks exploded all around. Sheets of smoke were swallowed by the starry night. Pierre nearly engulfed me in his arms. Quickly I pulled back. We stood face to face on the rim of the gusty blaze, our faces now golden with firelight.

"Ha!" He gave a happy laugh. "You're wearing the ring I gave you."

"I always wear this ring. I like it."

"If Mozart knew how I felt about you, he'd never have set up this meeting." He tried to embrace me.

I leaned back, my hands on his chest. "Pierre, don't be ridiculous. You've just met me, remember?"

"No, at this moment, I don't remember anything. But if I were you, I wouldn't turn around. Here comes our man. And don't forget, Tiger, we're working together. I intend to protect you."

As a matter of fact, I had no intention of turning. I was looking straight ahead, at one of the groups of people surrounding the bonfire. Luis was observing us, though when he caught my glance he turned away. The air was still pierced with the delighted shrieks of young couples galloping through the blue-and-yellow flames, mixed in the band's lively *pasodobles* from the incandescent clubhouse.

From behind us, through the firelight at our side, Hans Lazaar said, in his low, emotionless voice, "Hello, Miss Griffith." Then he faced Pierre. "How are you, François? It's been a long time."

Pierre nodded coolly. The bonfire snapped explosively. Up above, the stars swam.

"What brings you to Madrid?" Lazaar's voice was friendly yet detached. I gathered he either did not like Pierre or did not know him well.

"I come as often as I can. Spain is one of my favorite countries."

The short plump man's monocle lit up like a brass coin stuck in his fleshy puckered face. The fire also burnished Pierre's thick hair and made him, I thought at that moment, still more attractive.

"You're not going to get away with your treachery, Lazaar." Pierre's entire attitude had changed. His eyes blazed in the glimmer of the flames.

"What are you referring to, young man? And what right do you have to talk to me in that tone? I hardly know you, outside of one evening in Paris which I would prefer to forget."

"I don't intend to put up with your acts of violence."

I wasn't sure I had heard right. It was obviously an unexpected remark for the German, also, but his words did not falter. "What are you talking about?"

Pierre actually hissed. "I know all about each one."

Lazaar remained rocklike, impenetrable. "You've lost your head."

"Have I?" The eeriest smile crossed Pierre's face. "Tell me about the Marquesa of Torrejón's death."

Lazaar stared at Pierre.

"Go on, tell me."

"You're rabid. What are you talking about?"

Pierre shifted position. "You know she was murdered. Tell us about it."

Lazaar raged: "What are you asking me for? If that eccentric old lady was murdered, you'd be the first one under arrest, because you seem to be the only one who knows about it. As far as I know, she died of natural causes."

Just then voices approached. "What's going on?"

Spinning around, I saw Gloria von Fürstenberg stalking up, with Niki Lilienthal on one arm and on the other my friend the swimmer, Serrano-Suñer.

"I've been looking for you, Hans."

Pierre pulled me away. Softly he whispered, "I must go now, but let me take you home. Meet me in one hour in front of the club."

I nodded. He ran off in the opposite direction.

Lilienthal came over. "Would you like to go inside, Aline?"

"Yes, that would be a good idea."

We all started to walk toward the chalet. Gloria had her arm in Lazaar's. "What were you three talking about, Hans?"

"Nothing important, Gloria. Absolutely nothing." He turned to me and winked. "Those youngsters were trying to make me run through the glowing coals."

"Did they succeed?"

"They succeeded only in igniting my thirst for a drink."

"There's plenty of scotch back at the club." She turned to Serrano-Suñer. "Ramón, why don't you and Hans and Niki go back to the party? I want to chat with Aline." As they walked away, she said to me, "On second thought, let's go back inside. This fire is a little too hot for my taste." She put her arm in mine. "I need to talk to you alone. Immediately."

She led me to a small deserted game room lined with trophies in glass cabinets. Her stride was so rapid I could hardly keep up. When she turned, I was seeing a Gloria von Fürstenberg entirely new to me. "I have to leave Madrid—to get out. Please help me. You're an American. You can do it." After a deep breath she calmed down. For a second the mask was back in place. She smiled and said huskily, "You know, in my heart I adore Americans. I'm a Mexican, after all."

Motionless, I continued to read her face.

"When I was growing up in Guadalajara, my mother used to say, 'Gloria, you are the most beautiful girl in Mexico, and you are smart. Never settle for anything in life that is second-best. You don't have to. You can have whatever a woman can want in this world.' If you heard that twenty times a day, Aline, I think you'd believe it, too. And you'd begin to want it, just as I did. Only the best that life has to offer, whether in Guadalajara, Hollywood, New York, Paris, Berlin, Madrid. I've had the best of each of those places, my dear, and let me tell you, I know what I want now.

"I want to go home to Mexico. I want my children to be safe. You must know influential Americans. I'll repay you generously. I have my jewels—whatever you want, you have your pick."

We were standing in the middle of the room, empty except for a few card tables, straight-back chairs, and one large leather sofa next to the wall. Gloria dropped beside me on the sofa. She ruffled her thick hair with her lacquered nails. No longer leonine, she seemed suddenly fatigued. "Yes, I might as well tell you everything. I want to get out of Spain. I want to start a new life." She sighed and played with the tassel on her evening bag.

"When I first met Fürstenberg in Paris, I was insane about him. Finally! I had waited for it all my life, and if I dabbled along the way it was because I was looking for the best. The real thing. A great love. I thought I had found it. Then the war came and ruined everything. He was shipped off to Russia and I . . . I became confused. After a year, I was lonelier than a soldier on the front and thought I would lose my mind if I didn't start to have a life again. I heard from my husband infrequently and spent every moment in the interim driving myself mad with worry, worry that I would hear he was missing or dead. I started to go out at night to take my mind off it. I guess I got lost in the social whirl—it was easy. But the bombings started, and Berlin became dangerous. I came here. There was a price to pay—there always is, don't ever forget that, Aline. I've paid—for everything I do—but then . . ."

A waiter came in and asked if we would care for something to drink. We shook our heads in unison. As soon as he left, Gloria turned back to me.

"How long have you known Francisco?"

Her question was a surprise. At the table when he appeared, she had given the impression she had never seen him before. Perhaps Pierre was the real reason she had dragged me in here to talk.

"I met him for the first time tonight. I don't know him at all."

"Beware, my friend. He's bad business. He'll make a play for you, but discount it. He's a liar, a cheat. His passion is money—women come second. He uses them, always for a purpose." Her voice had risen to an unusually high pitch.

"You know him well, then?" I asked.

"Too well. I met him in Paris a couple of years ago. I don't know much about his background. He pursued me. Well, there's no other way to say it—he fell violently in love with me. Perhaps he thought I was rich. I was, then. But something always made me wary of him. He was devastating, I had to admit, but I didn't fall for him." As she spoke, Gloria became more and more agitated.

"Have you seen him here in Madrid?" I had to know more.

"He had the nerve to appear in my room the other day. Frightening me to death—and with the children next door! What a time I had to get rid of him! And then when I went to Ana de Pombo for the last fitting on this divine dress, he followed me there. Let's talk of something else."

She tossed her head as if to rid her mind of him. "Look, I really do want to be your friend and a friend of the Americans, Aline." Her eyes were now wide and appealing—almost innocent, if such a word could be used in reference to anything about Gloria von Fürstenberg.

Very slowly I opened my purse. Very slowly I held it up to her. I don't think a muscle moved in my face. I dangled it. . . .

There was a moment and then her huge black eyes went molten.

"Where did you get that?" Gloria reached for the jeweled parrot. I handed it to her. "Oh, I thank you. I have missed my lovely pin. Where did you find it?"

"I found it on the sofa of René Blum's apartment. The night he was murdered. You were there that night. If you want any help from me, you'd better tell me about it."

For a second she looked baffled. Suddenly she burst out laughing.

"Your imagination is positively deranged. I adore it. I do." Without another word she took my hand and pulled me up and back into the dining room. "I have never been in that bandleader's apartment. That pin was stolen from me, and I suspect by someone you know."

I still wanted to know how she had lost the pin, but already she was in the arms of the handsome Miguel Primo de Rivera and about to whirl off in a dance. As her partner moved to swing away, she stopped. Treating me to a smile, she opened her evening bag, dropped her pin inside, and with a carefree toss of her thick black hair dedicated her attention to the dance.

I had to find Edmundo. For a half hour I searched every room of the chalet and every corner of the garden. It took some time. He was nowhere. Neither the Avilas nor Carola had seen him leave. I told them I had to work early the next day and had a ride home. I looked at my watch again. One-thirty. Pierre must have been waiting for some time already.

I went to the cloakroom, grabbed my wrap, and dashed down the front steps. The implications of the last hour were devastating.

Pierre was waiting in the shadows to the right of the entrance. His sly, eager smile hit me like a warm bath. He held his hands out.

"Come on, Tiger, I'll take you home and we'll talk. I'll explain everything. I've been waiting to tell you for a long time." He opened the front door of a black Renault. I jumped inside.

At the wheel, Pierre lit a cigarette and shifted into gear, and on the gravel drive the tires spun. But someone came running toward us, yelling, "Francisco! Francisco!" I turned to see Gloria von Fürstenberg clutching her draping gown as she raced frantically up to the car, her black mane streaming, her huge eyes wide. Pierre braked with a screech.

When Gloria looked in and saw me her expression turned to astonishment, then to a kind of spreading fear.

Pierre smiled slowly at her, inhaling his cigarette with keen pleasure. For whatever reason, he seemed to savor this meeting. I had observed many aspects of the countess's behavior, but this one was a novelty: she was speechless.

"What's your problem, Gloria?" Pierre said.

I watched the beautiful face at work and saw that she was thinking as if her life depended on it. She glanced at me. Then she took a step back, rose to her full height. "I would like to discuss something with you, *now,*" she said in her deepest tone.

"Jump in, Gloria, I'll take you home, too." His tone was affectionate, or so it seemed to me.

"That's impossible—and you know it. My problem is urgent—a matter of life and death. If you're as much of a man as you think yourself to be, you'll come inside."

She pointed a long, slim finger at me. "There are plenty of chauffeurs in the parking lot who can take that girl home."

Pierre turned to me. "I *am* sorry. Evidently this is an emergency. But I will find a chauffeur for you right away." He jumped out and walked toward the parking area. Gloria went to the steps and turned to wait for Pierre. He spoke to a group of drivers at the entrance of the parking lot. He returned with a short stocky fellow whose face I could not see. Gloria had disappeared into the clubhouse.

"No problem," he said. "This man will take you to Madrid." He leaned in to give me a kiss on the cheek. "Be on guard until I see you tomorrow," he whispered. Then to the driver, he said, "Take the señorita to Monte Esquina 37, see her safely inside, and bring my car back here."

Without a word the man took the seat next to mine and put the car in motion, and we began to wind down the hill toward the main highway below.

I asked if he knew where my street was. Only a guttural *"Sí"*; not *"Sí, señorita,"* which would have been the usual courteous Spanish response. But I was occupied in trying to calculate what was going on between Gloria and Pierre. Evidently they knew each other well. Not only had she said so but he had complied with her appeal immediately. I was upset, to say the least. When we arrived at the highway, the driver turned left, taking a different road to the city, I supposed. Then his strange detour brought me back to the present with a jerk.

"Why are we taking this road?" I asked.

"Shorter," he replied.

I looked out at the open country of the unpopulated northwestern border of the city. Some instinct warned me even before he pulled the car to the side of the road.

As he came to a stop, I jumped out and started to run and in a second was in thick underbrush. I heard him following, and although it was pitch-black I feared he would hear my steps racing through the crackling underbrush. As I ran, I grabbed my Beretta .25, letting my bag fall. His pursuit, thrashing through the bushes, became louder each second. My long dress was catching on thorny branches, my heels were sinking into the sandy earth, making it difficult to run. I knew I had to do it.

I turned and without hesitating crouched and shot at the shadowy form rushing at me, fifteen feet away. I must have missed, because he lunged for me and grabbed my throat. He was strangling me! Using my last bit of strength, I shoved the gun at him, not knowing or caring where I was aiming this time. I was sinking into unconsciousness when I heard the sound of a shot. My own! But now it seemed to echo from afar; then there was silence.

It must have been only seconds later. My breath came in deep gasps, but I was alive. We were both lying on the ground, his body partly on top of mine, the revolver still in my hand. He was difficult to move, heavy and limp. Had I killed him? I couldn't take the time to find out. Searching his pockets, I found some papers, cigarettes; then a knife strapped to his inner calf. No other weapon. I ran toward the lights of the car, glimmering beyond the bushes. My feet were scratched, my arms, too, but I felt no pain. Just the exhilaration of being able to move, of being alive. Without much difficulty I turned the car around and drove back to the main highway.

As I drove I was dazed but trying to think. Who had put this thug onto me? If Gloria had not appeared, Pierre would have taken me home and I would have been safe. Someone had hired him, probably to wait in that parking lot to follow me home and to finish me off there when I was alone. Pierre's request for a driver just made it easier. But who? Edmundo? Lazaar? Gloria? Even that man Serrano-Suñer could be the guilty one. Or Lilienthal, if his tip had just been a ruse. They were all there together.

As I reached the Plaza de la Moncloa and turned down Cea Bermúdez, I began to wonder where to leave the car. Someplace near enough so I would not be seen in the streets in an evening dress spattered with blood, but not near enough to connect the car to me. After all, the man who had been seen driving it might be found—dead.

Three blocks from my house, in the shadows of the leafy branches of two acacias, I parked and ran home barefoot.

Whom could I call? I didn't even know Pierre's last name nor where he lived, so the only person I could trust at this point was unavailable. Belmonte was probably on his way from Granada to Cádiz for his next fight. Everybody else was a possible enemy. There was no choice. In case he was the mole, I would be on guard—but I had to call the boss.

Chapter 25

Twenty minutes after my phone call, Mozart knocked on the front door. When I opened it, his tiny eyes dilated.

"What happened? You're a wreck."

"I'm all right. Come in." I led him into my small living room; every step was an effort but I hid the strain as much as possible. For the second time—the chief had not entered my apartment since the night of Marta's death—the big angular man faced me from a chair while I sat on the sofa.

"Tonight the dinner dance at Puerta de Hierro proved full of surprises. The biggest of which is that on the way home someone tried to kill me . . . and I had to shoot him."

"Is he dead?"

"I don't know."

"Whom did you shoot?"

"I don't know." I handed Mozart a package of black tobacco—Ducados was the brand name—a driver's license, an identity card in the name of Jorge Iglesias Suárez, and the stiletto. "These were the only things I found."

"I must say, Aline . . ." When had he ever called me by my first name? "As long as you haven't blown your cover, everything will be all right."

"I don't think I have."

"Tell me in detail what happened."

"To begin with, I met Pierre."

Mozart nodded. "Good. You will be my contact with him from now on."

I hoped the boss did not notice my surge of joy. Quickly I said, "Pierre was going to drive me home but was stopped by the Countess von Fürstenberg, who insisted he stay. He then found a driver to take me. The driver is the one who tried to kill me." I gave Mozart the details as well as I could remember them.

"Where did Pierre find the guy?"

"At the entrance to the parking lot, almost in front of us. There were several chauffeurs chatting together, and this fellow was one of them."

"Did Pierre appear to know him?"

"I don't think so."

"Too bad—that would have helped."

"Who saw you with the man you shot?"

"No one except Pierre that I know of. Gloria was too far away when he approached to see him clearly."

"Where did you leave the car and the body?"

I told him, and he pondered for a minute. "May I use your phone?" Mozart went into the hall. On his return he said, "I've sent someone to find the car. If the man is dead—that's a bit of incriminating evidence —it also may be the clue we're looking for. We need to know who you're up against. I'm going to the office to call Spider, something I rarely do. It's not easy. Takes hours, and overseas calls are the only ones they tap. If Pierre contacts you tomorrow—and I hope he will—tell him what happened. Maybe he knows the chauffeur or could identify him or find out who his friends were. Is there anything else?"

"A lot, I'm afraid." And I began to narrate: Gloria von Fürstenberg's elaborate overture, and her scene with Pierre. Pierre accusing Lazaar of having murdered the Marquesa de Torrejón. Edmundo's gift of Gloria's pin and then his mysterious disappearance. Last but not least, my embarrassing discovery that I had known Ramón Serrano-Suñer for months.

At the end of my account, the chief was silent. Finally he stood up to leave. He paused. "I do hope you've told me everything."

"I believe so."

"Have you? I have reason to doubt that." Producing a piece of paper from his pocket, Mozart fastidiously unfolded it and handed it over. The cable from Spider stated that Prince Lilienthal had tipped me off about the mole. Before I could react, Mozart went on quietly, "We'll discuss this later. We have enough troubles for one night. You had better get some rest." Then he was gone, leaving me alone to think.

Spider's cable indicated Mozart was clean. That was a help, even if I had to suffer the humiliation of the boss's realizing that I had suspected him. I bolted the doors and went to my room, now accustomed to all windows being shut and shutters locked. For a while I couldn't sleep. Had I killed a man? Who? It had been so quick! Where was Edmundo? My list of suspects had become shorter—by one only. I still had all the rest . . . and no answers.

———

At eight o'clock in the morning, the phone rang. Mozart's voice.

"Your friend has expired. Now don't worry. Our radioman found your bag and sandals, and we imagine not a word of this matter will leak out. He was a hired hand, no doubt about that. The papers are false. Let me know after you've seen Pierre. He's sure to call you today."

The shock that I had killed a man seemed much greater now than last night when it had occurred. Who was he? Whom did he work for? Did he have a wife and children? The thought made me miserable, and I got up and started to dress. While I was in the tub, the phone rang, and I went dripping along the hallway to my room.

"What happened last night?" Pierre said. "That devil never returned my car."

I suggested we meet in the rotunda of the Palace Hotel so I could tell him, and find out what he knew about the driver.

He was standing on the steps when I entered. The concierge, Pepe, greeted me with his usual friendly smile. He was on our payroll. Probably on that of the other powers as well. No matter. I couldn't help liking him. Pierre looked more handsome than ever; then I remembered last night's conversation with Gloria. He kissed my hand and led me to a corner banquette. "What's the matter, Tiger? Don't you like me today?"

"I'm miserable and have serious matters to discuss. Also few illusions about you. Gloria told me you were in love with her."

He laughed. "Gloria! You're jealous. That's great. How could that man-eater have my heart? No, my dear, I have other reasons for pursuing her. Now tell me what your serious matters are."

We both ordered tea, and I recounted the events after he left me. His expression of consternation and incredulity grew.

"Tiger, I *put* you in the car with that fellow. I'm responsible. I should never have let you go alone with him. You saw me looking for a chauffeur to take you to Madrid. He was standing there and happened to be the first to offer his services. I bet Lazaar's the guy who hired him, but I never thought that bastard would dare to harm you after seeing you with me and realizing I knew all about him. He's an assassin, a vulgar, heartless assassin."

Pierre was truly agitated. I had to pull my hand from his. The waiter was watching us.

"Just think how I feel, Pierre. I've killed a man."

"It was in self-defense. Anybody would have been obliged to do the same. If you hadn't killed him, he would have finished you off. Stop thinking about it. After all, most of our training was preparing you for this sort of thing. This is war, Tiger. What do you think your brothers and friends feel when they kill people? Nobody likes it."

"Pierre, do you believe Lazaar killed Mimosa Torrejón?"

"I have no proof, of course. But I have my reasons for suspecting him. He's capable of anything."

"Do you think Lazaar could be Himmler's top man here?"

"Himmler has lots of people working for him here. Apart from the Gestapo personnel in Spain, he now has all the Abwehr employees and agents under his command. Why would he have one top man?"

"Evidently he does have one—some person who has special influence and a special mission for him. Probably working on information about the landing in southern Europe."

"What news do you have about that landing? Although I'm glad to be here and to see you, where I really want to be is back in France behind the enemy lines. That's real action!" He changed his tone, became more intense. "Tell me, what does Mozart say about me?"

"He said to tell you everything and that I'll be your contact with him. Did you know that?"

"No. I was told to go to that party and arrange to meet you there, nothing else." He thought again. "Operation Anvil must be about to begin, and I don't want to miss it."

"All cables in the code room refer to that right now."

"Have they designated Anvil's location yet?"

"Not in a way I could understand."

"Tiger, tell Mozart I intercepted a courier of the German high command. General Botho Elster, commanding the German First Army, is heading for the Biscay region, having deviated from his earlier route, changed direction completely, with seven hundred and fifty officers and eighteen thousand eight hundred and fifty men, plus an undetermined number of Mark III tanks. It is urgent Mozart get this information."

"Okay. I had so many things to ask you, Pierre. We've lost three agents here—and I've had two close calls myself. You can help us unravel all this, especially since you know Lazaar and Gloria. Two of our suspects."

"Neither of them trusts me. You heard what I had to say to Lazaar. But I'll do what I can. You'd better get this information on to your boss quickly. I'll wait for you to call me."

I stood up to leave. Pierre did the same.

"Tiger, now that we are going to work together, I consider it's no longer against the rules to fall in love." He put his hand on my arm as we walked down the marble steps. The same magnetism in his voice, his touch. "You can call me here in room four forty-two."

Only when I was halfway down the street did I realize I still did not know his last name.

———

When I gave Pierre's message to Mozart, he seemed pleased, although again formal and stiff. I was beginning to find him more comfortable that way. "Pierre is considered one of our most effective agents, Tiger. His record is exceptional. You're lucky to work with him."

"Pierre believes Lazaar is the one who hired the thug to kill me," I said. "But this doesn't help us know who the mole is, does it?"

"You must remember that no one knows about the mole except you and me—and the mole himself, of course. Work with everyone just as you have up until now. Not the slightest indication that your attitude has changed can be apparent."

"And Top Hat?" I asked. The *pícaro* was now at the top of my personal list of suspects.

"Especially Top Hat."

He toyed with the pencil for some moments as if considering how to express his next thought. "Spider has asked me to tell you he regards the first phase of Operation Bullfight completed and to congratulate you. He thinks Lazaar *is* the guy, and we will now take the proper measures."

"What about Serrano-Suñer? Now that I know him personally—"

"Unnecessary. He's not involved in our current preoccupations." The pencil was twirling in his fingers. "Tiger, you have a new mission." He looked up. "Phase two of Operation Bullfight and the success of the invasion depend on it."

He waited. I breathed deeply. What was coming?

"The experiences you have had up to now will help you be successful. I can't explain everything yet. Sometime in the next weeks you will receive a top-secret cable from Spider directly to you. I will advise Jeff that you will decode all top-secret cables from now on. As soon as you get that particular one, we have to act fast—bring it to me immediately. I'll be constantly on call. Not one word I tell you can be confided to anyone—not to Jeff, not to Top Hat, not even to Pierre—unless I say so. You'll begin by delivering a top-secret message.

"Call Pierre in the hotel and ask him to meet you at the street café in the Castellana two blocks down from here. Tell him he has my orders to be attentive to the Countess von Fürstenberg, with the purpose of finding out where the Germans *think* the next Allied invasion will take place. Be quick about it. You can tell him you're needed here because from now on you alone will be decoding all top-secret cables. Tell him you will call him in a few days, and not to contact you."

No message would have been more disagreeable to deliver. Pierre laughed when I told him so. Sitting across the small metal table sipping an icy cold *horchata*, I watched him beaming with pleasure.

"Don't look so worried, Tiger." His tone became caressing. "She's the last woman I'd be interested in. But I must admit the job is a respite from blowing up bridges."

We chatted for a while, then I got up to leave.

"Why so soon?"

"I'm the only one allowed to decode top-secret cables, so I can't be away. I'll call as soon as Mozart gives me something else for you." My heart was heavy. When I looked back he was still sitting there smoking and sipping *horchata* as if the war had nothing to do with him.

―――

"How did you make out with Pierre?" Mozart was waiting for me at the top of the stairs when I returned.

"He seemed delighted."

My voice may have betrayed me, because Mozart glanced at me curiously as he indicated I should follow him into the office. Once there, he said, "Take a seat."

I was still thinking about Gloria and Pierre.

"I'm sending you to the Costa Brava—tonight." His big fingers tapped the bare desk. "The information you will carry with you concerns Anvil. Now that you've got your travel permit, you should have no trouble."

In his ceremonious manner, he produced a roll of microfilm. "We're going to place this in a belt for you to wear. You won't go out of this building again until the hour for the train. No one must know you are leaving Madrid. My driver will take you to the station. Tell your maid you won't be home, that you are on duty tonight. I'll take care of informing her tomorrow that you will be out of town for two days."

My astonishment made him smile. "Don't worry, you'll have a toothbrush. At least we can provide that."

"What about the top-secret cables?"

"The one for you won't come in for several days yet. Any others I'll do myself."

Opening his drawer, he lifted up one half of a hundred-peseta bill and handed it to me. "Match this up to the other half, which is in the possession of the owner of a yacht called *El Vega,* awaiting your arrival in the port of Lloret del Mar. Deliver the microfilm to him."

He stood up and began to thump across the small room. His manner had changed. For once he seemed nervous, unsure. "This is a massive job of teamwork, Tiger. People from Washington to the farthest corners of Europe and Africa are pulling together to make it work. Keep that in mind."

I remained in my chair watching him. "Pierre's expecting me to call him at the Palace Hotel."

"We'll have an important job for him soon. When you come back, you must contact him again. But the only thing you have to worry about now is delivering this information without mishap. You'll like the yacht. I'm sure of that. And the owner is a nice fellow, too." He grunted. "Oh, yes. The yacht will take you out to an American PT boat."

Chapter 26

Miraculously the night train to Barcelona, despite the rocking and jolting of the ancient coach, provided me with a much-needed night's sleep, a respite from the events of the past hours.

In Barcelona, I hired a taxi to take me to Lloret del Mar. Mozart had warned me the road was treacherous, a two-lane, hairpin-curving ribbon bordering jagged precipices that plunged three hundred feet down to the rocks and sea below. The taxi was polished and well cared for but older than I. The driver was younger. He chattered away while I gazed at the Mediterranean, glistening as though glass, a sprinkling of whitecaps out on the sea, and farther up the coast waves spraying the shores. Reaching the summit of a cliff, I could see the entire coastline for miles, and the colors alone were breathtaking, bright blue bays carved into walls of red-and-gold stone. When we reached Mataró, the driver insisted I try the famous golden sugar-covered rolls for which the town was known. I told him I was in a hurry, but it was no use—obviously *he* had been looking forward to those buns.

Impatiently I submitted while he pulled into the main square. Excusing himself, he disappeared into a café. From the backseat of the taxi, I hardly had time to survey the town when a battered old car pulled up at the opposite side of the plaza. Three men whose faces I could not see but who were as shabby as their vehicle got out and walked toward a table shaded by large trees. I sat at a table near my taxi and ordered coffee and the famous buns. When the waiter returned with my order, he bent close to my ear.

"Those men"—he indicated the table in the distance; the men sat with their backs to me and were the only other customers—"are following the señorita. At least I heard one of them tell the other to keep his eye on you. They don't look"—he searched for the word—"reliable."

I was already on my feet, running toward another cab. As I lunged inside, my facial expression must have alerted the driver before I spoke. He immediately stepped on the accelerator. "Hurry up! As fast as you can!" I commanded. *"Sí, señorita,"* he said. And then it began.

My taxi sped up the hill. I watched out the back window as the three men ran for their old dark sedan. "Faster!" I implored. "I will reward you well."

"I am going as fast as I can, señorita." But he managed more.

We were approaching the summit of a steep hill. I looked down the cliffs to the rocky shore below—and swallowed. I looked back. The car behind seemed to be gaining ground. "Do you know the people following us?"

"No, señorita. Usually I know everyone on this road—but I've never seen that car before."

We tore down the mountain, taking curves that threw me from one side to the other. I fell to the floor and scrambled up, grasping the back of the front seat. The descent was with such speed I was sure we would go off the road and crash onto the sharp rocks below. The tires screeched on each hairpin curve, yet the old sedan behind pursued us relentlessly.

"What are you doing, for heaven's sake?" I cried above the racket. "At this pace we'll go off the cliff."

"Señorita," said the driver quite placidly, "first you are displeased because I am going too slow. Now you are displeased because I am going too fast. Here I can do nothing else, because, to be frank, señorita, I have no brakes."

I looked out the window. Sea, sky, trees—all seemed to be zigzagging in different directions. Maybe it was the tension—whatever it was, I burst out laughing. The car was a roller coaster, swerving and then dashing down, farther, missing each precipice by inches, while we were pursued by assassins for miles. And no brakes!

We finally reached the flat beach at the foot of the mountain. Respite for a moment. Far back the dark sedan was still pounding along. As we climbed a mountain road again, I lost sight of my pursuers every time we turned a curve, only to see their vehicle swing into view a minute later. We rattled through Arenys del Mar, then Caldetas, where a pine forest covered the seaside cliffs, up the mountain to Balnys, finally descending to Lloret del Mar, where I saw the long pier jutting out to the sea.

As soon as the taxi pulled up to the pier I tossed a fat wad of pesetas to the driver and raced down the wooden landing past several small craft until I saw *El Vega* painted on the bow of a large yacht at the end of the dock. The pursuing car was just screeching to a stop at the pier's entrance when I leaped on the gangplank and crashed onto the deck.

"Get out of here quick," I pleaded.

I was aware only of the yacht's motor roaring in my ears as *El Vega* surged out to sea. Strong arms pulled me to my feet on the windy deck. A pleasant weatherbeaten face framed in a frizzy gray beard smiled at me.

"It's fortunate you landed on deck and not in the water. Do you always arrive in such haste?"

I laughed. Now that I was safe, my mission almost completed, I felt great. "A car with three thugs inside has been following me since I got off the train this morning."

"You're not in danger now, and we'll make certain you have a safe return."

He led me inside. As soon as we were seated, each with a cool drink, he put his hand in a pocket and withdrew his torn half of the peseta note. I matched mine to his, and then handed over the microfilm from the belt at my waist.

My host excused himself and went out on deck, where I could see him scanning the horizon with binoculars.

Now I had time to think again about the morning's events. Who knew I was on this trip? Only Mozart. Or had I missed someone following our car in Madrid or trailing me on the train?

After a while I went out on deck. Leaning on the railing, I watched the coastline become smaller as we moved ahead, as well as up and down over the choppy water. It might have been about an hour later when the gray-haired yachtsman said, "There it is." In the blue distance, a dot made its way in our direction.

Eventually, the dot became a PT boat. After delivering the microfilm to its captain, we sat down to a dinner of lobster and crayfish in the small cabin while the yacht headed for Barcelona, where my host told me he was obliged to go. I slept on board and took the train the following day to Madrid.

This assignment was accomplished, but who was the mole? Everyone was always warning me to take care, to watch myself, to be alert. Good advice. But I'd need more than advice. What would my new mission entail? What was the top-secret cable I was to receive *about*? And how had those three men known I would be in Barcelona that morning?

When I arrived in Madrid after a peaceful train trip, life resumed and soon seemed almost humdrum. It was August 8, the middle of almost everyone's summer vacation. Mozart ordered me not to call room 442 in the Palace Hotel until he gave his permission. I worried that Pierre was having such a good time with Gloria he had forgotten me entirely. Then some red roses arrived with a nameless card. "Meant to be eaten" were the only words, signed with an F. Juanito was in the middle of his busiest season, but his carnations and telephone calls arrived regularly. José Heredia, the Gypsy, was impossible to find. Probably following his favorite bullfighters around the country, I imagined. A note from Edmundo arrived, accompanied by tuberoses that perfumed the entire apartment: *"A-dor-ada,"* it began. "Just to let you know my devotion never changes. Will call. Your *pícaro*." How could a guy with such charm be a mole? The Avilas and Carola were in San Sebastián. Yet the atmosphere in the office was tense. We all knew Operation Anvil had to take place —soon.

Then suddenly everything became shot with electricity—the critical cable arrived! As I decoded my blood pressure soared.

FROM JUPITER TO TIGER STOP   TOP SECRET REPEAT TOP SECRET STOP
ADVISE MOZART TO PUT PHASE TWO INTO EFFECT IMMEDIATELY STOP
TO TIGER FROM JUPITER

I rushed into Mozart's office without knocking. The cable still left me in the dark.

The sun came out. Mozart sat back in his armchair with a broad smile on his jagged face. He brought a radio out of his desk and turned it on, to make it impossible for anyone to overhear our conversation. Although the procedure had been explained to us at the Farm, it was an unusual precaution for Mozart to take now. Whom was he suspicious of in the office?

"Tiger." His sigh was one of relief. "This cable means that the invasion will take place near Marseilles. A piece of information which could mean the end of the war or the deaths of thousands of our countrymen."

He fiddled with the radio again. "This is the reason we brought Pierre to Madrid." I was still standing. Mozart walked to the wall, drawing up the only chair in the room. I sat down.

"Contact Pierre. Tell him his orders are to move his subagents to the Marseilles area. They should be in a position to assist our troops when they land. He must act surreptitiously with his own people. Information on the location of the landing is so secret it cannot be leaked, cannot be made known, even to those who have been risking their lives for us these past years. Can you make that clear to him?"

I nodded.

"In fact, this news is so vital we cannot risk Pierre being caught returning to France by his usual route through the Pyrenees. Too many German and Spanish spies roam those paths. I'll have to find a way to get him to Algiers, from where he can be parachuted in."

Mozart picked up the telephone and asked for the ambassador. Once he had Carlton Hayes on the line, he asked, "When do you have a plane going to Algiers, Ambassador?" There was a minimum of words exchanged before he hung up.

"We're in luck. Pierre can fly to Algiers tonight on an embassy plane. Tell him my Packard will be at his hotel at nine o'clock. You know the license number?"

I nodded again.

"Impress on him the gravity of the job. Pierre must be thoroughly aware of the importance of this news." Mozart's beady eyes never left mine. "OSS London handled Operation Overlord with high colors, and we cannot do our job less well."

He stood up and paced the room in slow heavy thumps.

"You had better get moving. Pierre must not miss that plane to Algiers. I don't know exactly when he will be parachuted into France, but whenever the drop occurs, I'll let you know so you can listen in with us to see if he arrives safely."

After months of transcribing and dispatching messages concerning the drops, I still found them the most exciting experiences of the war. On bright moonlit nights our agents were parachuted into enemy territory. They were greeted by friendly resistance fighters, the Maquis, their flash-lights pinpointing the landing zone. Sometimes a small plane could land, drop the agent, and take off without turning off the motors. This meant that many people prepared for each drop; everything had to be coor-dinated, and those involved had to be totally reliable.

Chapter 27

When I faced Pierre a few hours later, in the dimness of the Palace Bar, he reached for my hand. "I had hoped you'd call me when you saw my flowers. Didn't you like them?"

I laughed. "Much more than my bullfighter's carnations. In my hometown, carnations are usually sent only to funerals."

"And where have you been? I've called several times."

"Mozart sent me to the country to rest and forget that terrible night —far away from everyone." This was what I had been ordered to say.

"What about the top-secret cables?"

"He said he would do them himself—but I don't think any came in during the short time I was away."

"Well, your rest seems to have agreed with you. Since you killed that thug you look more beautiful than ever to me."

"You mean I should kill people more often?"

"I told you, it was your life against his, that's all. And miraculously, you're alive. The narrower the escape, the greater the thrill of tricking death. For the time being, at least. That's why we're paid. Well paid. To do the job. The 'hazardous risk,' it's called."

"I never think about the money. Do you?"

A coy smile played on his face. "I like the money, yes, and the risks, too. I've been in many tight spots, but I always survive. Someday I'll tell you everything."

"Famous last words. You said that the night you left me in the car at the country club."

"You said you had important news for me." I noticed he had avoided talking about Gloria. Mozart had told me to ask him for whatever information he had been able to obtain.

"Tell your boss it wasn't easy. They don't tell her anything, or at least that's what she pretends. She did say that General Tresckow, chief of staff of the Second Army now on the eastern front, plans to move the Fourteenth Panzer Corps and the Fourth Panzer Division, if their current attack on the Russian front is successful, to southern France. She said her husband is in the Fourth Panzer Division and that's how she knows this. I have to be careful that she does not suspect I am working with American intelligence. Mozart must understand that."

I wondered how many times he had seen her to get that information.

He was impatient. "Tiger, my love," he said, his voice waxing affectionate, "tell me the reason you had to see me so urgently."

"Mozart has a special mission for you. Just received. Top secret."

He still held my hand. I didn't remove it as I gave him Mozart's orders. This might be the last time we would meet. He was going on a dangerous drop at a critical moment. The orders pleased him. "Finally." His tone was exhilarated. He pulled a cigarette from the pack on the table and took a long sip of sherry. "When do I leave?"

"The black Packard with diplomatic license plate CD 406 will pick you up at nine at the steps of the hotel. Your plane takes off as soon as you arrive at the military airport of Getafe."

"Who would have guessed at the Farm that one day *you* would be delivering my orders for a mission? The day we studied the maps of France . . . that one day *you* would be sending me there? Do you remember?"

For a moment we were in the dusky library again, the coved ceiling looming above us. I looked at Pierre's face, skin, hair, arms, frightfully aware of his magnetism.

"You do care for me, Tiger?"

Our eyes met. The room suddenly felt overheated. His thick lashes nearly hid his pupils.

"What about your friendship with Gloria?"

"You're still worrying about that! I told you I'm not interested. That wasn't a love scene. Gloria and I once knew each other in Paris. Before I met you. Gloria is frightened of Lazaar, as everyone is, and wanted me to help her get out of Spain." He peered at me, concentrating all his appeal into a single gaze. "You're the one for me, Tiger." He stood up. "You must trust me. I'll be back. And I am going to miss you."

I got up from my seat. "I'll miss you, too."

We walked out of the Palace lobby onto the street.

"Tiger, I want you to know that since I met you, I've tried to change —a lot of things. I'll tell you one day."

"Good-bye, Pierre." I started to turn around.

He spun me to him, his hands on my shoulders. His parting look was so deep it cut through all our recent words and transported me beyond the bounds of time or space. The next moment he released me and turned away, striding in the opposite direction. I watched his retreating back and felt the temperature cool, degree by degree.

=====

The next day the telephone rang just as I was going out the door to the office.

"Your *pícaro* appearing for duty."

"About time, Edmundo. Where have you been? What serious matter has gotten you out of bed at this shocking hour—or haven't you been there yet?"

"A bit of both, my dear. You are growing up quickly, thanks in great part to my efforts."

"Edmundo, I've been longing to see you since the night of the dance at Puerta de Hierro."

"I'm grateful to learn you truly appreciate me. Your own disappearance has caused me alarm also. However, I must admit my time has been productive."

"With the princess?" I couldn't resist asking.

"Tsk, tsk. Oh, I see you *have* become fresh. Well, it was bound to happen in the devious web of Madrid. And of course it's only natural that the pupil should try to compete with her master. My dear, I must see you tonight. I can't say a word on the phone. But I will tell you this: Edmundo Lassalle has solved the mystery! Oh, it's too delicious. I did. Yes, of course with help from you. No, I won't be greedy. *We* did it. Oh, Mimosa has been avenged. My darling beloved Mimosa has not died in vain."

"Do you know who killed her?"

"Not another word on the phone, pet. I'll pick you up at midnight. Be prepared for surprises, *mi amor.* Oh, by the way, did you have a lovely night at Puerta de Hierro? I'm dying to hear about that dashing stranger you were dancing with. You looked devastating, and so young on the dance floor. Oh, well, it's nice to see you've retained at least a vestige of your innocence. And what have you been doing since?"

"I'll bore you with the details when I see you."

"Remember—the witching hour. You must be punctual."

"That means we're in for one of our eventless evenings."

I heard his high-pitched giggle. "You will have to wait to find out what this Aztec genius has in store! Viva Mimosa!" Edmundo hung up.

=====

I knew better than to ask him where we were going. His sense of drama forbade it. In the backseat of the taxi, I let the sultry night breeze lap at my face through the open window. In the pale streetlights, couples could be seen strolling along the peaceful Castellana. Few cars, two carriages going in the opposite direction. At the corner of the Plaza de Colón, some tables under the great trees were occupied by customers taking after-dinner coffee or a *copita* of anise, enjoying the coolness of the late hour. I glanced at the fountain in the middle of the plaza below the statue of Columbus. Madrid was, I thought, more serene, more captivating than ever. The driver leaned out his window, recognizing a friend. He slowed down. *"Vaya con Dios,* Pepe."

"Nothing can make these people hurry," Edmundo said, laughing, breaking the silence. He liked the pace of the city too. "Now, tell me everything. What have you been doing?" The glass window between the driver and us was shut.

"Not much. On my way home from the dance a chauffeur tried to strangle me. And I killed him." Following Mozart's orders, I mentioned nothing relating to the mole or phase two, but his reaction to the details I did declare was important. Where had he been when the paid assassin had gotten into Pierre's car?

Edmundo watched me like the cat he was, shrewdly, insatiably curious. After I had given a little more, he said in his soft growl, "Seriously, Aline, life must be a deadly bore for you to concoct such fables. Though I do admire your adolescent imagination."

I just looked at him.

"Tell me you're kidding."

"My sense of humor doesn't include murder."

"Jesus." He sighed. "The pupil *has* superseded her master."

The taxi now turned up the Calle Hermosilla—and I realized where we were going. Sure enough, it came to a halt in front of number 14— Ana de Pombo's shop! Before I could ask anything, Edmundo jumped out. "Come on, let's go." Cool efficiency in his voice. The street was deserted. On the sidewalk, he checked his watch. "That's odd. José Heredia should have been here by now."

"Why?"

"He's the one who gave me the tip. Thanks to your having ordered him to watch certain people. Well—come on. We can't wait." From inside his jacket he pulled out a shiny snub-nosed revolver. I produced mine.

He picked the lock in seconds. Total blackness inside. "Follow me," he whispered. "The *portero* won't bother us. He's not around after midnight."

Edmundo crept down the black hall, then up a rickety back stairway. At each squeak we froze. He prowled as if he had navigated this route before. My worries increased. I had not told Mozart about this meeting. Was I taking too great a chance being alone with Edmundo? At least I was behind him—revolver poised.

On the third floor he paused in front of a door under which filtered a crack of light. It was locked—but not for long. Edmundo applied what seemed his greatest professional skill and in silent seconds turned the doorknob so slowly I thought my heart would burst. The next moment he threw it open.

Someone lunged. "Don't move or I'll shoot!" Edmundo hissed. The figure stopped.

I could barely distinguish anything at first, because the room was lit by candles. Then from behind Edmundo's shoulder I made out a familiar figure—and gaped. In the corner was a huge radio transmitter. Overwhelming in comparison to anything we had. What a find! Not even the British had been able to locate a transmitter this size in the country.

Edmundo, revolver in one hand, reached for the light switch with the other.

"Why do you think I am using candles, Edmundo dear?" said a sultry voice from the shadows. "The electricity is cut. It always is when one most needs it. The drought, you know."

The heat from so many candles was stifling. Frozen in front of me, in a thin muslin robe, stood Gloria von Fürstenberg. The perspiration had left her hair curly and streaming like Medusa's. In one uplifted hand she held a stack of paper. The crimson polish on her long nails was chipped. Unusual for her.

Edmundo's gun was aimed point-blank at her heart. Gloria just stood there, like a petrified rock, the whites of her eyes gleaming in the candlelight.

"You bastard, Lassalle!"

Edmundo purred, "Relax, Gloria."

With swanlike majesty, she lowered her arm, and, keeping her wild eyes glued to us, placed the sheets of paper on a table at her side.

Edmundo lowered his gun. I did not. "Do forgive us for interrupting you in the middle of a fitting," my partner meowed. "Or should I say, a fit. Surely this is not the usual manner in which you spend the late hours, my dear Gloria."

As if ignoring Edmundo, she turned to me. "What an unexpected pleasure, Aline. We haven't met since I saw you leaving Puerta de Hierro."

"Frankly, this encounter is a surprise to me also, Gloria."

Standing there, staring fiercely at me, she seemed more enigmatic than ever. I wondered about the relationship Pierre had with this woman. Did he know she was an enemy agent? Now there was no doubt about that. We had caught her red-handed. Looking around the room, I recognized it all—code boards, the safe, stacks of cables.

The fine line between control and abandon in her voice was uncanny. "It is always a pleasure to see you, Aline. But I cannot say the same for your companion."

Her glance at Edmundo would have reduced him, were it possible, to ashes.

"Dear Countess," Edmundo said. "Won't you please sit down."

Languidly, insolently, she obeyed. There was a table and several chairs. We sat facing her. The candles sputtered, cast shadows like waves. The room was more suffocating by the minute. There was no window and only the door through which we had entered.

"For a beginning, what kind of work have you been doing? And for whom—for Heinrich Himmler? Or is it Schellenberg? I do want to keep the names straight."

Gloria was mute.

"You see, Aline," he went on, turning to me, "our friend works for all of them. She is their best pupil. You might even say she's the teacher's pet."

Running her fingers through her hair, she remained silent and with not a sign of subservience.

"Gloria, it would be laudable of you," he said in a sarcastic tone, "to tell us what information you send and receive from your professors in Berlin."

"Special messages went out from here," snapped Gloria, "but I never knew what they were. I just brought them back and forth from Wizner, the Gestapo chief in the embassy. He told me there was certain information he didn't want passed through the embassy code room. How would I know what they meant? I had to do it—it was the price I had to pay to get out of Berlin and to earn a few cents to feed and clothe my children."

Edmundo approvingly shook his head. "Such a devoted mother. It tugs at my heartstrings. I could weep. Truly I could."

Gloria's glance scalded him. Then she turned full force on me, though miraculously modulating her voice to a musical whisper. "Do you remember our little tea party? At El Morisco? When Lazaar marched in and announced his room had been searched? I knew who you were at once. In fact, I warned Francisco about the charming—and very nosy—American girl. When he met you at Puerta de Hierro, he already knew you were working for the Americans. That's why he asked you to dance and wanted to take you home. He thought you had influence. He needed to get money out of the country."

Evenly, Edmundo said, "That's rubbish. You wanted to eliminate Aline that night at Puerta de Hierro. You knew she was suspicious of you."

Edmundo's prey looked as if she would strike him. Instead she replied coolly, "What ridiculous statements you make."

"What about Lazaar, Gloria? Did you help him murder Mimosa?"

"That's a childish question, Aline! How did the Americans send such a naive girl on this kind of work? It is amazing how such a credulous country could win a war against the cleverest men of old Europe." She gave me an almost affectionate glance. "Hans wouldn't dirty his hands with that kind of activity—and certainly not mine."

"But Hans *is* a good Gestapo agent, yes?" Edmundo's gun lifted, and he cocked the trigger.

Gloria still did not have a defeated air, but she was subdued. "Almost everyone in Madrid suspects that. They're wrong."

"And why is that?"

"For example." She shrugged her shoulders. "Himmler has always been jealous of Goering—especially the way in which he has been, shall we say, picking up art treasures throughout Europe. And he knows that Hans has been helping Goering to get these paintings shipped to South America. A *good* Gestapo agent would never dare to defy the supreme boss."

"I don't believe a word you say. But what were you looking for in René Blum's apartment? Because you were *involved* in his murder. You threw caution to the winds when you accompanied your colleague Lazaar there."

Her anger was aroused. "Neither Lazaar nor I tried to kill that bandleader. I know nothing about that."

"Then who killed René?" Edmundo was acid. "Tell me, Gloria."

"My friends do not include killers," she snarled.

"You know, my sweet, you may have a point there. I suspect you paid others to do your bidding—particularly the one thug with extremely strong hands who killed Mimosa, strangled her with his bare hands. What do you know about that?" The gun teetered.

"Nothing. I swear."

"I'm getting terrible urges from Mimosa right now. She is speaking to me from her grave. Oh, my dear, she's hissing dreadfully. 'Pull the trigger, my *pícaro*. Pull the trigger!' " He shook his gun. "What do you know about Mimosa?"

"Nothing," she murmured, apparently unimpressed by his threats.

"Tell me." The severity of his voice frightened me.

Gloria glanced back and forth at Edmundo and me. But then I saw the familiar gesture. She swelled. Ran her fingers through her hair. She arched, as if for retaliation. Though she never moved an inch, the myriad candles all at once rose and swelled, flickering like stars brightening the room.

At that same moment, Edmundo and I glanced behind us.

"Well, well, well," my colleague had the presence of mind to remark. "Ana de Pombo is going to join the party."

From a hidden door in the wall, now ajar, the bizarre red-haired designer peered at us like a mute figure in a painted fresco.

"Well, well, yourself." The frizzy-haired designer's voice was a near cackle. She had not yet seen Lassalle's weapon. "Welcome to my mouse-trap, Mickey. Tsk, tsk, tsk. What a surprise to see Mickey Mouse here. I don't think Walt Disney . . ." Her voice faded when she came closer and saw the revolver.

"You'd better take a seat also," Edmundo said, an invitation edged with threats.

With becoming majesty Gloria now stood up and strode center stage, her motion disturbing the candle flames again, playing each successive gesture for everything it was worth, creating the maximum suspense. For once Edmundo was without a *bon mot*. He just stared at what, by any theatrical standard, was surely a memorable performance. She looked pious, bountiful, enlightened. "My friends . . ." Her husky voice was extraordinarily low, like a supplicant's.

Edmundo and I waited.

"My friends, why not work together? We could end the war like that." She snapped her fingers, though she spoke slowly. Ana de Pombo remained mute. Now they were both facing us. "I want to make a deal with you," Gloria began. "No one knows about your visit except Ana and myself. We will both work for you in the future if you promise not to send us back to Germany when it's all over."

"Surely you jest," Edmundo answered, recovering his wits. "What kind of deal would we make with two Gestapo agents? How could we trust you?"

"Because I could make you the most famous Allied spy of World War II. You'd go down in history with the information I can supply."

"You've heard of *Camille,* Aline," Edmundo scoffed. "Well, what we're watching is the Countess von Fürstenberg in her most honest role —*Chameleon.* Well, tell us, my dear, just why we should be foolish enough to believe you won't inform your German friends of everything."

"Consider my career. I've been a winner all the way through. Back in Guadalajara, they all thought I'd marry a fat prosperous old sugarcane merchant and deliver a brood like a big sow. None of them had a clue to who I was—not my father, my sisters or brother. They didn't know Gloria Espinosa. My mother wanted me to have the world. I wanted the stars. And I got them." The candles behind her seemed to wink in accord.

"One night in Berlin, at a party. Amazing—there were a dozen parties every night then, even while the bombs fell. We danced and sang and flirted and wore the best we had. It was wild—wild. One night after the opera, I was at a party when Schellenberg walked in. Well, one look at him and I thought, My God, what is Gary Cooper doing here? Gary was a friend in Hollywood." She paused to smooth her hair.

"Do go on," Edmundo encouraged.

"Schellenberg saw my style at once. Every bovine Fräulein in Berlin was wearing her mother's moth-eaten velvet with enough gold brocade to choke a horse. I had on a pure white off-the-shoulder sheath—one diamond on a platinum chain—and of course there was the matter of my body. Well, he gawked like a baby. That was the beginning. In a month I was dining with Himmler and even Hitler himself."

"Don't stop there, Countess." Edmundo was obviously enthralled.

Suddenly I realized that these two belonged onstage. Supreme exhibitionists who should be at the same altar, the same shrine, the fatal religion of glamour, drama, and intrigue. Unscrupulous—both—and obviously Ana de Pombo also. Now Gloria and Edmundo were exactly attuned to each other, entrenched in their respective roles. I wasn't there for them.

"Of course I worked for Schellenberg, for Himmler. But today they are losing the war. I merely did what was necessary to escape." She directed her gaze at me and then back to Edmundo. "You think my hands are stained with blood? What about your own?" She raised her long slim fingers in the air. "What have I done that either of you hasn't?"

Did she know about the man I had killed only a few days ago?

"We've just been on different teams, that's all. Don't you see? I can help you. Whether or not you believe me is irrelevant. There is one reason even you should understand. I want to survive for my children. They're everything to me."

Eyeing her sharply, Edmundo said after a second, "What do you think, Aline?"

Whether or not there was a word of truth in what she said, obviously there was now no other way out for her.

"What about it, Aline? Shall we give our star her last chance to shine?"

I smiled. "You know only Washington can give this permission."

Gloria listened, then said, "You must protect Ana and me!" The carrot-topped woman nodded in agreement. "If the Gestapo discovers our duplicity . . . There is a saying around the embassy when anyone is suspected of defecting—'Remember the piano crate.' Wizner had two defectors killed and shipped out that way. Can you *imagine*?"

Edmundo and I resisted even glancing at each other.

She shrugged as if to remove the worry. "What about the blacklist? Can you get us off it?"

"If you cooperate with us, we'll ask Washington what can be done," he said.

Gloria sighed deeply. "Thank you, my friends. You've made a wise decision, one you'll never regret. Copies of all these messages"—she indicated those on the table—"and whatever future cables we receive will be at your disposal."

Edmundo stood up. "You are amazing. Living proof that you can have your cake and eat it too. Consider yourself lucky."

"The price for my luck has been high. I have just given up several influential friends."

"Knowing you, I'm sure you'll get over that in no time. You can replace Schellenberg and Himmler with others much better—like myself, for example."

"You're so clever—it must be our Aztec blood that unites us."

———

It was two in the morning when Edmundo and I walked down from the deserted street toward my house. No water sprayed from the fountain in the plaza, but the sky sprayed stars happily at us.

"We did it," Edmundo said. "We have discovered one of Himmler's best spies. Oh, I am proud of us." He turned to me. "I want you to know, Aline, neither of us could have done it alone. Absolutely not."

Would Gloria turn out to be Himmler's special agent? The one Operation Bullfight referred to? Somehow I couldn't believe that the kind of work she had been doing was that important, but I dared not confide any of my thoughts to Edmundo.

He took my arm as we walked down the street. "Think of it, love. We now have some pieces to work with. We must find the killer, and we will. Lazaar undoubtedly is still a suspect. I don't trust Gloria, but we can get more information from her little by little."

We continued in silence for a while. In my mind there were huge questions. How well did Pierre know Gloria? Had she been involved in the attempt to kill me? Premonitions also made me resist mentioning Francisco to Edmundo.

A lone figure approached us from the Plaza de Colón. It took a moment to realize who he was. His clothes were in shreds, and he was staggering. "José!" cried Edmundo, hurrying toward him. He tried to give him a hand, but José stood before us, suddenly standing straight, as if oblivious to his wounds.

"Señor, señorita, tonight I am a free man," he said in his gravelly voice. Blood matted his thick gray hair, smeared his lined cheek. "I have avenged my daughter. On the man who goes—there." He pointed toward the building from which we had just departed.

"What man?" Edmundo and I asked together.

"The man who works the radio. The man who works with that—lady. That is how I knew about this place."

Edmundo turned to me. "You see, José is the one who discovered the radio station."

"I followed the man to and from an apartment where he lives, around the corner from the German Embassy. You see, after that night at Villa Rosa—when that pig raped my daughter—I began to go there, night after night. It took thirty nights before he came back. When he did, the bartender pointed him out to me. That is when I began to follow him. While I was waiting for you tonight, Don Edmundo, he came out of the building. My blood boiled. I couldn't resist following him through the streets until we were alone. When he passed an alley, I took care of him. Gypsy-style."

Edmundo swallowed audibly.

"What is Gypsy-style?" I asked.

José Heredia hesitated. "That's not for the ears of a señorita. But I am avenged."

"José, you're badly hurt. Let me help you," I said.

"No. These wounds are my pride. I am happier tonight than in a long time."

"You've done useful work for us, José. I am grateful."

The Gypsy bowed his head. *"Vaya con Dios, señores."*

As he walked off, I asked Edmundo, "What's Gypsy-style?"

"Do you really want to know?"

I nodded my head insistently.

"It means to cut off a man's testicles," he replied.

———

Mozart was obviously satisfied when I told him about discovering the transmitter in the dress shop. He leaned forward enthusiastically, his gangly arms almost falling off the desk.

"Good work! That's the station we've been looking for. It's so powerful that it transmits all the way to Tokyo. Tell Top Hat I congratulate him also."

"What about the countess working for us? We more or less agreed to that last night."

"She can be useful, no doubt about that. Defections are frequent these days. In England, OSS is using some of Germany's most dependable agents, who are helping us to feed false information back to Berlin. That dressmaker can be useful too. But I'll have to get approval from Shepardson and Donovan himself."

"Do you think Gloria and Ana de Pombo can help us uncover the mole?"

Mozart flinched. I had touched upon a sensitive subject. Still, the flinch had been almost imperceptible. When he answered, his tone was emotionless. "Don't worry about that. We have the problem under control."

Such a response annoyed me. Mimosa and Lilienthal had information that coincided—a mole in American espionage in Spain. It had to be someone I knew. If Mozart would have enough confidence in me to tell me who it was, I could protect myself better. Unless . . . it was Mozart himself.

"Will I be the contact with the countess?"

"No." His response was quick this time. "I don't approve of women working together when not absolutely necessary."

That made no sense at all. Didn't I have his own orders to put up women in my house and to form a women's chain? By the time I left his office, I was having doubts about everyone again, and despite Spider's cable, especially about Mozart.

Chapter 28

It was eleven o'clock at night, July 1. Two full days had passed since Pierre left. I sat at the dressing table, brushing my hair, thinking how dangerous a drop in southern France would be at this stage of the war. The Germans had powerful antiaircraft searchlights placed all along the coast. Outside, the night was hot and strangely silent, as before a cloudburst. Soft rays of a full moon gleamed on my windowsill. I wondered if Pierre in Algiers was looking at the same sky. The phone rang. Edmundo, you *pícaro*! I prepared to say. Angustias had told me he would call. Instead, I heard the gruff, abrasive voice of Mozart.

"Can you come to the office right away?"

"Of course."

Twenty minutes later I climbed the narrow steps to the top floor. In the empty halls my heels echoed: click, click on the barren tile floor. In the taxi I had thought, Everybody is finishing dinner or out dancing or home asleep, and Pierre could be in a plane over the Mediterranean. My intuition warned me: This is the night.

The door was bolted. Mozart opened it. He said nothing. The offices were dark and still as we passed them, going into the transmitter room, where Jimmie, one of the radiomen, sat at the radio. "Have a seat, Tiger." By the time the chief closed the door of the dimly lit room, my premonition had become a certainty.

"Pierre will be making his drop in thirty minutes," Mozart announced, his tiny eyes on the wall clock. "I thought you should be the first to know what happens. The fate of Operation Anvil depends on his not being caught."

I watched the second hand wheel in its slow arc; my heart seemed to follow it. Mozart's voice was lower than ever. "If Pierre lands without mishap, Jimmie will hear his familiar staccato about ten minutes later. If he hears nothing, well, he may have been shot on his way down or ambushed when he got there."

I knew that each agent had his own manner of jiggling the transmitter and could be recognized by the receiver just as someone's voice is on the telephone. Often this helped us to know when one of our men was captured and an impostor was sending us messages.

The shuttered room sealed out the noises of life like a tomb. I kept staring at the clock and telling myself there was nothing to fear. Only five minutes had passed. Twenty-five more to go. Then there would be ten more before Pierre could make radio contact.

I was with him on that plane. I felt its rumble, heard its drone, high above the Mediterranean, then over the landmass that is southern France. I remembered Pierre sitting next to me on the train to New York, his physical presence like an electric current. Dancing with him at El Morocco. Fifteen minutes. I stared at the transmitting equipment as though it could talk. Its knobs and levers were mute. Jimmie sat in front of it like a statue, Mozart nearby like a sphinx. I was surprised my heartbeats didn't deafen them.

The wall clock struck twelve. Midnight. Pierre would be in position, strapped in his parachute, in the belly of the transport. Ten minutes.

The three of us watched the clock. The silence was so intense it made me more anxious. I drew on every resource to maintain self-control. I saw Pierre plunging through space. It was an eternity. Three minutes. Two minutes. One minute. Nobody said a word. I imagined the Maquis with their flashlights illuminating the spot where he should land, then dashing back behind the bushes and underbrush until the plane had passed and dropped its burden. They would come out, help Pierre disentangle from the red-and-green parachute. I could see Pierre folding it, another burying it, so no evidence would be found. Then the process of setting up the small transmitter. Any moment now Jimmie would turn to us and smile, nod his head. The wait began again.

The minutes ticked by. How strange that silence could be so meaningful. I willed the transmitter to sound its staccato. I willed Pierre to be safe. Ten minutes. Twelve. Fifteen. Twenty. Twenty-five minutes. Jimmie kept jiggling his machine, trying to make contact, but we could tell nothing was coming from the other side. Mozart was uncontrollably nervous. He paced back and forth, thumping from the desk to the table in the corner. He finally said, "I brought some champagne in case we could celebrate," but his voice was despondent. "Would you like some sherry instead, Tiger? Jimmie?" I flinched. Pierre had been caught, maybe shot on the way down. Something had gone wrong.

The chief poured three glasses. *Come on, Pierre,* I pleaded. *It's not too late. You can contact us. Come on. Please.* The chief handed me a glass of sherry.

Holding his, he proposed the grimmest toast I'd ever heard: "To Pierre." He sipped.

"To Pierre," Jimmie echoed.

Silently I drank.

"It is to be surmised that phase two has failed. We must find another way—and quick," Mozart growled.

As he was speaking, we started to hear the clicking of Jimmie's machine —weakly, then a stronger tat-tat-tat.

"He's there!" yelled Jimmie. "He made it after all!"

I sank into a chair, thoroughly exhausted. Mozart went mad, crashing his sherry glass in bits all over the floor, raising the champagne bottle in the air, shouting, "You did it, Tiger! It worked! Anvil will be a success!"

I didn't understand, but I was too happy to care. My mind and heart reeled. I was remembering Pierre on that long eternal fall day in New York when we walked through Central Park. I had fallen in love then —or maybe before that—in the first moment I looked into his fathomless dark eyes.

He was alive!

Sunday. The phone call was urgent. It was Belmonte's *mozo de espadas* calling from La Clínica de los Toreros, the Bullfighters' Hospital, in Madrid. His voice chilled me. "Señorita, Don Juan this afternoon has been gored." I had been on duty in the code room, unable to go to another of Juan's important *corridas*. The man's sobs made it difficult for him to talk. "He was operated on . . . by Dr. Tamananes . . . and is still unconscious." The man of swords now cried at random.

"*How* serious?" I asked, terrified he would tell me my friend was dying. Since the man was unable to answer, I hung up. Minutes later I flew out the door into the warm night.

With good reason I had expected a crowd outside Belmonte's room, but I wasn't prepared for pandemonium. Not only reporters and a few photographers, but fans and friends who'd heard of the calamity over the radio were thronging the hospital corridor, despite protests from guards, doctors, and nurses. The room was cordoned off, but fortunately the man who'd phoned me was outside, still in his satin, silk-embroidered *banderillero*'s costume, his eyes red. I feared the worst. When he saw me, he ushered me through the mob into the room.

Belmonte's mother, Doña Consuelo, stood up from the chair next to the narrow hospital bed and came to greet me. Although her expression revealed strain, she was surprisingly beautiful, as Juanito had told me. Huge brown eyes, a perfect oval face, black hair pulled into a knot at the nape of her head—like the women in the paintings of Romero de Torres.

"*Gracias* for coming, Aline. Juanito has been asking for you ever since he came out of the operating room. He is still . . . groggy, but *gracias a Dios,* his wound is not as serious as we thought." I looked down at Juanito in dismay. The pain and loss of blood had drained the color from his face, which looked like a wounded child's. I reached for his hand. It took a minute for his eyes to connect with mine, for he was drugged and still in shock. Standing there, I watched as he pursed his lips for speech. Through the open window, the city lights shimmered suggestively on that exotic summer night.

"Aline." He motioned with his hand, then grimaced in pain as he tried to change position. "Would you care for some chocolates?" On the table next to his bed sat a box of our favorite chocolates wrapped in pink tissue paper. I smiled at him and shook my head.

"Well, in that case, would you mind feeding me one? To tell you the truth, ever since I came to, I have had a terrible longing for a chocolate. Please?"

I selected a piece and obliged him, holding it while he chewed in thorough agony. Who could ever understand these Spaniards? They were children, spontaneous, passionate, unruly children. I knew better by now than to question Juanito's logic or disobey his harmless request.

"Now could I have some water?"

From a pitcher on the table I poured him a glass and held it while he took small sips from a bent straw.

"Chocolates and water. What else does a man need? Surely not bulls. Will you be my Florence Nightenberg?"

"Nightenberg?" I laughed. "Of course I will."

=====

When I finally prepared to leave the hospital, I was relieved. The doctors had discovered that no main arteries were affected and he would be all right in two weeks, more or less. This was to me incredible, but Juan explained that wounds from a bull's horns cured more quickly than others because the horn went in with such speed that it was like fire and such wounds rarely became infected. The Spaniard's explanations did not convince me, but I knew he would be in the ring as soon as he could walk, no matter how weak, because this was the height of the season, and he lost a fortune every day he missed a fight.

When I went out, three men standing at one side of the hospital entrance drew my attention; perhaps it was the fumes of the heavy black tobacco they were smoking. One of the faces illuminated by the overhead light looked familiar. Then the short stocky figure and the drab baggy suit of another also rang a bell. *Definitely*. I stood still a second, while people passed up and down the steps. Of course, I recognized the man who had gotten on the train in the Atocha Station going to Málaga months before. Nothing would stop me now from finding out who he was. And the other face—I could swear he had been in front of my door on the Calle Monte Esquina.

I walked over, pointing to the short fellow in the middle of the group.

"Didn't I see you on the train to Málaga sometime ago?"

A kind smile lit his face. *"Sí, señorita."*

"Who are you?" My voice was unfriendly.

"But señorita, you don't know us? We work for Don Juan, and we have seen you often."

I still did not understand. What work did they do for Juanito, and why did they know me so well?

I turned to the other. "And I think you have been in front of my house once or twice."

"Not once or twice, señorita," he answered respectfully. "Almost every night. Well, we changed sometimes, but more often I took that part."

"But why would you be in front of my house?"

"Don Juan wanted us to protect the señorita and to inform him who the señorita went out with, to make certain the men would bring her to no harm."

I threw my hands up, shaking my head in disbelief. How had I been so oblivious to the fact that Juanito could be jealous enough to have me followed?

Suddenly I grabbed the arm of the short stocky man. "Since Don Juan wanted you to protect me, why didn't you see that no one entered my room in Málaga?"

"Señorita, I knew nothing about that until the next day."

"But where were you when that happened? You had better tell me," I warned. "I can inform Don Juan how badly you have protected me."

"Señorita, I will tell you all I know—which is not much." He scratched his head nervously, and I wondered if he would tell the truth. "The trouble is a beautiful Gypsy girl I know in Málaga. She dances at a bar near the Club Náutico, and once I saw the señorita was safely in her room I went there for the rest of the night. She is a good dancer."

"But didn't you hear that my room had been searched? Everybody in the hotel seemed to know what had happened when I came downstairs the next morning."

"Yes, I did hear about that. And I am sorry. But I don't know who could have done such an ungentlemanly thing."

"Did you see the German with the monocle while you were there?"

"Yes, señorita, he was in the same flamenco bar with us that night."

So it wasn't Lazaar after all. Unless he had hired a mercenary.

"Well, don't follow me anymore. Do you understand? It has been kind of Don Juan to protect me, but it is not necessary. I will speak to him about this, but I want you to stop immediately."

"Oh, no problem, señorita. We told Don Juan when we came back from the Costa Brava that it was much too dangerous. We nearly got killed on that trip. The señorita really should not take so many chances, racing like that in the car." The three shook their heads in unison.

I had to burst out laughing. "So it was the three of you who followed me that day?"

"*Sí, señorita.* We told Don Juan that it would be less dangerous to return to our jobs as *peones* in the bullring."

As I walked to the waiting taxi, I was still smiling. I wondered when Juan's men had begun following me. And all along I had thought it was Lazaar's men. Although I knew there had been others, I had no intention of confessing my stupidity to Mozart.

Chapter 29

In my hands was the July 22 ABC newspaper with the grisly details of Colonel Klaus von Stauffenberg's aborted assassination plot on Hitler. In retaliation, the Führer had a number of army officers suspected of involvement in the plot filmed for the public to see while they were slowly strangled on meathooks. Constantin von Weiderstock's famous godfather, Wilhelm Canaris, had been imprisoned and was probably facing a similar fate in the near future. "Like lemmings, annihilating themselves. Mind-boggling atrocities. Edmundo, are you listening?"

During a temporary slack in the flow of messages, I had met my comrade in an outside café on the sunny, desert-dry afternoon. The crowd around us was lazily occupied in observing the passersby. Edmundo was sipping sherry; newspapers were strewn all over the tiny table. I had decided to take advantage of every opportunity to observe Top Hat. Mozart had designated him as the contact with Gloria, and now the envelopes I carried back to the office were sealed. Edmundo no longer suggested that I read them. Suspicions of both Mozart and Edmundo continued to plague me. The fact that Anvil, which had been expected to take place a month ago, still had not occurred made me worry even more.

"Aline," he said languidly, "I may ask Ratibor to marry me."

"Edmundo, how can you do that? *You* put Ratibor on the blacklist. If you married her, you'd have to resign from the service—Washington would never allow it."

"My dear, I ask you, what else can a man do but obey his heart? And, frankly, what is more important, I ask you: espionage or a title? Didn't a king abdicate his throne for a woman? Well, what can I do? What is a court of law when I, Edmundo Lassalle, bow as a humble petitioner before the court of love? Besides, I must do something. I am bored. I need something to pick me up."

"Try another sherry."

"Very funny. Don't be peevish."

"Edmundo, are you serious? Would you marry Ratibor? Are you really in love with her?"

"Aline, think of my future. What does it hold for me after the war ends? Can you see me shuffling papers behind a desk in some American company? A consultant for General Motors, perhaps, with a wife and two children in Grosse Pointe? Look at me and tell me, is that how you see the destiny of Edmundo Lassalle? Or perhaps you would have me imprisoned in the Pentagon, working for the Army. No, my darling, remember: 'Edmundo Lassalle. He danced not in vain.' As Ratibor's husband—consort, if you will—the world of society is mine. We'll live between Mexico City, New York, Paris, Deauville, the Italian Riviera." He gave a long sigh. "I tell you, I must do something—I'm so, so bored. This war is unexciting lately. Nothing unusual happens. Nobody's been murdered for too long now. I used to have something to look forward to. No, I *will* do something! I must. I'm even tired of inventing the reports I give to you. My imagination is as dry as a prune."

I looked at him. "How is it that working with the devastating countess has not given you exciting information for Washington?"

Edmundo was stroking his mustache. His smile was evanescent. "She avoids me as much as possible. Every day I trust her less. But I make a valiant effort to keep those old fogies in Washington interested. Why, it makes their day just to receive one of Top Hat's delicious concoctions. We must amuse them, my dear. You know that as well as I. After all, they *are* our employers."

"Edmundo." I shook my head. "If Mozart knew!"

Edmundo preened. "My dearest, as my prized pupil who will one day undoubtedly share my firmament in the galaxy of immortal spies, I tell you from the bottom of my heart—on Judgment Day we will not be accountable to Mozart. I, for one, intend to be accountable only to . . . Venus."

I rolled my eyes, went back to the newspapers. A moment later I was startled to hear Edmundo mention the person I was thinking about.

"Do you know, my pet, the handsome fellow you danced with at the country club has had a long romance with Gloria? You can probably write them up as doomed lovers. I don't believe half of what our new colleague, the countess, has to say about him, because my princess told me she saw them dancing together in Berlin."

"Berlin?" I asked, incredulous. "When would that have been?"

"Last New Year's Eve, to be exact. The night I met you. Do you remember?"

"Berlin?" I repeated. "Only months ago." A chill was coming over me.

Edmundo was still talking. "You can be sure that romance has lasted a few years at least. You don't seem to be listening to me. I hope I'm not wasting my breath. Please remember to treat me decorously, for the sake of my princess."

I left Edmundo, hardly saying good-bye, and rushed to the office. Either Edmundo or his princess was a liar, or what I had just heard opened terrifying possibilities. By now Walters had left, and I was fortunately alone to code my message to Jupiter. My haste was such that I worded the cable as I coded.

FROM TIGER TO JUPITER STOP   PHASE TWO IN DANGER STOP   MOZART
REFUSES TO GIVE IMPORTANCE TO RUMORS OF MOLE STOP   TOP HAT
INFORMS PRINCESS RATIBOR SAW PIERRE WITH VON FURSTENBERG IN
BERLIN JANUARY FIRST THIS YEAR STOP   AM BEGINNING INVESTIGATION
ON MY OWN CONCERNING RELATIONSHIP BETWEEN PIERRE AND FUR-
STENBERG STOP   PLEASE ADVISE FROM TIGER TO JUPITER.

Paco Aylagas promised to have someone meet me at the station in El Escorial and take me to the prison to see Pilar. "I can't understand why a nice girl like you would make any effort to see someone like that woman—a communist conspiring against the government," Paco said.

"Nevertheless, in this country we try to do what we can for a friend. Have a good trip and let me know about your visit when you return."

When we reached the foothills of the Guadarrama Mountains the wind blowing through the window was cool and refreshing despite the dry July heat. Instead of concentrating on the lovely view of green *retama* bushes filled with yellow blooms, the live oaks and fascinating stone formations, I went over the questions I intended to ask Pilar.

A woman official led me into the warden's office, which had been vacated for my convenience. A few minutes later Pilar appeared, looking just the same as always. Her prison garb and shoes were no more dreary than what she had worn each day she came to my apartment. She was enthusiastic.

"Señorita, have you come to get me out of here? I knew you could do it."

Even when I told her that was impossible she claimed that if I wanted I could get her released. "You don't understand, señorita. Just insist. Now you are winning the war. Those damn fascists will be anxious to do anything you Americans say. I have to get out. The war will soon be over, and I must organize my women to tell our compatriots in France, Mexico, and Russia to send us money so we will overthrow this fat pig."

"That's just why they won't release you," I answered. "They know you will continue to try to overthrow the government."

I gave Pilar the box of goodies Cecilia had prepared and some books. Her myopic eyes blinked behind the thick lenses. "You are kind, señorita. What a pity I cannot be helping you right now."

"But you can, Pilar. Do you remember any of your informers on the countess mentioning a handsome young man?" I described Pierre as objectively as possible.

"Yes, in the last report—which I never was able to deliver, because I was picked up by the police—I mentioned that fellow. He saw her a lot that week. I myself saw him leave her hotel with her several times, and I always suspected he was the one who denounced me to the police. Mr. Lazaar had a quarrel with him in front of the hotel one night."

"Pilar, do you know his name?"

"The name was foreign. I don't remember."

That was all the information I could get from her, but it was a beginning. Pierre was in love with Gloria and he had lied to me. Did he work with her also?

Operation Anvil could begin at any moment. There was no time to be lost in getting to the bottom of this, in getting reliable answers. Did Mozart suspect any of this? Or was he the mole who set these situations up? Whom could I turn to? Whoever the mole was, he would certainly be more interested in eliminating me now if he knew what I had discovered. I sensed that I had never been in such danger before.

=====

I called the countess and asked her to meet me in the great hall of the Hotel Ritz, where the Spanish ladies met for a *copita* before lunch, where we would appear to be discussing any frivolity—the current parties or fashion shows.

Gloria was especially well dressed for her new role of double agent. All the women turned to look as she entered, then buzzed to each other, surely commenting on her chic purple-and-black linen suit, the tiny purple hat, the matching shoes. Even the parrot pin was in place as she seated herself in a decorative position in the large armchair facing mine.

"I have a little gift for you." She opened her bag and brought out a large box. "Perfume, straight from Paris, courtesy of the German Embassy pouch by way of Berlin, Lufthansa to Barcelona, and Madrid. I do hope you like Chanel No. 5."

I thanked her and then said, "Gloria, I've been asked to get information on your friend Francisco. Could you tell me his full name?"

"To tell you the truth, I know very little about him. We met in Paris two years ago. He used an exotic title, Comte de la Perla, although I always suspected it was false. Francisco likes to impress people. So handsome, and Paris in 1942! We had a glorious time for ten days. Then he disappeared. That's about all I can tell you."

"But what has he been doing in Madrid?"

"Wouldn't I like to know! I know he's desperately in love with me, because he pursued me all over Madrid when he first arrived."

"When was that?"

She raised a red-lacquered fingernail to her cheek. "Oh, let me see. That must have been about the beginning of May."

She was lying—he had been in my house before that—but I pretended to believe her.

"Was he working with you for the Gestapo?"

"Certainly not. He hated the Nazis."

"But we have a reliable informer who saw you dancing with him in Berlin last New Year's Eve."

"Whoever says that is not reliable. That's a lie. I *was* in Berlin on New Year's Eve. That's a fact, but I never saw Francisco there."

"What was Francisco's business?"

"He had a factory near Nice. I don't know what kind—but he came to Paris frequently on business trips."

"Did he do business with the Germans in Paris?"

"I don't know. He had financial difficulties, but they are almost over." She paused a moment. "In fact, I just happen to have a note here in my bag that he left me weeks ago. What a coincidence."

She snapped her purse open, then handed me a wrinkled sheet of Palace Hotel stationery.

I read: "Gloria, *guapa,* I have to leave unexpectedly—just wanted you to know that I'll repay you soon. I'm going to be a free man and in a position to give you whatever luxury you wish. Don't turn too many heads in the meantime. F." The signature was the same one that had accompanied my roses, and the handwriting seemed the same also.

Gloria explained. "He came here to get a large sum of money which he had difficulty in claiming—and I helped him with some pesetas until he could repay me."

Try as I might, that was the extent of the information I managed to pry from her. When we left the hotel, each to a different taxi, she slipped me an envelope. "Perhaps this information about the Germans' latest antiaircraft installation in southern France may be useful. We'd better not see each other often—Lazaar will become suspicious."

As the taxi circled the Plaza de Neptune and turned up in the direction of Alfonso XII to the house of the Avila sisters, I pondered who else might give me more information on Pierre. José had been watching Ana de

Pombo's shop during the time Pierre was in Madrid. But I would have to wait. I had called all around Madrid for three days and José was nowhere to be found. At least one thing was now certain. Pierre was having some kind of a love affair with Gloria. Thus his flirting with me had to have a purpose.

Chapter 30

T hrough his indomitable will, Belmonte recovered more quickly than expected, and his daily progress received as much coverage in the press as D-Day had. The goring in the arena was elaborated in numerous versions and in graphic detail—the depth of the gash, which muscles and which tissues were lacerated, how much he'd bled, and the prognosis of several eminent physicians, as well as the list of celebrated luminaries who had made the pilgrimage to the renowned hospital room.

Then something happened that swept even Juan Belmonte off page one. It happened before I got an answer from Jupiter, before I could talk to Heredia, who I had trailing Gloria, Lazaar, and even Mozart. And it held for me what seemed like, at that moment, the most discouraging news of my life.

Walking out of my house on the morning of August 15, I heard the *portera*'s radio blasting: "Ninety-four thousand Allied troops are landing near a fishing village called Saint-Tropez." I couldn't believe my ears. Saint-Tropez was near Cannes—far from Marseilles, the information in the message I had delivered to Pierre. I rushed to the office. Everyone was jubilant. By now Jimmie was in radio contact with our OSS transmitter there. General Truscott's VIth Corps had been the first to go ashore, followed by General de Lattre de Tassigny with the French corps. The U.S. Seventh Army led by General Alexander Patch completed the group. Despite some resistance, the Germans had been taken unawares, and there was no fighting as destructive as that encountered in Normandy a month and a half before. Operation Anvil was a success.

Nobody could understand why I wasn't celebrating. Nobody except Mozart. He called me into his room.

I couldn't wait for him to explain. I was indignant, hurt—finished with espionage, as far as I was concerned, for the rest of my life.

"Why did you not have faith in me? Why did you think I was not reliable enough to know that you were having me give false information to Pierre?" Now I knew: the mole had been Pierre, and my bosses knew that by feeding him the wrong landing location, they would misinform the Germans, who would act accordingly.

"Don't take it so hard, Aline," said Mozart. "The success of this invasion is also yours. If you had not done your job so well, we might be counting casualties today instead of this victory."

I just stood there shaking my head. No matter what he said, nothing would make up for his lack of confidence in me.

He seemed to sense my thoughts. "We did it that way for one reason —to protect you. Pierre would have killed you if he had had the slightest inkling you knew he was a double agent. And he would have known. You didn't have to tell him, he would have smelled it. And as far as the place of the actual landing, no one, including many generals involved in this war effort, including the head of OSS London, was allowed to know the exact date or place. That was an order from Eisenhower, and we had to obey." He came around the table and put his arm on my shoulder for the first time. "So why not go back and join the others in celebrating your own success? You deserve it."

Somehow I just couldn't. The news was what I had been waiting for during eight months, but discovering that Pierre was a traitor made it a tragic day for me. With what I hoped appeared to be a grimace of pain, my hand pressing my stomach, I explained to my ecstatic colleagues outside in the hall that the excitement had given me a sudden case of "Madrid misery," and I went home to think about the many unanswerable questions. Had Pierre been the one who hired the thug to kill me the night of the dance at Puerta de Hierro? Had Pierre come to my house that night so many months ago with the intention of killing me then, only the uncalculated arrival of Edmundo had thwarted his scheme? Had Pierre strangled Mimosa, René Blum?

A few days later when I entered my apartment, Angustias announced, "Señorita, a gentleman has been waiting to see you. He says he is an old friend, but refused to give his name."

Immediately suspicious, I entered the living room cautiously. My shock was total.

"Hello, Tiger. You're looking well."

Jupiter! John Derby! He was standing, and I rushed to shake his hand. "I can't believe you're really here, in front of me. What are you doing in Madrid? How are you?"

He looked the same—eternally scrubbed. Short-cropped silver hair, fresh fair skin, hawklike eyes. It was almost a year since we had met. "I'm fine. And the main reason I'm in Madrid is to see you."

"Please sit down. What can I get you to drink?"

"Nothing right now. I have too much to tell you." We were both seated on the sofa, side by side, regarding one another with as much curiosity and affection as if we were long-lost friends. In a sense, we were. "Where do I start? First of all, Whitney Shepardson sends his congratulations. He's heard about the good work you've been doing, and now credits himself with having discovered you." Jupiter winked.

His words somewhat soothed my demolished ego, still stunned from the revelations of the past few days. I listened attentively.

"Also, I've just come from southern France, where two of your colleagues send you their warmest regards." My heart jumped. Had he seen Pierre? "Whiskey and Magic told me that as soon as the war is over, you're all going to have one hell of a reunion. It was Magic, actually, who prepared this report." He handed me two folded sheets of paper from his pocket and, lowering his voice, said, "Read it. It may hold some answers you've been looking for."

Somewhat confused, I unfolded the papers and looked at the small print of an ancient typewriter. Jupiter walked over to the window, as if to give me privacy while I read. As soon as I saw the first words, I understood why.

REPORT ON OSS AGENT PIERRE NUMBER 333
François Ferronière, born July 17, 1916,
Nice, France.

My heart quickened, uncontrollably. I raced through the lines.

. . . son of Josef Ferronière and Cecilia Alvarado, daughter of Francisco, Marqués of Torrejón of Madrid.

So Pierre was Mimosa's nephew! I looked up at John Derby's stalwart back, thankful he couldn't see my face.

Magic's report continued:

François Ferronière's father was representative of American Radiator for southern France. Politically he was aligned with the fascist groups, especially with the Milice, whose leader, Marcel Darnan, placed it at the disposal of the Gestapo, providing the names of those willing to serve as collaborators.

When Ferronière, who had studied English, obtained a minor clerical position at the American consulate in Vichy, Darnan offered him modest sums for information on American war plans. François's quick intelligence, knowledge of English, and winning personality made him a popular employee and facilitated his obtaining useful data.

After the North African invasion, the American Embassy personnel moved from Vichy to Algiers, occupying the Villa Magnol, where François continued to work. The Villa Magnol housed all American governmental agencies, including the first OSS recruits.

Through Axis contacts of Darnan in Algiers, Ferronière was offered larger sums and managed to be sent to Washington for intensive intelligence training. Later he was shipped to England and to Algiers, from where he was dropped into southern France in December 1943.

When it became apparent that a traitor operated inside Pierre's area, he became suspect along with others. But after surveillance, Pierre's guilt became more obvious and he was called to Madrid with the pretext of overseeing agents' crossing the frontier. In actuality he was being kept there to be used at the proper time to feed false information to the Germans on the Anvil landing location.

This mission was accomplished by OSS Madrid, but Pierre disappeared during the August 15 invasion and has not yet been apprehended. His name has been listed for war crimes trials.

The report, dated August 18, Marseilles, confirmed my fears. Pierre was not only a traitor but an assassin as well. It seemed undeniable to me now that he had killed his aunt, Mimosa. Undoubtedly, Pierre had been one of the men she had seen conspiring the day she was sitting in the "hand chair." She was startled precisely because her own nephew was involved in the dirty plot. Most likely he had killed her too in order to inherit her fortune. Gloria said Pierre was only interested in money. And the other murders—Marta, René—were probably his doing.

I mustered a huge effort to murmur, "A hard lesson to learn."

Jupiter walked toward me. "You were at the Farm with him. What did you think of him then?"

"Charming" was all I could say. I was anxious to change the subject and said so.

"I don't like to think about him either. Pierre's case depresses me, but in the end he became one of our means of befuddling the Germans about the landing in southern France. And we have you to thank there, Aline. The importance of your contribution is incalculable. We were manipulating others to confuse the enemy at the same time, but personally, I think the decisive information that convinced the enemy was that which you passed on to Pierre. Obviously he never suspected you would give him false information. And fortunately the Germans had full confidence in him."

Jupiter paused and sat down. "I've come here for other reasons—important ones right now." He smiled. "You've done great work, Tiger. Mozart has informed me of your accomplishments—and I must say, your rather unusual exploits, all over Spain, have converted you into a real professional."

When he mentioned the name of Mozart, I shuddered, remembering the cable I had recently sent without his orders. Jupiter understood. "You've nothing to worry about. Mozart may seem a cold guy, but I assure you he is your most enthusiastic admirer. In fact, if he were not appreciative of your work I would not be here today for a purpose I can tell you now."

Few words could have made me happier. That Mozart considered mine a creditable job was the highest compliment I could receive.

Jupiter continued, "You work hard and you deliver. That's what we need if we're to end the war. But it's still going on, as you know. And there's a lot to be done.

"Also, no one knows how the world will be divided after the war, what new political factions and threats to democracy will occur. That's why I'm here."

He walked to the window looking down into Monte Esquina again, where the streetlights illuminated the *sereno* starting his rounds. He beckoned me. "I want you to take what I am going to say very seriously, more seriously than anything you have considered so far. Sit down and relax. You're going to have to make an important decision."

I took a seat on the small sofa while he drew up a chair. Relax? His last words had left me tense. But I tried to appear cool.

Jupiter's gold-flecked blue eyes were full of purpose.

"I have another mission for you, Tiger—if you'll take it, that is. You don't have to, you know. You can keep working in the Madrid office as long as you want. There is plenty to do here."

He paused again. I tried to control my curiosity.

"But this is really something special, and if you think you have seen excitement in Spain . . . well . . ."

He leaned toward me, his hands crossed on his knees. I concentrated my attention on him alone. There was much to consider. I remembered Pierre—and felt the heartache. Yet, to think that this moment could be a beginning was compensating, stimulating.

"If you're not still willing to volunteer for hazardous duty, speak up."

I just waited for him to continue. He leaned back in the chair and grinned.

I said nothing, knowing that in my silence I had chosen to seal my fate. Then I listened as attentively as he had expected.

I continued to work for the OSS in Spain until the end of the war. I was ordered to obtain a new job and a new cover in Europe. In Washington, meanwhile, the OSS was struggling with other departments of the government to maintain control of foreign intelligence in peacetime. I continued to do undercover work in France and Switzerland until 1947, when I resigned from the service in order to return to Madrid and marry. I had not only fallen in love with the man who appears in my story as the Count of Quintanilla, but also with Spain. Later, due to the Spanish system of succession, our title changed to Romanones, a name of great eminence and tradition in Spain. No doubt many Spaniards, on reading this book, will be at pains to believe the bizarre path that led me to such an honor.

Epilogue: El Salvador, 1984

The black hair was thinner and gray, the reddish-tan skin was sunbaked with deep creases, yet the smile and that dark penetrating gaze had not changed. In El Salvador, he was the last person I had expected to see.

For a long moment, I was too stunned to speak. He had the same reaction. We just stood there, almost unaware of the sound of the pool and the soft swish of the palm leaves. Beyond the hotel's glass walls, a few men in colorful short-sleeved shirts moved about, but in that secluded patio, encircled by flowers and exotic leafy plants and memories, we were alone.

He took both my hands in his, and I became aware of the night air caressing my cheeks. "Tiger, you've hardly changed in all these years. How is that possible?"

I laughed. "I was thinking the same about you."

"What are you doing here, of all places?"

"And you?" The last time I had looked into those smoldering eyes had been on the steps of the Palace Hotel in Madrid in the summer of 1944. Had it really been so long ago?

He offered me a chair at a table nearby. Still in a daze, I sat down. He took a seat facing mine. He held out a pack of cigarettes to me. "Do you still not smoke?"

I shook my head. Not the moment to explain that I had and had stopped. My brain was flooded with recollections, reawakening emotions, and qualms.

He leaned back in his chair, smiling that magical grin. "Where should I start? I owe you a few explanations, Tiger."

"For years I wondered about you, Pierre. I thought you probably had been killed during the invasion without anyone on our side knowing about it."

"I dared not contact you at the end of the war. And by the time I was able to, you were married." He stared absently at the orange bougainvillea covering the wall next to our table. I sensed he was struggling with the same jumble of emotions I felt. The sounds of footsteps caused him to turn toward the approaching waiter. Then he looked at me.

"We must celebrate, Tiger. How about some champagne? Remember that day at the Stork Club?"

The waiter was standing patiently at his side. "Your best Moët et Chandon, Pedro. And make certain it's cold."

The fellow bowed. *"Sí, Señor Alvarado. En seguida, señor."* Pierre was a familiar and important customer.

"Why does he call you Señor Alvarado?"

"My mother's name. I've been using it for years."

"Wasn't your mother Mimosa Torrejón's sister?"

"Yes. And if I had gotten to my Aunt Mimosa in time, perhaps I would have been able to set my life straight. I wanted to change—for you, Tiger. But luck was not with me."

There was no sense putting it off. I had to ask him. "Did you kill Mimosa?"

His head jerked forward. He leaned across the table toward me. "My God, Tiger, did you think I had killed her?"

"Everybody in our office did. And that you killed René Blum also. And that you tried to kill me."

"But how could you have thought that? I was in love with you."

"Gloria seemed to think differently, and our information proved you had an affair with her. I believed your stories then, Pierre, but not now."

The waiter had reappeared with a bucket of ice, twirling the bottle of champagne. Pierre dismissed him and poured the drinks himself. Not a word passed between us. When he raised his glass, I did the same.

"To Tiger and Pierre." His voice was melancholy, and for a moment he looked almost his age. "And to what might have been." We both took a sip.

The cold bubbles intensified the atmosphere of unreality. He raised his glass again. "And to my Tía Mimosa—who could have put us together if she had read her cards correctly." His dejected mood had disappeared . . . with the same engaging smile that had captivated me so long ago.

"What are you talking about, Pierre?"

"My plan was to ask my aunt for some money and one of her titles, one that would eventually have been mine anyway, so I could become a Spanish citizen and get out of that war entirely."

"What went wrong?"

"I got there too late. After managing to get into her house through a back window—with difficulty, because the Germans were watching it every minute—I arrived too late—only minutes too late." His brow creased. "She was lying on the chaise longue. Jesus, I can see the scene right now—as if it had happened yesterday." He took a handkerchief out of his pocket and wiped his brow.

"When I tried to wake her, she was dead." He looked up at the palm tree above his head and exhaled audibly. "At that very moment, her old maid Salud came into the room. Of course it looked as if I had done it. The person who had committed the crime must have left a few moments before I arrived. The maid became hysterical, and rang for the other servants. I had to escape as fast as I could."

I *wanted* to believe him. At first I had been skeptical, but now I sensed he was telling me the truth as well as he knew it.

"I knew the maid wouldn't denounce me to the authorities. That would have brought scandal to the family name, which meant everything to her, since she had been born in the house. But I had to find the assassin to convince her I was not the guilty one."

He studied his glass. "I tried to for a while, but time was against me."

"Who do you think murdered her?"

"Lazaar was my suspect at first. That's why I accused him the night of the dance at Puerta de Hierro. Too late I learned it was Lazaar's Gestapo chief, Wizner . . . a ruthless monster."

"What about Gloria?" I swallowed, thinking how near I had come to wasting my life on this still-attractive man.

"Gloria was frightened of Lazaar. He threatened to send her back to Germany. She tried to help me, but never could get from him the information and proof I needed."

"Who tried to kill *me* that night?" Despite the warm humid climate, a chill went down my spine as I remembered the feeling of fighting for breath almost forty years ago.

"One of the Gestapo's mercenaries, maybe the same one who killed Mimosa."

"But Gloria stopped you from taking me home. She must have been helping them to get rid of me."

"No. She liked you and was incapable of anything like that." He spoke resignedly. "She didn't know about the guy planted there."

We had both left our glasses untouched for many minutes. The waiter appeared to refill them, but Pierre waved him away. My questions had dissipated the joy reflected in his face during those first moments. He was now slouched in his chair and pushing his hands through his dark gray hair. But I had to know more.

"What happened to you after you parachuted into Pau?"

"That was only a few weeks before the invasion. I had to go into hiding when Anvil did occur, because then I realized the Americans had been on to me all the time." He let out a profound sigh. "The only friends I could count on were two Spaniards who worked for me in the resistance. One was a socialist who had been on the Republican side during the Spanish civil war, a Catalán from Barcelona. The other was a communist from San Sebastián."

While he spoke, I didn't move.

"We were trying to save our necks and took the only road open to us—slipping across the border into Italy, where the communists gave us jobs and protected us. I lived in Milan for the next eleven years."

He loosened the collar of his *guayabera*. There was no movement of air at all, and I too became aware of the uncomfortable humidity. He paused, but I gestured to him to go on.

"By that time François Ferronière had ceased to exist, as had my dreams of living in luxury in Spain—going to partridge shoots, flamenco parties, and bullfights. I became Pedro Alvarado, a Spanish communist working for the KGB, not daring to return either to France or to Spain, except surreptitiously, which I did from time to time."

I could hardly believe what he was saying. Abruptly, he sat up.

"I'm spoiling our party, Tiger. Don't worry, my life hasn't been all a bed of cactus. I've had a great time. One also becomes accustomed to difficult situations. I can't complain. Money, good cars, and yachts—I've had all that and more."

He had misinterpreted my mood entirely. "Please tell me," I said. "How do you happen to be here in El Salvador?"

"I'm here on business. I come frequently. I married a Milanese girl, and we moved to Miami, where we still live. I have an office here."

Pierre's manner recaptured his former vitality. "Pep up, Tiger. Drink the champagne and change that expression. We should be grateful that we are here to talk about these things after so many years. What happened to our old colleagues? Did you ever see Mozart or Jupiter again?"

"I never saw Mozart, but I know he's well and living someplace in California. Jupiter has been a close friend always."

"Do you know that your friend Top Hat committed suicide? He certainly picked on a strange way to do it, I must say. He stuck his head in the kitchen oven and turned on the gas."

Pierre's words made me feel a profound sadness. "Not so strange. An OSS girl killed herself the same way in Lisbon in '44. Top Hat, I remember, was impressed by that and spoke about it often. Did you know that he married Agata Ratibor, and after she divorced him in Mexico, he came to the United States and married an attractive American girl and had some children? It's strange that he would commit suicide just when it appeared his life was becoming stable for the first time."

"He was caught lifting two cans of sardines in Harrods in London. That's why he did it. But what a reason. He had two hundred thousand dollars in his checking account when he died."

"If that had been a diamond brooch he would probably be alive today. His problem was that he was a kleptomaniac."

"What about your admirer, the bullfighter?"

"He married a girl from a great Spanish family about ten years after the war, and they had three children. But unfortunately he died of a heart attack very young before his children even grew up."

Pierre snapped his fingers for the waiter and ordered another bottle of champagne. "I saw Gloria years later in Mexico; she was beautiful still. She had married an Egyptian who soon died, but when I saw her she had finally found, she said, the perfect man and married him."

"Tell me, Pierre, what happened to Lazaar?"

"He escaped from Spain in a monk's habit just before the war ended and went to Brazil, where he died several years ago. But what happened to Niki Lilienthal and his beautiful daughter Carola?"

"He's dead. Carola and his other children are all flourishing in Spain."

"And Casilda Avila?"

"She's one of Spain's most important duchesses today."

"Well, Tiger—how about that marvelous Madrid? It was so beautiful in 1944."

"You wouldn't know where you were if you went back. All those lovely palaces on the Castellana have been torn down and replaced by ugly modern office buildings. The traffic is unbearable. Four million more people have moved into the city. Some of the old places like Villa Rosa, Horcher's restaurant, the Palace Hotel, and the Hotel Ritz still look pretty much same. In Puerta de Hierro, they even have the same dance on the Eve of St. John and the same bonfire."

Pierre took my hand in his and gripped it so tight it hurt. "Tiger, you must believe that I was not the one responsible for those murders."

I couldn't answer. Instead I asked, "Why did you work for two sides at the same time? How could you betray so many people?"

His eyes squinted; his face took on a heartbreaking expression. "I never intended to. But . . . if you make one big mistake in your life, it usually leads to others, until you find yourself caught in a trap with no way out. That's what happened to me. I have always—"

"Señor Alvarado." The waiter had appeared, cutting off the rest of the sentence. "Miami on the telephone, señor."

Pierre stood up. "I'll be right back. Wait for me, Tiger."
The minute he disappeared through the door, I left.

═══

Since then, I've off and on tried to supply the words of his unfinished sentence, to twist the meaning into something that would help me preserve at least one lovely memory of him. But instead what always comes to my mind is the vision of the honorable Spanish man I did finally fall in love with and marry, the first Spaniard I met that day coming into the Palace Hotel, who carried my bags up to my room.